Sheri Bauman
Linda R. Shaw

group work
WITH PERSONS
WITH DISABILITIES

AMERICAN COUNSELING
ASSOCIATION
6101 Stevenson Avenue • Suite 600 • Alexandria, VA 22304 • www.counseling.org

group work
WITH PERSONS
WITH DISABILITIES

AMERICAN COUNSELING ASSOCIATION
6101 Stevenson Avenue • Suite 600 • Alexandria, VA 22304

Associate Publisher • Carolyn C. Baker

Digital and Print Development Editor • Nancy Driver

Senior Production Manager • Bonny E. Gaston

Copy Editor • Celia K. Nelson

Cover and text design by Bonny E. Gaston

LIBRARY OF CONGRESS CATALOGING-IN-PUBLICATION DATA
Names: Bauman, Sheri, author. | Shaw, Linda R., author.
Title: Group work with persons with disabilities/Sheri Bauman and Linda R. Shaw.
Description: Alexandria, VA : American Counseling Association, [2016] |
    Includes bibliographical references and index.
Identifiers: LCCN 2015049586 | ISBN 9781556203404 (pbk. : alk. paper)
Subjects: LCSH: People with disabilities—Counseling of. | People with
    disabilities—Mental health services. | Group counseling.
Classification: LCC HV1568 .B38 2016 | DDC 362.4/0454—dc23 LC record
    available at http://lccn.loc.gov/2015049586

This book is dedicated to our teachers and colleagues—
the many caring and compassionate souls
who inspired us, taught us, and modeled
exemplary counseling skills and values,
and to our clients and students,
who together have made us
the counselors and educators
that we are today.
• • •

TABLE OF CONTENTS

PART I
General Principles

ACKNOWLEDGMENTS

The authors gratefully acknowledge the following people, all of whom contributed their ideas and experiences for this book:

Amanda Easton
Lia D. Falco
Gabrielle Ficchi
Michael T. Hartley
T. Gregory Kopp
Teresa Mayle
Jayci Robb
Toni Saia
Kristi Thomas
Allison Thorbergson
• • •

ABOUT THE AUTHORS

Sheri Bauman, PhD, is a professor and director of the counseling graduate program in the Department of Disability and Psychoeducational Studies in the College of Education at the University of Arizona. Prior to earning her doctorate in 1999, she worked in public schools for 30 years, 18 of those as a school counselor. She is a licensed psychologist (currently inactive). Dr. Bauman conducts research on bullying, cyberbullying, peer victimization, and teacher responses to bullying. She also studies group work and is past editor of the *Journal for Specialists in Group Work*. She is a frequent presenter on these topics at local, state, national, and international conferences. She is the author of *Special Topics for Helping Professionals* and *Cyberbullying: What Counselors Need to Know* and is lead editor of *Principles of Cyberbullying Research: Definition, Measures, and Methods*. Her most recent book is *Mental Health in the Digital Age*, coauthored with Dr. Ian Rivers. Her vita includes more than 50 publications in peer-reviewed scholarly journals, numerous book chapters, three training DVDs, and other publications for a general audience. She has been the recipient of two grants from the National Science Foundation and is now the principal investigator on the research team funded by a grant from the National Institute of Justice to investigate how school resource officers (SROs) affect school climate and safety and to test the added value of an enhanced model for training SROs. Dr. Bauman lives in Tucson, Arizona, with her husband and three golden retrievers.

• • •

Linda R. Shaw, PhD, is a professor and department head in the Department of Disability and Psychoeducational Studies at the University of Arizona. Prior to her current position, Dr. Shaw was the director of the Rehabilitation Counseling Program at the University of Florida. She has more than 35 years of experience as a rehabilitation counselor, administrator, and educator. Her counseling and nonacademic administrative experience includes specializations in spinal cord injury rehabilitation, brain injury rehabilitation, and psychiatric disability. Dr. Shaw is a licensed mental health counselor and a certified rehabilitation counselor. Dr. Shaw currently chairs the Code of Ethics Revision Committee for the Commission on Rehabilitation Counselor Certification (CRCC) and was a member of the American Counseling Association (ACA) Ethics Revision Task Force, which completed the 2014 revision of the counseling *Code of Ethics*. She is a past president of the Council on Rehabilitation Education (CORE), the national accreditation body for rehabilitation counseling programs, and a past president of the American Rehabilitation Counseling Association (ARCA). She represented CORE on the 20/20 Visioning Group cosponsored by the American Association of State Counseling Boards and ACA. Dr. Shaw has served as vice chair of CRCC and has also served as chair of the CRCC Ethics Committee, presiding over that committee throughout the process of a previous revision of the *Code of Professional Ethics for Rehabilitation Counselors*. Dr. Shaw has published and presented widely on issues related to disability-related job discrimination, the correlates of professional ethical behavior, professional issues in rehabilitation counseling, and neurological disability. She is the author of two coedited books and many publications and presentations. Currently, her research is focused on disability harassment in employment and on professional ethics.

• • •

part I

GENERAL PRINCIPLES

chapter 1
INTRODUCTION

The need for this book became apparent when we were searching for a suitable supplemental text in group counseling for graduate students in a counseling program with a rehabilitation emphasis. A thorough search revealed that no such book existed, despite the fact that approximately 19% of the U.S. population reported a disability on the 2010 census, with more than 50% describing the disability as severe (U.S. Census Bureau Reports, 2012). The *Occupational Outlook Handbook* (2014) indicates that in 2014, 120,100 rehabilitation counselors, who specialize in working with people with disabilities, were employed in the United States, with a projected growth of 9% by 2024. In addition, many counselors who are not trained as rehabilitation counselors serve clients with disabilities. Persons with disabilities may participate in groups to assist them in adapting to an acquired disability, but they also may seek groups to help with the many issues for which able-bodied persons participate in groups. Groups are helpful to survivors of abuse and trauma, family problems, social concerns, career decisions, and myriad other topics. Whether the facilitator is a specialist in working with people with disabilities or a generalist counselor with standard training, conducting effective groups that include members with disabilities requires additional knowledge, attitudes, and skills over and above what is typically covered in the basic group counseling course. This book is designed to provide those needed components.

DEFINITIONS AND FRAMEWORKS

We use the term *disability* to refer to a physical or mental condition that results in significant limitations in one or more major life activity. Limitations could be difficulties in mobility, communication, sensory processing, cognitive processing, and many others. This definition is consistent with the concept of disability used in the Americans With Disabilities Act of 1990 (ADA), a critically important disability civil rights law passed in 1990. However, it is important to emphasize that this definition is not intended to convey the notion that a disability is a deficit.

We subscribe to the disability model that frames disability as an interaction between the physical or mental condition of the individual with a disability and the attitudes, policies, and contexts that create limitations. In other words, disability is a socially constructed concept. The disability rights movement in the United Kingdom uses the term *disabled* "to denote someone who is disabled by society's inability to accommodate all of its inhabitants" (Disabled-World.com, 2016, ¶13). There are many types of disabilities, including mobility or physical impairments, spinal cord injuries (SCIs), vision or hearing disabilities, psychological disorders, and cognitive or learning disabilities. Some disabilities are readily apparent to others, whereas others are invisible (such as epilepsy or diabetes). We include this definition because members of groups may bring up the social discrimination they experience, and because their own view of the limitations associated with their particular disability (or disabilities) may become issues to be addressed in treatment.

We also choose to use "person-first language" (Dunn & Andrews, 2015, p. 256) in the title and throughout the book not only to be consistent with the American Psychological Association publication style guidelines but also because we want to convey that the disability is one aspect of a multifaceted person. A useful guideline for using person-first language can be found at http://www.cdc.gov/ncbddd/disabilityandhealth/pdf/disabilityposter_photos.pdf.

However, we recognize that there is an opposing viewpoint that prefers "identity-first" language. From this perspective, for some people, the disability is the focus of their identity. For example, Emily Ladau (2015) believes that person-first language separates the person from his or her disability and "implies that 'disability' or 'disabled' are negative, derogatory words. . . . [Person-first language] essentially buys into the stigma it claims to be fighting" (¶ 7). She points out that when referring to the racial or ethnic identity of someone, we do not say, "a person who is Latina" or "a person who is Jewish," we say, "She's Latina" or "He's Jewish." She feels that saying "She's disabled" is equivalent. However, though we acknowledge this position, we use "person with a disability" rather than "disabled person" in this book, recognizing that this is not a universally accepted choice.

We use the term *group* or *group work* to include all types of groups: task, psychoeducational, counseling, and therapy. The needs and concerns of persons with disabilities exist in all of those formats and in all settings (schools, community mental health facilities, hospitals, rehabilitation centers) in which groups may be offered, and we provide material that will generally be applicable to all contexts and formats. Although the distinctions between types of groups and settings are important, we believe that the concerns related to disabilities transcend those distinctions. In those cases in which the material is specific to a type of group or setting, we make that clear.

CLIENT RIGHTS

The passage of the ADA in 1990 was an important step toward ensuring the rights of people with disabilities (see http://www.ada.gov and http://aaidd.org/home for additional information). B. Brown (1995), in the spirit of that legislation, proposed a "Bill of Rights" (p. 71), which provides a foundation for this book. We include below those rights that are most pertinent and urge readers to view the original article for the complete list:

- The right not to be discriminated against on the basis of a disability when being referred to or requesting participation in group work.
- The right not to be discriminated against on the basis of being regarded as a person with a disability.
- The right of individuals to be judged for inclusion in group work on their own merits.

- The right to request and to be provided with reasonable accommodation that is not an undue hardship.
- The right not to be disqualified from group membership on the basis of the inability to perform nonessential role functions.
- The right not to be discriminated against as a direct threat to the safety or health of others, unless certain standards are met.

B. Brown (1995) also highlighted rights that focus on the prospective group member:

- You have the right and responsibility to initiate discussion with the facilitator about any accommodation needs.
- You have the right to reveal a disabling condition to the group leader and to members without being discriminated against.
- You have the right to expect the development of group norms that recognize the value of diversity within the group. (pp. 72–75)

With these rights in mind, we draw on a model proposed by Merchant (2013) for multicultural groups to provide a framework for this endeavor. She proposed that groups might be culture specific, which in the case of disabilities would mean that membership in the group would be restricted to persons with a specific disability (e.g., deafness, AIDS, cerebral palsy, SCIs), with the goals of providing support, information, and resources for persons with that disability and of helping members accept themselves and their lives with the disability. A second type of group would be one designed to increase understanding of, and sensitivity toward, persons with disabilities in a group comprising a mixture of persons with and without disabilities (or with different disabilities). We do not focus on such groups in most of this book, although we touch on them in the training and resources sections. Finally, there are groups for a variety of issues (e.g., family violence, substance abuse, grief and loss) in which persons with disabilities participate although the focus is on the issue rather than the disability. In each of these types of groups, the facilitator must be knowledgeable about the particular challenges of including persons with disabilities as contributing members of the group. These challenges may be related directly to the disability, but they also may include other health issues, relationship difficulties, family-of-origin issues, abuse, and so on. Facilitators must also have a basic understanding of the disabilities to anticipate and prepare for the needs of those members while helping all members have a positive experience in the group and a deeper appreciation of the psychosocial context of the member (or members) with disabilities. Finally, it may be that the group facilitator is a person with a disability; the nature of the disability and the composition of the group may present unique leadership issues whether or not the members have disabilities as well (Bauman & Thorbergson, 2011).

IMPORTANCE OF GROUPS FOR PERSONS WITH DISABILITIES

On a very basic level, groups provide a social support network for members. For those with disabilities, this may provide a necessary ingredient for growth. The skills that form relationships in the group can be applied to social settings outside the group with the confidence that one has been successful using those skills in the protected context of the group. Groups provide a safe and supportive environment in which members can gain deeper self-understanding and develop a more nuanced understanding and appreciation of others. The well-known therapeutic factors in groups (Yalom & Leszcz, 2005) can be particularly powerful in the case of groups with persons with disabilities (Ellis, Simpson, Rose, & Plotner, 2015).

One of those factors is *universality*, which refers to the recognition in the group that one is not alone in her or his situation. For persons with disabilities, being in a group with others who have the same challenges can reduce the sense of isolation that often accompanies such circumstances. This phenomenon is powerful in groups for parents who have children with disabilities (Seligman, 1993). Parents may struggle to adjust their parenting to meet the needs of the child with a disability and may experience negative reactions from others in the community; sharing and learning from others who share these challenges can be very therapeutic. In groups with others who do not have disabilities, the person with disabilities may find he or she shares feelings and struggles with others regardless of their disability status, which is also a vehicle to reduce the feelings of loneliness and disconnection from others. In such groups, the person with disabilities may find that experience facilitates the transition into other settings (e.g., work, social activities) with nondisabled persons. Groups provide an opportunity to exchange ideas about common problems (Livneh, Wilson, & Pullo, 2004), often generating new perspectives on perceived challenges.

In a group, the opportunity to be helpful to others, or *altruism,* can increase the members' feelings of self-worth. When others in the group acknowledge or appreciate a member's contribution to the group or to individual members, he or she feels valued and important, essential ingredients for self-esteem. When members encounter others at different stages of dealing with an issue, they may develop a sense of hope that they, too, can make progress and feel more satisfied and fulfilled. For those whose disability may limit their opportunities to join with others, the feeling of cohesiveness that develops in groups can provide that sense of belonging that is so essential for optimal human functioning.

Groups also provide a place where members can express their emotions without fear of judgment, a process known as *catharsis.* This experience often precipitates feelings of relief from the effort to bottle up strong emotions, and it allows members to shed feelings of shame and guilt that are frequently associated with those emotions. Groups also provide a context in which one can learn from others, by giving and receiving feedback, modeling the behavior of other members, and exploring existential issues of freedom and responsibility, mortality, and loneliness. Although these factors are present to some degree in all effective groups, the potential for profiting from these therapeutic factors may be enhanced among those with disabilities, particularly those disabilities that may be associated with social isolation or that are particularly heavily stigmatized.

In groups led by a professional, the leader has the opportunity to observe and assess the client's interpersonal style. In individual therapy, the counselor must rely on the client's self-report; in the group, the clinician can observe and assess the psychosocial needs of the client directly, which provides much more authentic data.

ORGANIZATION OF THIS BOOK

The book is organized into sections to facilitate the location of pertinent information. All chapters include a section on Key Terms and Recommendations for Practice. References are in a separate section at the end of the book.

Part I

Part I includes chapters whose information is most general. For example, in Chapter 2, we discuss themes that are likely to be prominent for groups with a focus on disability concerns. For some people whose disability had a recent onset, it is likely that issues of adjustment and adaptation to the disability will arise. There may be a need for information sharing regarding managing the disability, as well as social concerns about relationships (including intimacy, friendships, family, and professional).

The variety of group formats, including those using technological platforms, is discussed in Chapter 3. In many ways, groups using technology can be particularly helpful for persons with mobility or transportation difficulties, those with rare conditions, and those with concerns about being judged by their appearance. In Chapter 4, we examine issues of diversity that interact with disabilities to present complex issues. Demographic factors such as race, ethnicity, age, sexual orientation, and cultural context combine to create unique profiles even among those who share the same disability. Moreover, we consider the case of persons with multiple disabilities or a history of polytrauma and discuss how those factors affect the process and content of groups. In Chapter 5, we examine more closely decisions that must be made regarding the composition of groups. For example, we consider whether a group should be homogeneous or heterogeneous and on what basis and characteristics that choice should be made.

Chapters 6 and 7 address significant topics that bear close attention. Chapter 6 focuses on ethical considerations. The importance of concentrated focus on ethical concerns cannot be overstated. As professionals, we adhere to the ethical standards of our professional organizations and must be sensitive to specific situations that can engender ethical dilemmas. Chapter 6 focuses on ethical considerations specific to facilitating groups with members who have disabilities, rather than ethics in general. Chapter 7 reviews special training needs and brings attention to logistical and other accommodations that may be necessary to include clients with disabilities. In this chapter, we illuminate psychosocial concerns that may not be at the forefront for clinicians not specifically trained in rehabilitation, and we discuss points of general etiquette that must be observed to treat all clients with dignity.

Part II

Part II focuses on group work with specific populations. Each chapter is designed to stand alone, so that a counselor doing a group session with persons with that type of disability can use it as a guide. In some cases, we suggest accommodations that might be necessary to enable full participation by a person with a disability. For example, a person who is blind may need braille room or floor numbers; a person who uses a wheelchair needs an accessible location with ramps and doors that are wide enough to allow wheelchair passage. However, we wish to stress that group counselors should see these adaptations not as burdens but as opportunities to embrace universal design principles. Universal design is a movement that promotes the design of physical spaces and products to make them usable by everyone (http://www. washington.edu/doit/universal-design-vs-accommodation). This includes having wheelchair-accessible buildings and restrooms but also providing written materials such as intake forms in large print.

Chapters in this part cover sensory disabilities, behavioral and emotional disabilities, cognitive disabilities, physical disabilities, chronic illness and disabilities including AIDS/HIV. Each chapter provides focused and in-depth discussion of needed information for counselors working with individuals with these disabilities in their groups.

Part III

Part III summarizes and integrates the information presented in previous chapters and includes additional resources that will be useful to readers of the book. Readers will find lists of books and other media and information about organizations that provide information and services to persons with disabilities. There is a glossary to assist readers in developing an understanding of the terminology used and training activities for those who are counselor educators.

We hope that counselors at all levels of training will find this book useful. We believe strongly in the power of group work, but because of the potential power (that, when mishandled, can be harmful), it is critical that groups be facilitated by a well-trained and prepared counselor or therapist. That is particularly true for those who serve clients with disabilities. Conducting groups with persons with disabilities (many of whom have multiple disabilities or additional issues) takes knowledge and skill but also an accepting, inclusive attitude.

We believe most counselors are likely to encounter clients with disabilities in their career—recall that persons with disabilities are the largest minority group in the country. We hope this book will inspire confidence so that if a counselor learns that a client interested in a group has a disability, he or she knows that he or she can return to this book for information.

KEY TERMS

Disability: a condition that limits a person's ability to engage in one or more major life activity (school, work, travel and movement, recreation). Disability is a social construction, because the attitudes, policies, and lack of accommodations in the environment create the limitations rather than the disability creating them per se.

First-person language and disability-first language: When referring to someone who has a disability, there are two competing beliefs about the most respectful and appropriate way to do so. One camp uses a phrase that first notes the person and then the disability (person-first language, e.g., person with a hearing loss), and the other prefers to acknowledge the centrality of the disability by saying "deaf person" or "hearing-impaired person."

Group dynamics: patterns of interaction among and between members and between members and the leader.

Group work: a generic term that includes all types of groups, primarily task groups, psychoeducational groups, counseling groups, and therapeutic groups. Classroom groups and athletic teams are sometimes studied as examples of task groups, as are committees in the workplace. The dynamics of interactions are similar in all groups.

Therapeutic factors: Also known as *curative factors*, this concept originated with the work of Irvin Yalom and refers to characteristics of groups that promote beneficial outcomes in members.

RECOMMENDATIONS FOR PRACTICE

1. Locate a copy of a well-validated measure of attitudes toward persons with disabilities. Take the inventory honestly, and evaluate your own performance. If it is not what you would like, consider how to get additional experience to become more accepting of this population. One such measure is available online at https://implicit.harvard.edu/implicit/. Log in as a guest and take the disability measure.

2. You may wish to ask clients whether they prefer person-first or identity-first language as part of establishing norms at the beginning of the group.

3. A discussion of what the term *disability* means to you (and members) can be very enlightening.

4. Be sure to explain why groups are the treatment of choice for this population.
5. Be conscious of the meeting space and ensure that it can accommodate persons with a variety of disabilities.
6. Observe or survey your groups to determine which therapeutic factors are most prevalent. Reflect on how you can maximize these experiences to enhance the growth of group members.

chapter 2
COMMON THEMES

Sheri Bauman and Amanda Easton[1]

In this chapter we focus on themes that are common in groups specifically for persons with disabilities. Understanding why these issues are important, and being informed about these topics, will help the counselor facilitate more productive interactions and growth among members.

Although we mentioned the social or minority model of disability in the Introduction, it is relevant to this chapter as well and bears some amplification. We also review disability identity and culture because of its general significance and as a backdrop for the more specific topical issues. Because many groups for persons with disabilities have a goal of assisting clients to adjust to life with the disability, we provide an overview of a model of adaptation to disability so that the counselor can conceptualize the members' progress within a well-known framework. Then we turn to specific topics of social relationships and dating, sexuality, overprotection, abuse, substance abuse, maintaining health, and accessibility issues.

---

[1]Amanda Easton, PhD, is an assistant professor of practice in the Department of Disability and Psychoeducational Studies at the University of Arizona in Tucson, Arizona.

MODELS OF DISABILITY

Historically, disability has been viewed through several lenses, and there are lingering remnants of those views today (Olkin, 1999). The *moral view* of disability suggests that disability is either a punishment for or evidence of moral failure or sin. When this view prevails, those with disabilities are shunned and shamed. The flip side of the moral view, however, paints disability as a marker of a model family: "God only gives children with disabilities to those who are up to the challenge." In addition, some cultures have viewed disability as evidence of extraordinary powers (e.g., ability to foresee the future).

A later theoretical development was the *medical model* (Olkin, 1999), which focused on the defective bodily or mental systems. This perspective focused on the individual, who was seen as abnormal or pathological. The goal of treatment was to repair the defective systems to the extent possible while also learning to adapt to the condition and to the inhospitable environment.

A contemporary perspective is the *minority* or *social* model, which situates the problem in the environment, emphasizing that problems occur when the environment does not accommodate persons with disabilities and holds negative attitudes toward those persons (Olkin, 1999). These environmental obstacles and the attitudinal barriers presented by some nondisabled persons are the focus of this perspective. Only since the passage of the Rehabilitation Act of 1973, and the later development and implementation of the associated regulations, has the minority model become a prominent perspective. The persistence of negative stereotypes of persons with intellectual disabilities (IDs) is such that they have been excluded from full participation in many important activities (e.g., meaningful work, independent living; Special Olympics, 2003). As a result, the Special Olympics organization emphasizes the importance of advocacy and self-advocacy for this population.

The World Health Organization's (2011) global report on disability pointed out that the medical model and the social model are not mutually exclusive. In fact, this organization espouses a *biopsychosocial model*—which considers the interaction of the health condition, categorized as impairments (physical conditions), activity limitations (difficulty or inability to conduct basic activities such as walking or eating), and participation restrictions (problems with access or discrimination), and contextual factors in the environment (in both the person and the environment)—as the most useful model.

Cultural Views

These perspectives on disability are expressed in different cultures to a greater or lesser degree. We discuss the cultural implications in Chapter 4. There are cultures in which the moral or medical models are the dominant view, and for Americans whose parents or native community still subscribe to ancestral cultural beliefs, their growth and development can be marked by incidents in which those attitudes are influential. For example, Grace Tsao (2000) described her childhood experiences as a female Asian American with a disability. She recalls a time when she protested that she was not allowed to attend certain significant events in the cultural community; the reason she was given by her parents was that if she were to attend, the elders would look down upon the family because her disability would be evidence of their misdeeds.

Although the role of environmental factors in disability is now widely known and generally accepted, negative attitudes and misinformation about disabilities persist in many settings. That means that clients who come to a group probably have experienced overt discrimination and microaggressions that lead to frustration in many areas of life. For example, TS, a woman with cerebral palsy, reveals that strangers have voiced surprise to see her in a bar where many young adults congregate, have asked personal questions about her sexual functioning that they would never ask an able-bodied person, and have assumed that her boyfriend must also have a disability (surely an able-bodied man would not find her attractive), along with numerous other insults.

Although we have a law that requires businesses to be accessible to persons with disabilities (the ADA), many businesses meet the letter of the law by providing some sort of access, but those entrances may be "around the back," so that those accommodations separate and demean persons with disabilities. For example, there is a local pizza and beer establishment that has bar-height tables and stools for seating. Although the eatery does have a separate, albeit inconvenient, entrance that accommodates a wheelchair, the table they have available to a person using a wheelchair is at standard table height, meaning that the person in the wheelchair would be below the other members of her party.

The skilled and sensitive facilitator must recognize that these experiences are hurtful and common, and group members may need to talk about them in a safe and supportive climate in which they believe they will be understood, regardless of the focus or theme of the group. Because these themes are the canvas on which other issues are projected, it is important to allow these issues to be explored and not to treat them as distractions or story-telling behaviors that need to be cut off.

TS attended a group at her university with other students with cerebral palsy, facilitated by a counselor who had both cerebral palsy and an SCI. This counselor brought the additional perspective of someone who had to adjust to a disability at a later point in life. Although all members had cerebral palsy, they differed on many other factors: how they were treated by their families and culture, how salient the disability was to their identity, and in the types and severity of their symptoms. For TS, her disability does not define her, but it does affect her life. She found this group to be valuable because she was accepted easily and found people who could relate to her experience as a new college student with a disability.

Counselors should encourage self-advocacy and should be well-informed about mechanisms that clients can use on their own behalf. For example, ADA complaints can be filed online at http://www.ada.gov/filing_complaint.htm.

A Model of Adaptation

As with other processes that are associated with common experiences (e.g., grief and loss, response to natural disaster), there is a model of adaptation to disability that helps the clinician conceptualize the experience of clients in a group. We emphasize that models never apply universally, and individuals are often not linear in their progression. Stages occur in a different order than the theory describes, or recur, or individuals get stuck at a given stage. However, understanding the tasks involved will enhance the group facilitator's ability to manage the varied responses that are likely to emerge in the group setting. That is, the responses to the same circumstance are likely to vary among group members because they are different people in different stages of adaptation, and the facilitator should be prepared to point that out. It might even be appropriate to do a mini psychoeducational piece about the stages to illuminate the dynamic in the group.

Although more than one model has been proposed, we summarize the one developed by Hanoch Livneh (1986). This model applies to disabilities that are acquired rather than congenital, although even those who were born with a disability may experience some of the same reactions as they develop and mature and realize how their disability affects them.

The first stage, *initial impact*, occurs when someone has a sudden physical trauma (e.g., amputation, SCI) or an unexpected diagnosis of a serious life-threatening disease (e.g., cancer, Huntington's chorea, amyotrophic lateral sclerosis). During this stage, many persons experience a state of shock, during which their responses are numb and detached. Their thinking may be disoriented by the situation, and their energies may turn inward rather than toward others. As the shock dissipates (at different rates for different clients), people are likely to experience intense anxiety and demonstrate thinking disturbances, and they may display many symptoms of intense anxiety or panic.

The next stage is *defense mobilization*, in which people utilize psychological defense mechanisms to protect themselves from becoming overwhelmed. This stage is reminiscent of the model applied to grief and loss. The person often will engage in bargaining, mentally trying to negotiate with God or an ancestor to repair the lost function or to take away terminal disease. They may promise to change in some way in exchange for removing the present disability. They may also deny the situation entirely by convincing themselves that the situation is not as it seems, that they can recover or restore full functioning. People in this stage may seek multiple medical opinions, believing that the right doctor will reverse the situation. They may also increase their religious involvement, hoping to convince God of their sincerity and worthiness for a reprieve.

In the stage of *initial realization*, the individual is beginning to come to terms with the reality of the disability. *Mourning and depression* is the stage during which people accept the circumstance and experience grief over the losses (of limbs, functions, activities, etc.) and during which the psychic pain is intense. Grief (emotional), mourning (behavioral rituals), and depression eventually subside. However, when depression lingers for much longer, and when it becomes a barrier to progress, it may require clinical attention. The withdrawal and lack of energy that accompanies a prolonged depression may make it difficult for someone to commit to being in a group, but if they can be persuaded to attend, finding that others have had similar struggles can be very therapeutic.

For example, WA, a counselor who works with clients with visual disabilities, describes a client who came into her agency after just having lost a significant degree of vision and learning that the condition that caused the vision loss would ultimately lead to blindness. She refused any rehabilitation services that would develop skills she would need to function with her condition. This client was scared of blind people, and reluctantly agreed to attend the group, although she insisted that her husband remain in the building because she expected to leave before the group was over. She took a seat in the farthest corner available to distance herself from the others in the group. WA said that her level of fear was extreme, but by the end of the first 2-hour session, she was beginning to engage with others because she understood that they could relate to her experiences and feelings. At the end of the 7-week group, she asked, "Now, what can I do next?" Her husband thanked the facilitator for "giving me my wife back." WA commented that the group was an important place for the client to get her mind to a point at which she was ready to learn rehabilitation skills. She believed that her connection with the group was instrumental in that process.

Along with mourning and depression, clients may experience *internalized anger*, blaming themselves for their current situation and often experiencing guilt as a result. This is a personal version of the moral approach to disability. These feelings can inhibit progress toward integration if not contained.

Retaliation may follow, which is a period during which anger and hostility are turned outward rather than the inward focus of previous stages. Clients may appear bitter or resentful of able-bodied others and be prone to outbursts of intense anger. They may project their previously internalized blame and guilt onto others, or displace their anger at the universe onto others in their environment. Understanding this stage is essential for group facilitators, because the anger may emerge in group or even be directed toward the group or the facilitator. The reader might wish to consult the following article on working with difficult group members for additional tips: http://ct.counseling.org/2014/02/the-toughest-kinds-of-groups/. Understanding allows the facilitator to avoid taking the anger personally and to help the group also comprehend the dynamics at play, to reflect on their own processes, and to help the individual move beyond this stage to the final one, which is described next.

The final stage is one of *reintegration*, which has the goal of adjustment to the disability. At this point the person has acknowledged to him- or herself the nature of the disability and the implications it has for his or her life. The person at this stage is developing a revised self-concept, evaluating resources both internal and external. This does not imply that all the challenges have been mastered, but rather that the person is approaching the disability with a rational understanding and a desire to integrate the changed reality into future plans.

The facilitator of groups with the goal of adjustment or adaptation to the disability may find this model helpful in understanding the different stages exhibited by clients. If the group is not homogeneous in the stages, those who are closer to the reintegration stage can be models for those who are in earlier stages and can inspire hope in members who cannot yet imagine learning to live with this disability. One client said to her therapist at the end of the life of a group, "When I came here I thought it was the end, but it was really the beginning." She learned from others in the group that her life was changed by her suddenly acquired disability, but it was not over, and she eventually embraced the idea of finding a new life that included her disability.

Now we turn to more specific themes that are likely to emerge in groups as members work toward the goal of reintegration. Not every theme will come up in every group, but we have selected those that will surely come up in some groups, and the facilitator can be prepared to handle them when they do arise.

FREQUENT TOPICS IN GROUPS THAT INCLUDE PERSONS WITH DISABILITIES

Social Relationships and Dating

In this and the following sections, examples generally reflect heterosexuality; that is not meant to suggest that homosexuality is ignored or disrespected. Social relationships and dating, and sexuality, are important areas of functioning for persons with disabilities, regardless of sexual orientation. In fact, these topics are too infrequently discussed in general, and attention to sexual minority issues and disabilities is almost absent from the literature (Harley, Nowak, Gassaway, & Savage, 2002). Harley and her colleagues (2002) noted that in the college environment, students receive accommodations for their disability but "are simultaneously marginalized based on their sexual orientation" (p. 525). We discuss the issues of multiple minority identities in Chapter 4, but we wish to be clear that the information below applies to persons with disabilities of all sexual orientations.

Research has consistently found that more men with disabilities than women with disabilities marry. TS believes that may be because women are socialized to nurture and help others and would then be less concerned with the need to help their partner than might a man. The particular difficulties experienced by women with disabilities have been ascribed to several factors: the importance in the society of physical perfection in women, and the perceived role of women as caretakers. Regardless of career aspirations, women are still expected to be mothers and wives and caretakers of the family. There exists a biased notion that women with disabilities are unable to fulfill this role (Gill, Kerotoski, & Turk 1996) and are therefore less desirable romantic partners. That is, women with disabilities are erroneously thought to be dependent and requiring a caretaker, which contradicts the image of the mother as caretaker for others.

Women are expected to be beautiful (or to do everything possible to become so). Despite recognition that this is a seriously flawed ideal, the shift in attitudes and beliefs is slower to occur. Women, absorbing this unrealistic standard, strive to be thin and fit, use cosmetics to conceal flaws in their complexions, choose clothes and specially designed undergarments to flatter their shapes, and so on. That is, both women and men have difficulty looking beyond the physical or surface qualities of a potential partner; getting past the initial reaction to one's physical presentation takes effort that few people expend. Add to that a visible disability, and the challenge is clear. For example, TS shares that when she is sitting at a bar or table without her wheelchair close by, men will approach and flirt until she gets up, and then they either retreat or switch to a friendly rather than romantic style. She believes that men view women in a wheelchair as "dead from the waist down" and thus unattractive as a romantic partner.

Men also experience challenges in the dating world, because they are expected to exemplify strength and independence; thus, men with physical disabilities may be viewed as less than "real men." This perception hinders their ability to profit from typical social opportunities to meet potential partners.

These stereotypes may explain why many persons with disabilities find online dating to be a more acceptable way to meet dating partners. Some individual profiles do not mention the disability, but this information is typically shared once an initial contact has been made to avoid surprises should they decide to meet in person. Others using the sites mention the disability in their profile so that they do not chance a rejection if a person finds out later; if they are put off by the disability, they simply will not initiate a contact. There are also dating sites specifically for persons with disabilities, although some singles do not want to restrict their search to only others with disabilities. Others find the prospect of dating someone with a disability to be more comfortable because there is no need to prove one's abilities. They can enjoy the other's company without feeling judged solely on the disability.

A personal story told online described a scenario in which an able-bodied man (the author of the piece) attended a dinner party. He arrived late, and others were already seated at the dinner table by then. He noticed a very attractive woman at the other end of the table, and they exchanged glances and behaved flirtatiously toward each other throughout dinner. When the meal was over, the writer was eager to approach the woman; when he did, he saw that she was in a wheelchair and had disproportionately short legs. His initial reaction was fear: He was not sure that he wanted to approach her after all. He did overcome his own reluctance, and the tale has a happy ending. The couple has now been married for 15 years.

Although this story is heartwarming, it is unfortunately not typical. It is realistic to suppose that many, if not most, men would have ended their approach when they saw that the woman had a disability. If the man were the one with the disability, the situation would probably be the same. In this manner, many people with disabilities have been shut out of the dating world or have experienced rejection so often that they choose to withdraw. Developmentally, for young adults, finding a romantic partner is a basic task, and feeling as though one is unable to participate is a very disturbing experience. This is common enough that it is likely to be a topic in many groups with persons with disabilities, especially in those groups that are targeted toward adolescents and young adults.

Among lesbian, gay, bisexual, and trangender (LGBT) young people, those with developmental disabilities may not be adept at interpreting social cues. Thus, if a gay or questioning person with a disability is treated kindly by a same-sex individual, he or she may interpret this as romantic interest and ask for a date (Harley et al., 2002). The person may respond angrily or rudely, resulting in an awkward and uncomfortable situation.

Sexuality

Sexuality, according to the World Health Organization's (2006) working description, is

> a central aspect of being human throughout life [that] encompasses sex, gender identities and roles, sexual orientation, eroticism, pleasure, intimacy and reproduction . . . sexuality is influenced by the interaction of biological, psychological, social, economic, political, cultural, legal, historical, religious and spiritual factors (p. 2).

Historically, sexuality is a topic that has been ignored, neglected, and given little merit in relation to disability. This is because people with disabilities have often been viewed as individuals who do not engage in sexual behaviors or romantic relationships or as people who cannot and should not be viewed as sexual beings. In addition, they often receive little, if any, sexual education (Aunos & Feldman, 2002; Tepper, 2000). Furthermore, the negative attitudes associated with sexuality and disability also stem from a legal perspective in which laws throughout the world, both presently and historically, have stifled personal choice for people with disabilities around childbearing, marriage, and engagement in sexual behaviors with persons with and without disabilities. However, recent efforts to include sexuality and disability in a multicultural framework have aided in building more positive attitudes toward sexuality and disability.

More important, the type of disability one experiences can often dictate how sexuality is expressed and experienced. For example, on one hand, there have been considerable efforts to protect people with IDs against sexual abuse but limited efforts to provide sexual education (Cuskelly & Bryde, 2004). On the other hand, people who have experienced traumatic brain injury (TBI) or SCI have been given much attention in the medical literature, exploring physical sexual functioning and sexual impulsivity (Sakellariou, 2006; Sandel, Williams, Dellapietra, & Derogatis, 1996). As described by a parent of a child with autism spectrum disorder (ASD), "If my child had a physical limitation or something other than autism, she would be at less risk, have access to more information, and I would feel more comfortable discussing sex with her" (Easton, 2013). This parent's view is not uncommon. In fact, there are more resources on sexuality available for disabilities such as SCI, physical disabilities, and other acquired disabilities (http://www.sexsci.me, http://www.disabilities-r-us.com), but few resources exist for congenital disabilities outside of medical references that focus primarily on sexual functioning.

The information one receives regarding sexuality is also important to consider. The first exposure to sexual information for most children and adults with disabilities comes from family members (parents, guardian, siblings), from support staff, or from sexual education that is provided in school. However, for many individuals who take part in special education programs, limited sexual education is provided, and parents and guardians often opt out of those programs. Though there have been efforts over the past 20 years to improve sexual education opportunities for people with disabilities, there are concerns that the emphasis is placed on information transmission rather than on building more positive attitudes toward sexuality and disability (Whitehouse & McCabe, 1997).

Given the limited dissemination of sexuality-specific information to people with disabilities, the lack of emphasis on building positive attitudes related to sexuality and disability, and the reality that people with disabilities experience sexuality in both similar and unique ways on the basis of the type of disability, means that a group context can better facilitate both the procurement of information and the development of more positive attitudes around sexuality and disability. When discussing sexuality in a group setting, a number of factors need to be considered because of the sensitivity of the topic. *Sexuality* is a broad term that is used to capture experiences, thoughts, fantasies, beliefs, attitudes, and values related to roles and relationships (World Health Organization, 2006). The facilitator needs to be alert to not only the attitudes and values of the group but also any potential signs of sexual abuse that may not be raised directly. This can be accomplished at the beginning of the group by surveying group members about what they hope to gain from the group, while establishing ground rules that support respect and privacy for all members.

In being aware of the values and beliefs of group members, it is common that individuals who partake in sexuality-based groups are there to learn about sexual safety, while attempting to ascertain their sexual orientation and sexual preferences. Awareness of the personal attitudes and values present in the group will enrich the conversation around topics that may provoke negative reactions from some members. In situations such as these, the facilitator must be sensitive and empathetic and help to uncover the origin of the negative reaction. Also, in efforts to promote knowledge acquisition and increase accepting attitudes, it is best practice that a group facilitator address the needs of the members of the group in terms of the language used within the group. For example, it is commonly appropriate for young children to refer to their genitalia as "wee wee" or "pee pee." However, it is recommended that anatomical terms be used in place of slang terminology when discussing body features.

Topics covered in a sexuality group may include a focus on historical assessments of sexuality and disability, hygiene, contraception, reporting of sexual abuse, survivors of sexual abuse, sexual orientation, gender orientation, masturbation, and sexual behaviors, along with sexuality in the workplace. In each category there are likely to be a range of feelings and reactions displayed by the group facilitator and group members. Facilitators of groups need to be knowledgeable about different types of disabilities and be both competent and comfortable using language that is specific to sexuality. Facilitators must always be aware of any personal beliefs or biases associated with sexuality so as not to impose those on the group.

It may be helpful for such a group to be homogeneous on disability so that members are able to provide more detailed accounts of sexual experiences that have been complicated by disability. The group context serves a normalizing function in that members learn that others have similar concerns. The group also provides support from others as they struggle to understand and accept their sexuality (Mackelprang, 1993). Having members in the group who have adjusted well to the disability, including the sexual aspects, can provide hope to other members, and those members may increase their self-esteem as they assist others. Mackelprang (1993) also suggested that doing couples groups, with both partners participating, can be particularly useful so that both members of the couple learn the same information and skills.

Mackelprang (1993), writing about persons with physical disabilities, suggested that groups to help persons with such disabilities, congenital or acquired, should include several necessary components: basic sexual anatomy and physiology, the physical effects of their disability on sexual activity, the emotional aspects of the sexuality, practical suggestions for navigating sexual activity with a physical disability, and strategies for attaining a positive sexual adjustment.

Mackelprang (1993) pointed out that the facilitator needs not only to be knowledgeable about sexuality in general, and the disabilities that group members have, but also to understand the physiological and neurological mechanisms that are involved in sexual arousal and performance. She or he also should be familiar with the effects of medication on sexual functioning.

Mayers (1978) described a group for mostly single adults with chronic and severe physical disabilities. Although the reader might be concerned that the material is outdated, her description of the group and her recommendations ring true today. The group included 10 members (six women), ages 22–29 years, with a variety of physical conditions. One husband who was able-bodied attended with his wife. The facilitator was also able-bodied. Although some members had acquired disabilities, all members had been disabled for 14 years or more.

Although the group was advertised and explained as a group on sexuality, members were still nervous and uncomfortable talking about these topics. Mayers (1978) found that the initial focus on parents' and doctors' lack of attention (or outright resistance) to sexual matters was an important way to develop trust in the group. Early on, there was also considerable discussion of the difficulties of being a person with a disability in an able-bodied world; a novice facilitator might cut off such discussion, but Mayers recognized the function it served: establishing trust. As the group progressed, however, Mayers intervened when members tried to steer the conversation away from the sexual issues.

The reader is encouraged to read the complete article; the descriptions of group dynamics and her facilitation are instructive. We summarize her lessons learned here:

- Experiences are easier to disclose than are feelings. Experiences are likely to be the focus at earlier stages in the group, but as group cohesion develops, the facilitator should help members access and express feelings.
- The facilitator must intervene when members avoid discussion of sex. By allowing the tangential discussions, the facilitator would be colluding with the member and conveying that sexual topics are not appropriate to talk about.
- In screening and orienting members, and at the initial meetings, the facilitator needs to stress the importance of confidentiality. At those times, the possibility that members might be attracted to one another and form relationships should be mentioned, along with how that will be handled in the group.
- Sexually specific information should be presented in a respectful manner that does not convey that members are inferior because they do not know the information.
- The facilitator should be aware that much of the literature on sexual matters for SCIs and other disabilities focuses on men, and the facilitator needs to ensure that the concerns of both genders are discussed.
- Mayers pointed out that some members whose social skills need improvement tend to avoid discussion of their social errors and ascribe any failures to the disability. The facilitator needs to assist the member, with the group's input, in distinguishing between what is the result of the disability and what is the result of his or her interpersonal interaction style.

Because this topic is both important and overlooked, we refer to sexuality in one other population: hearing-impaired adolescents. Laitmon (1979) pointed out that deaf and hard-of-hearing adolescents have the same developmental interest in sex and relationships as do their hearing peers, but they may lack the education and experiences their hearing peers gain, both formally and informally (sometimes from overhearing ambient conversations). The group milieu provides the opportunity for them to engage with peers as they develop their sexual identities. Laitmon provided suggestions for facilitators of such groups. For example, she used an exercise to develop a vocabulary of feeling words early in the group to enable members to be more precise in their communications. She also used lots of hypothetical situations to encourage group discussion, such as "Someone points to your breasts and says 'beautiful,' or a boy unzips his pants on a bus and watches you," and so on. Members talk about how they might feel and how they might respond. She used a hands-on activity (creating collages of the many aspects of self) and completion of a very useful sexual attitude survey that members take individually and then discuss. There are 50 items, but the facilitator is encouraged to select the ones most appropriate for the particular group. The group includes instruction and practice around problem solving, which also revolves around scenarios developed by Laitmon for this purpose. Many of these could be used by hearing students as well, but are particularly effective for deaf and hard-of-hearing teens. As the group progresses, there are scenarios to role-play, and eventually group members could bring their real problems to the group for support.

Both articles by Mayers (1978) and Laitmon (1979) were written some time ago, but the need is still high for groups addressing sexuality in persons with disabilities, and the principles and activities designed by these group workers are still relevant today.

Counselors and group facilitators must not ignore the needs of LGBT persons with disabilities. These persons belong to two minority groups that are often stigmatized in society, and this experience should not be replicated in groups that focus on sexuality. The facilitator also must be mindful that there is a widespread misconception that persons with disabilities are asexual (Bauman, 2008), which is patently false. Although there are events that can be a source of pride and community building among LGBT persons, sometimes these events have limited accessibility (Webb, 2014). The need for a safe space to discuss these issues is illustrated in an interview with a 28-year-old gay man with spastic quadriplegic cerebral palsy who uses a wheelchair for mobility (Rosenberg, 2013). Regarding how he has been treated by the homosexual community, he said, "While they haven't 'looked down', the community has been unable to embrace me because of a lack of exposure and lack of knowledge" (Rosenberg, 2013, ¶3). He goes on to say,

> To be 100% honest with you, my disability has completely affected my dating life. When I came out at 15, my family was very accepting. It was when I was 19, and trying to navigate the LGBT community that I found to be the most difficult. The first time I was intimate with someone, they told me they had done so because [I was in a] chair and that it was, in effect an act of pity. Many guys have told me, "I can't handle your chair" or "it scares me". In my youth and sometimes [even in adulthood] those words really, *really* hurt me. What this has caused me to realize is that the LGBT community needs an education on the LGBTD (Gay, Lesbian, Bisexual, Transgendered, and Disabled) community. They need more exposure in gay themed media, at clubs, on-line. From that, perhaps our ideas of what constitutes "body beautiful" will start to shift. (Rosenberg, 2013, ¶4)

Overprotection

There is an understandable—and biologically encoded—desire on the part of parents to protect their children from harm, and this instinct may be amplified when the child has a disability. As a result, some parents of children with disabilities may become overprotective, so that as children grow and develop, this overprotection may take the form of lowered expectations for independence and fewer opportunities for self-advocacy and decision making (Sanders, 2006). These lowered expectations often exist in other spheres in a child's life, such as school and play, resulting in reduced achievement, reduced socialization, and a lack of understanding of the options available to them for future pursuits. Sanders (2006) pointed out that when parents are overprotective, the child is not given the opportunity to learn the consequences of his or her actions and may become isolated from nondisabled peers. This parenting style often persists into adolescence and young adulthood, and teachers and other school personnel may be complicit in this strategy. Albeit overprotection is intended to spare the child from danger and harm, it frequently results in lower self-esteem and overdependence on parents.

Carla Lohr is a blogger. She was born with spina bifada myelomeningocele and has a son with spina bifada occulta. She has experience both as a person with a disability and as the parent of a child with a disability. She writes passionately about the importance of not overprotecting or limiting the experiences of a person with disabilities:

> Everyone has basic human rights to pursue happiness. To do this, children with disabilities need to be exposed to the same life experiences as other kids. They need to be exposed to a variety of people and situations. The children must learn to deal with anger, disappointment and frustration, just as any other person would. They must also learn how to deal with people who ask questions, including people who may not be comfortable around them or those who act like complete jerks. The child should be given the opportunity to learn how to gauge the appropriate response to all these things. To deny this is to deny them their basic human rights. (Lohr, 2012, ¶6)

Another blogger, Shaimaa Ibrahim, who is blind, believes parents who overprotect their children with disabilities "are actually damaging and destroying this valuable treasure they have" (Ibrahim, 2012, ¶3). He offered advice to parents: "Don't be afraid to teach your blind daughter son to use the stove; don't be ashamed to introduce your blind child to the society" (¶6). He says the outcome of doing everything for the blind child is that "they will be pampered and really become disabled and helpless" (¶5).

A group member who comes from a family that has been overprotective may bring the learned helplessness and inexperience in exercising autonomy to the group context. Skilled facilitators will use the group milieu to help such members discover their areas of strength and encourage them to expand their view of their abilities. Facilitators must model for members that it is not only acceptable, but important, to provide helpful feedback and to challenge beliefs that reflect their learned helplessness.

Another manifestation of overprotection that may appear in the group is the anger that some members may feel at being deprived of the chance to have the range of experiences that they believe were denied to them. This anger may be expressed directly, by talking about it in group or expressing the emotions forcefully and fully. It may also surface indirectly, with the facilitator (the parental figure) being attacked for any perceived attempt to "control" or guide the member in the group. The skilled and sensitive facilitator should recognize the origin of the anger and, with the help of other members of the group, help the member understand when the anger is being displaced.

It is also important that the group help the member move past the anger and helplessness that the overprotection may have engendered. As with any client whose past infringes on the full experience of the present, the group is an opportunity for the member to decide how to use the energy from the anger to determine a course going forward or to make a decision that he or she is in control of the future and will make decisions to ensure optimal growth. The group also provides a laboratory for the member to practice new skills in a safe and supportive environment.

Abuse

Numerous studies have documented the disproportionate prevalence of all types of abuse among children and adults with disabilities (Baladerian, Coleman, & Stream, 2013; Heasley, 2013; Kvam, 2004; National Center on Elder Abuse, n.d.; Thornberry & Olson, 2005). An extensive discussion of the topic is beyond the scope of this book. However, it is important to understand how being victimized or abused can manifest in a group and how a facilitator can be prepared to respond.

First, the facilitator should make certain that she or he is well versed in the signs and symptoms of potential abuse so that appropriate steps can be taken to ensure the safety of the client. People who work with individuals who have been abused typically are thoroughly and continuously trained and updated in that field. It is also true that those who work with people with disabilities receive comprehensive training. What may not be happening is the cross-training for both groups. Because persons with disabilities have higher rates of abuse than does the general population, both professionals need to be well informed on both issues.

In a support or adjustment group for persons with disabilities, the issue of abuse may not be raised directly, but some of the psychological sequelae may influence individual responses in the group. For example, TM had a client in one of her groups with a history of abuse. Shortly after a group session ended, TM received a text message from this client asking whether the facilitator had been offended during the meeting. TM could not recall any incident that could have given the client this impression. She realized that as a child who grew up being abused by adults, the client became hypersensitive to anything that could signal the adult might be upset, which would mean abuse was likely to follow. It could be that some nonverbal behavior of TM (the parental figure in the group) elicited this fear, and the client was attempting to avoid any repercussions from the anger.

For many clients, the abuse has been a secret, and the life-saving practice of not talking about something that so profoundly affects their lives is a survival behavior that is difficult to relinquish. Furthermore, abuse victims often blame themselves for their mistreatment, and their self-esteem suffers. In a group, the member will have difficulty trusting others and may perceive his or her own potential contributions to be inadequate. This sets up a dynamic of being reserved or quiet in the group, which may cause others in the group to question the person's commitment to the process or to pressure the person to share more. The facilitator needs to assist the member to learn how to manage these requests for disclosure and help the group learn how to appropriately express their interest in the member without violating her or his right to privacy.

If the group is a psychoeducational group for persons with disabilities, it may be helpful for the facilitator to mention the high rates of abuse to perhaps open the door to the topic, if it is one that members are ready to explore, but the treatment needs of persons with disabilities who have a history of abuse probably are best addressed in a group that is homogeneous for that experience. Depending on the location, it may well be that there could be sufficient need to form a group to address abuse in persons with disabilities, which would be ideal. If that is not possible, attending a group focused on abuse is likely to be most helpful, provided the facilitator is well informed regarding the client's disability. Individual therapy is often provided in conjunction with the group.

When conducting psychoeducational groups for clients with disabilities, it would be useful to include a component on abuse. Persons with disabilities may lack information on how and to whom to report if they are abused. This topic must be presented carefully, because caregivers could be the abusers, which adds to both the impact and the lack of confidence in the system to protect them. Data have suggested that their fear is not unfounded (Sobsey & Doe, 1991). Information must be presented in understandable language and in sufficient depth that clients are able to act on their own behalf if abuse occurs. One hopes that they will have the support of the group as they develop agency and self-advocacy in this important arena.

Maintaining Health

The acquisition of accurate information regarding one's disability is an essential requirement for self-understanding and for empowering people with disabilities to take control of both their physical and their psychological health. People with disabilities often do not utilize, nor do they have ready access to, adequate health care (cf. Smeltzer, 2010). We use the term *health care* to encompass not only the medical needs associated with the disability but also the routine prevention and health screenings that should be part of everyone's health and wellness protocol. Health maintenance activities may not be part of the life of persons with disabilities for a variety of reasons: They may not be aware of the importance of these activities (exercise, not smoking) and screenings (mammograms); the person or the providers of these activities and services may perceive that the disability prevents them from participating; health care providers do not provide sufficient guidance and support for these activities; and there may be a general lack of information about the strategies for overall health and wellness (Smeltzer, 2010). Furthermore, health care insurance may be elusive for persons with disabilities (National Council on Disability, 2009), although it is hoped that this may be alleviated to some degree by the Patient Protection and Affordable Care Act (2010). Medicaid or Medicare are available to some people with disabilities, but persons using these mechanisms report long waiting periods and difficulty finding physicians who accept those programs; other needed services, such as vision and dental care, may not be covered. Copays and deductibles may cause health care to be out of reach financially, even for those covered by insurance. For persons whose disabilities are associated with communication impairments, this challenge may seem insurmountable.

In psychoeducational groups, health maintenance should be a high-priority topic, because this may be the only opportunity for members to receive and process this much-needed information. Smeltzer's (2010) article is complete with issues and strategies for health and wellness promotion that could easily be incorporated into a psychoeducational curriculum for anyone with a disability. The counselor should be familiar with local resources for adaptive physical exercise or athletic programs (e.g., http://www.family-friendly-fun.com/family-health/fitness.htm; http://www.disabled-world.com/fitness/exercise/) and perhaps encourage group members to share with others their successes in participating in these programs.

Using the group as a support mechanism to encourage physical activity, in whatever form, for persons with disabilities, can encourage them to acknowledge fears, stay motivated, and share successes. Obesity is a problem for many in our society, but being overweight or obese can exacerbate many other conditions that are often found in persons with disabilities (Better Health Channel, 2015). Persons with disabilities may be reluctant to participate in such programs as Weight Watchers®, and although the group does not need to be focused exclusively on weight, including a component that addresses this health need would be beneficial. The group is more likely to understand the barriers to weight loss programs for members, which will create a climate in which discussing this health issue is more acceptable and less threatening than in other settings.

TM, a licensed counselor who has worked with persons with a broad range of disabilities for many years, observed that in her experience health care is often neglected by her clients. She finds that they often need education on their own disabilities. Those with cognitive disabilities often do not understand how to take their medications and may show effects of inconsistent adherence to medication regimens. She finds that the information or education they receive is often presented in terms that those clients do not comprehend, and she finds that in her work with them in groups, she must devote some time to health education.

Substance Abuse

Substance abuse is as much as twice as prevalent among persons with disabilities as in the general population, and they get treatment about half as often (Krahn, Farrell, Gabriel, & Deck, 2006). In this section, we briefly review the reasons why both of these situations exist by exploring the links between substance abuse and disabilities; we also touch on barriers to treatment, which is an area in which groups can be helpful. This section is not a comprehensive study of substance abuse in persons with disabilities; rather, we provide background so that our recommendations for group work rest on a foundation.

Krahn et al. (2006) investigated the issue by using a large database for Oregon, along with interviews with administrative personnel at agencies and with persons with disabilities. They compared the disability group with recipients of a variety of federal programs (including Medicaid and Medicare). Although their findings reflect patterns in one state, they are likely to be similar to those that would be found elsewhere. The age distribution of persons with disabilities differed from the other groups in that they had fewer people in substance abuse treatment in the 18–26 age group and more in the 46–55 age group. Men were more likely to be in treatment than were women in the disability group, as were Blacks, but Hispanics were less likely to have had treatment than were other ethnic groups. Referral sources also were different for the disability group: They tended to be self, family, or employer; legal services, or mental health agencies, whereas for the other groups, the order was reversed and included social services.

Substance use disorders are found at higher rates in persons with disabilities than in the general population (Disabled-World. com, 2013). Although the rate of substance abuse in the general population is estimated to be about 10%, rates of close to 50% of those with SCIs, TBIs, and mental illness are reported (see http://www.disabled-world.com/medical/pharmaceutical/addiction/severe.php and National Rehabilitation Information Resource Center, 2011 citation for reports on additional research).

People with disabilities who have substance abuse disorders may have significant complications (Substance Abuse and Mental Health Services Administration, 2011). Their abuse of substances may become more important than their rehabilitation services, potentially limiting their progress. Medications used for some conditions may interact with the substances of abuse (e.g., alcohol) and reduce their effectiveness or create additional medical issues. In addition, substances can negatively affect muscular coordination and control, cognition, and the ability to organize one's time and conduct necessary self-care activities. Some substances can lead to conditions in addition to the primary one (e.g., someone uses alcohol and develops liver problems in addition to a physical disability). As with all substance abusers, some will lose interest in, or become unable to function in, school or employment. It is important for counselors to recognize that a significant percentage of women with disabilities and substance abuse disorders also have a history of abuse, which may contribute to the complications for treatment. Counselors should also be able to recognize signs of a substance abuse problem so that they can follow up with further assessment when necessary. The Substance Abuse and Mental Health Services Administration document includes recommendations for screening procedures.

Barriers to accessing substance abuse treatment include stigmatization, low self-efficacy, lack of social skills, and limited mobility.

The interviewees with disabilities also did not believe substance abuse treatment was effective, or they denied that they had a substance abuse problem. The study also revealed that many of the substance abuse treatment providers were uninformed about substance abuse among persons with disabilities and were not prepared to accommodate the needs of persons with disabilities in their centers. The most salient theme was the negative attitudes toward substance abuse treatment, some of which were also held by the families and service providers with whom the person with disabilities associated. Another theme from substance abuse treatment personnel was that persons with disabilities and their families and caregivers were focused almost exclusively on needs related to the disability, and either ignored or enabled the use of substances. Treatment providers also observed that some treatment programs prohibit the use of any psychoactive substance, including prescription medication. For many persons with disabilities, medication may be necessary for functioning.

It is clear that substance abuse is not receiving adequate attention in persons with disabilities. Group facilitators who offer psychoeducational groups to persons adapting to disabilities should include a discussion of substance abuse. They should also be aware of signs that this could be an issue for group members and explore the possibility in a nonjudgmental way. Given the high prevalence, it is likely that more than one member may need this information. One hopes that the group could help encourage those with substance abuse problems to get more focused treatment. Such feedback is much more powerful when it comes from group members rather than from the leader. Group facilitators may need to advocate strongly for their clients to be admitted to such programs, and they may need to remind treatment providers of their obligations under the ADA.

A challenge in facilitating a group and discussing the possibility of a substance abuse problem in a member is that several members may unite in their denial or in their complaints and justifications for not getting treatment or acknowledging that this is a problem. Members may turn on the facilitator if she or he confronts anyone with obvious behaviors; they may defend another member because they realize their similarity with that member. The facilitator must be clear that offering information and suggesting further attention to substance abuse is necessary and appropriate, but techniques from motivational interviewing might be useful to work with anticipated resistance. It may also be useful to be aware of online programs and alternative treatment programs (Bauman, 2008) so that objections to a particular approach to treatment can be redirected. Online programs for substance abuse have proliferated and allow participants to attend from home. The variety of formats for online programs was discussed by Bauman and Rivers (2015). These comments refer primarily to a general group for persons with disabilities rather than to substance abuse–specific groups. Given the unique needs of people with substance abuse problems and disabilities, it would be ideal to conduct substance abuse groups specifically for persons with disabilities.

Another concern related to substance abuse is that some members of a group may have not only used substances to excess prior to the onset of the disability but that use may also have been involved in the cause of the disability. "Alcohol has been identified as the predominant risk factor for injury and an obstacle to rehabilitation for both populations [TBI and SCI]" (Kolakowsky-Hayner et al., 1999, p. 571). In their review of the literature, Kolakowsky-Hayner et al. (1999) found that 57% of persons with SCI and 42% of persons with TBI diagnoses were identified as heavy drinkers prior to the disability onset. The presence of alcohol in excess of the legal limit was detected in 36%–51% of TBI cases and 17%–62% of SCI cases in previous research. More important, those with high levels of alcohol use preinjury are more likely to die, to have serious brain abnormalities postinjury, to have longer hospitalizations, and to deteriorate after the injury. However, significant proportions of these patients continued to be substance dependent or to use substances at high rates after the injury. Among young men, the group most affected by SCI and TBI, socializing with alcohol at clubs and parties is an important part of returning to a normal social life, and resumption of the use of alcohol and recreational drugs often is positively viewed as a return to normalcy. Often, however, alcohol and drug use takes on other important roles—an outlet for stress or even pain management—and may substantially interfere with rehabilitation and functioning in life activities.

In a study conducted by Kolakowsky-Hayner et al. (1999), patients with TBI and SCI (who were matched on demographics as closely as possible) were largely unmarried men whose injury was sustained in a traffic accident. They were mostly high school graduates who were employed at the time of the accident. Their sample had higher rates of heavy and moderate drinking than did the general population. Almost a third of the participants admitted illegal drug use prior to the accident or injury. The TBI and SCI patients were similar in their use of alcohol and other drugs (with the exception that TBI clients were more likely to use marijuana, and SCI clients were more likely to use crack or cocaine). About 29% in both groups used more than one drug. The researchers also discovered that persons with TBI or SCI who continue to drink after the injury are unlikely to be social drinkers; they tend to use alcohol frequently. This may interfere with their participation (and attendance) at group meetings. The facilitator may want to enforce a norm that members not be intoxicated when attending a meeting.

These findings suggest that groups with clients with either of these diagnoses are likely to include some members with preexisting problematic substance use; some may have sustained their injury while intoxicated. This means the topic should come up in the group. Depending on the situation, it may be possible to form a separate substance abuse group in addition to the general adaptation group, but if that is not an option, the facilitator will want to be prepared to address it without making it the sole focus of the adaptation group. Ideally, other members of the group will acknowledge problematic substance use predisability and share their experiences of attaining and maintaining sobriety and how this affects life with the disability. The facilitator will be much more effective if the screening interview for the group includes taking a detailed history, which serves two purposes. In addition to providing the facilitator with an awareness of concerns affecting group members, it also allows the facilitator to gauge the willingness of the member to acknowledge and talk about the problem, even if he or she has decided not to abstain. The facilitator can then anticipate some of the dynamics and prepare to manage them to the benefit of individual members and the group as a whole.

Dual diagnosis, or comorbidity of a mental disorder and a substance abuse disorder, is not uncommon. Kessler (2004), using large national datasets, found that someone who had a diagnosis of a mental disorder was 2.4 times more likely to have had an alcohol or drug use disorder than were those without a mental disorder. That is, about 51% of people surveyed who ever had an alcohol or drug use disorder had a mental disorder at least once in their lifetime, and a similar percentage of those with a history of mental disorders had a history of alcohol or drug dependence. It may be that the person with depression or anxiety or borderline personality disorder finds that substances (nonprescription) ameliorate some symptoms and that he or she overindulges in these substances to self-medicate. This makes treatment for both diagnoses more challenging, and the clinician must be on his or her toes when such a person is a member of a group.

Accessibility Issues

Despite the ADA, many locations are not accessible to persons with disabilities, so that on a given day, the person may meet with multiple frustrations, contributing to an elevated level of stress. It is safe to assume that most persons with disabilities have chronic or ongoing stressors related to their disability. Daily hassles contribute to distress and detract from overall well-being (Chamberlain & Zika, 1990; Serido, Almeida, & Wethington, 2004). Thus, it is important to allow group members an opportunity to talk about these frequent frustrations in order to be understood and for their feelings to be validated.

Even in buildings with accessible entries, one may still find service counters and restrooms that are not correctly designed. The toilet may be accessible, but the sink and paper towels may not be. Objects such as drinking fountains in hallways become obstacles to a person using a cane to navigate. Signage may be too high for someone using a wheelchair. Ramps may be too steep. Websites may not contain the code to allow use by persons who are blind, and audio components may not be captioned for those with hearing impairments (U.S. Department of Justice, n.d.). One faculty member in our department who is blind found himself practically impaled by a prickly Christmas wreath festively hung on a door.

In addition to the frustration of inaccessible facilities, the lack of understanding by some able-bodied people may exacerbate feelings of exclusion. The group may be a place in which members can talk about their frustrations without fear of being misunderstood. It may be that the group will help individuals to develop advocacy skills and will encourage members who take action to educate others about these issues (or insist that a particular violation be corrected).

KEY TERMS

Abuse: patterns of actions toward another that involve cruel or violent treatment, treating another (especially someone vulnerable or unable to adequately defend against the treatment) wrongly, improperly, or inappropriately.

Accessibility: the availability of a product, device, services, or physical space or environment to persons with disabilities.

Adaptation: changing in order to more effectively navigate the challenges that accompany a new or different condition because that condition is permanent or chronic.

Advocacy: actions that support a cause, in this case, rights for persons with disabilities.

Culture: a complex set of shared beliefs, traditions, behaviors, customs, values, food, music, and sometimes language that distinguishes a group of people from others. Culture may be based on race or ethnicity, national origin, age, disability, or other characteristics. Deaf culture and disability culture are examples.

Dual diagnosis or comorbidity: refers to coexisting mental illness and substance use disorders.

Health maintenance: practices that promote wellness and well-being and discourage illness and compromised functioning.

Models of disability: a model in the sense that it is used here that refers to a set of ideas or principles that describe a phenomenon, or a framework for thinking about a construct. The purpose of the model is to represent the concept in a parsimonious way that encodes the main idea. In this chapter, we discuss the moral model, medical model, social model, and biopsychosocial models of disability. We also look at a model of adaptation to disability.

Overprotection: providing more protection than the person or circumstance requires, depriving the person of autonomy.

Substance use or addiction: The publication of the *Diagnostic and Statistical Manual of Mental Disorders* (5th ed.; *DSM–5*; American Psychiatric Association, 2013) revealed changes in the definition of these disorders. There is no longer a distinction between substance abuse and substance dependence, and disorders are listed separately for each substance. Substance use disorders are now characterized from mild to severe. *Addiction* is frequently used synonymously with *substance dependence,* but *addiction* is a broader term that implies not just physical tolerance and withdrawal but behavioral and psychological symptoms as well.

RECOMMENDATIONS FOR PRACTICE

1. Develop a basic understanding of the issues discussed in this chapter. They are likely to come up in a group.
2. During your screening interview, make an informal assessment of where each potential member falls in the process of adaptation.
3. You may wish to raise the topics discussed within this chapter when you sense that there are unspoken concerns about them.
4. Build a professional library of the most useful articles and books on the various themes that are germane to these groups.
5. Create a climate in the group that encourages open discussion of difficult topics.
6. Encourage members to communicate with each other, to give feedback, and to share experiences and encouragement. In this environment, deeper exploration of sensitive topics is likely to occur.
7. If you are conducting psychoeducational groups around a disability, consider using the themes in this chapter as essential content.
8. Carefully examine the setting in which groups will be conducted to ensure access for all clients.
9. In a mixed-age group, dating may not be of interest to those in stable long-term relationships, but all can benefit from a discussion of relationships in their lives.
10. Be very clear on the law and ethical codes regarding reporting of abuse, and be sure to provide informed consent to clients about limits of confidentiality.
11. Be clear with clients with substance abuse disorders about your expectations for group attendance and the necessity of attending while not under the influence of a substance.
12. Be aware of the cultural factors that might be affecting members of the group, and be sure to acknowledge those influences.

chapter 3
TYPES OF GROUPS

There are many ways in which groups whose members include persons with disabilities can be configured. First, there is the format for the meetings, which can be in-person meetings or meetings using a variety of technological options, each with advantages and disadvantages. Although by definition, self-help groups (SHGs) do not use a mental health professional to facilitate the process, they are a popular and important type of group that professionals must understand and to which they may refer their clients. There are several types of groups facilitated by professional counselors or therapists: support, counseling, psychoeducational, family, and therapy groups. Each of these is described in this chapter, and their relevance to disabilities is discussed. Finally, we consider groups that are based on a particular theoretical orientation and examine how those orientations may apply to groups with members with disabilities.

SELF-HELP GROUPS

SHGs are organized, managed, and conducted without a professional leader. They typically comprise persons with similar goals, conditions, experiences, and challenges. Like support groups, SHGs espouse goals of inclusion and empowerment. Lieberman (1990) pointed out that there are two reasons why professionals should be informed about SHGs: They serve a large number of people, and they appear to be effective. They apparently emerged to fulfill unmet needs for help and support for a variety of problems (Finn, 1999). The best known SHG is Alcoholics Anonymous (AA, and its many 12-step derivatives such as Narcotics Anonymous, Adult Children of Alcoholics, Sexaholics Anonymous, Alanon, and Alateen). Arguably, AA started and has endured because the professional response to alcoholism failed to meet the needs of all individuals seeking help with substance abuse disorders (Lieberman, 1990). The little data available on AA suggest that from a third to half of its members have less than a year's sobriety and indicate that those who attend AA as an adjunct to other forms of treatment have better outcomes than do those whose efforts to achieve sobriety rely solely on AA. However, research has suggested that despite concerns that persons needing professional services may utilize SHGs instead, most SHG participants use multiple services. SHGs are usually free, so that financial resources are not required for participation.

On one hand, there are many similarities between SHGs and groups led by professionals. The sense of belonging or cohesion is fostered in both kinds of groups, and support, acceptance, and feelings of universality are identified by participants in both types of groups as helpful processes. Both kinds of groups create a setting in which strong emotions are experienced and expressed, and in both settings, members look to other members for alternative ways of managing their lives. In both settings, topics that are difficult to discuss (e.g., sexual functioning with disabilities) are important subjects of discussion.

On the other hand, the cognitive and emotional processing of the experience in the group are not addressed to the same degree in SHGs, given the absence of trained leaders. In many SHGs, inter-action between members is not emphasized (cf. 12-step meetings), whereas in professionally led groups, intermember interactions are an important process element that is encouraged and observed by the leader. Some SHGs (again, cf. 12-step groups) espouse a singular set of beliefs about the origin and nature of the problem that is the focus of the group. Trained professionals often have a broader view of the problem and are versed in a number of ways to conceptualize it. Finally, in SHGs, there may be no identified leader and hence no difference in status between members. In a professionally led group, the facilitator may be seen as an authority or parental figure or an expert. This difference will result in different group dynamics.

Because SHGs usually have a very specific focus, they may not be as well equipped to deal with corollary problems. For persons with disabilities, this may result in overlooking the unique aspects of their circumstances unless the group is specifically focused on disabilities. A professional leader, however, can integrate the complications that may attend the disability and provide a broader therapeutic experience, particularly when the specific focus of the group is not on the disability per se. For instance, to continue with the example of 12-step groups, that format may focus on alcoholism exclusively, without recognizing the complexity inherent in being an alcoholic with a disability. Furthermore, the emphasis on acknowledging one's powerlessness over alcohol (the first of the 12 steps) may conflict with the importance of developing self-advocacy and a sense of agency that is important for many persons with disabilities.

What, then, is the role of professional group counselors with respect to SHGs? First, counselors may want to recommend such groups in addition to the professional treatment they are providing. Given their wide availability and popularity, it is important to be supportive of those programs and to be aware of good sources of lists of such groups. Some sources cover numerous locations (e.g., meetup.com/topics/disability), whereas others are specific to particular geographic areas, so developing a working familiarity with SHGs within the local region is essential. The group counseling professional may also want to be available for consultation with groups; for example, perhaps an SHG for a specific topic discovers that one of the members displays a serious psychopathology with which the group is unable to cope. Many of the disability-specific SHGs combine support with an educational component, and professionals are often welcome contributors. Knowing that there is a mental health professional who is supportive of their goals and to whom they can refer or call on for informational meeting segments can be a valued service.

Some persons with disabilities will locate in-person SHGs, but for many others, that is unlikely. First, if someone has a rare condition, finding enough people interested in a group, who are located in a particular vicinity, is difficult. Second, if the disability results in restricted mobility, getting to a meeting could be daunting or impossible. We turn now to SHGs that use an online format.

ONLINE SELF-HELP GROUPS

Many SHGs (and other types of groups as well) are available in various online formats. This allows those with mobility difficulties—or perhaps accessibility challenges or fears of being seen going to therapy—to obtain the benefits of those groups. Online groups can be conducted in synchronous or asynchronous formats and can use video, audio, or text to communicate. There are many benefits to online groups for persons with disabilities: Members do not have to travel to the site, they have a wider choice of professionals than are available in a particular geographic area, and they do not have to fear being seen by others in the group or in a waiting room if they are concerned about their appearance or reputation. Those with communication difficulties can participate in text-based groups. Although some experts believe the online format encourages self-disclosure (the online disinhibition effect described by Suler, 2004), others suggest that the text-based asynchronous formats allow the clients to take time to compose their messages more thoughtfully. This is particularly beneficial to members with communication disorders or medical problems that include such difficulties (e.g., aphasia due to a stroke). In addition, many of the online platforms preserve the record of communications in the group, allowing members to review and reflect on content.

Additional advantages of online groups were discussed by Braithwaite, Waldron, and Finn (1999), who pointed out that the often large number of members who offer their unique experience and perspectives increases the quantity of information that members receive. These large groups may include members with the same disability, but from different cultural groups and other life circumstances. The large number also is a powerful message regarding the numbers of others who are part of the community, reducing the feelings of isolation that often accompany disabilities. In some groups with open access, nondisabled persons may observe the communications to increase their understanding of the experiences of those with disabilities. These "lurkers" may be family members, coworkers, and friends who want to develop a deeper understanding of people close to them who have a disability.

Finn (1999) used data from one online SHG site for persons with disabilities and identified the curative factors that were evident. He detected examples of catharsis, providing support and empathy for others in the group, universality, friendship (important for persons whose disability may keep them isolated), opportunities to talk about "taboo" topics that are troubling, requesting and providing information, problem solving, and cohesion.

Counselors may choose to recommend online groups to their clients when a local group is nonexistent because of a low-incidence disability, when transportation or scheduling to an existing group is difficult, or when the client is more comfortable in the online setting. We strongly recommend that counselors recommend professionally facilitated groups or those that are associated with reputable associations dedicated to the particular issue. The website http://www.disability.gov has links to many of these associations that offer online groups, as do http://www.parentcenterhub.org and http://www.cdc.gov/ncbddd/disabilityandhealth/people.html. Counselors who specialize in services for persons with disabilities should keep current on available online groups and check with clients who use those groups for recommendations.

SUPPORT GROUPS

Groups that are formed for the purpose of providing support to members with common concerns are called *support groups*. Most SHGs are support groups, but this format can also be facilitated by professionals. Support groups differ from counseling and therapy groups in that the focus is not on remediating or preventing developmental problems or treating mental illness but on building a social support system on which members can rely. The mechanism by which this occurs is mutual sharing, which builds a feeling of cohesion among members. A support group for women with a variety of disabilities was found to have a positive impact on members by providing experiences and relationships that counteracted the internalized oppression with which many members contended (Mejias, Gill, & Shpigelman, 2014). Mejias et al. (2014) found that the increased sense of belonging in the group led to decreased feelings of isolation; these findings were similar to those of earlier studies of support groups for women with disabilities. Hughes and Cohn (1990) recommended support groups for children who are hospitalized because of chronic illness. The children in their groups participated for the duration of their hospital stay (or for as long as their medical condition allowed). Some of the themes that emerged in the group were those of separation from family, adjusting to the hospital environment, sexuality, and relationships with other children, including those in the group. Hughes and Cohn pointed out that though hospital support groups can provide many positive aspects to children with chronic illnesses, the presence of children who are terminal or who otherwise present with the most extreme consequences of the condition might be traumatizing to other members. They recommend such children not participate in the groups but receive services in another modality. In addition, the age range of children in hospital groups can be wide, and although this can present challenges for leaders, Hughes and Cohn found that the advantages outweighed the challenges.

The nature of support was examined in a study of an email support group for people with disabilities (Braithwaite et al., 1999). These researchers coded 1,179 posts by 42 senders over a 1-month period. After examining the posts, the researchers concluded that there were approximately equal numbers of men and women and that most members had physical disabilities. Posts were classified as information support, tangible assistance, esteem support, network support, and emotional support. Emotional support was the most frequent type of post, with information next, followed by esteem support (compliments, validation, and relief from blame). Network support and tangible support were infrequent.

Many advocacy groups representing the needs of individuals with specific disabilities and their family members develop networks of support groups that fulfill an integral part of their mission. The organization's web pages often link to support groups that are located in a convenient geographical vicinity or provide a contact who can help to link individuals and their families with the appropriate group for them.

COUNSELING GROUPS

Counseling groups help members with life problems by using interpersonal support and problem-solving strategies. Livneh et al. (2004) asserted that such groups are particularly helpful for people with disabilities. In fact, in the early 20th century, Joseph Pratt, an important founder of counseling and guidance in the United States, incorporated groups in his treatment of tubercular patients' depression and isolation and later expanded the approach to include other chronic health conditions.

Livneh et al. (2004) proposed that counseling groups for people with disabilities address affective, cognitive, and behavioral goals. Affective goals include providing a safe space for catharsis (expression of intense feelings), providing emotional support, reducing anxiety that is often associated with adapting to a disability, and fostering universality. Cognitive goals help members increase self-esteem by accepting themselves as a person with a disability, assisting them in reality testing, providing information, and inculcating a more optimistic view of the future. Behavioral goals include increasing coping skills; improving interpersonal skills; establishing personal, educational, and career goals; and gaining a reasonable degree of independence. Livneh et al. discussed specific issues for groups with persons with sensory disabilities, orthopedic and neuromuscular disabilities, and other disabilities, including those for members with multiple disabilities. These are discussed in detail in Chapters 8–12.

A counseling group for senior citizens who had become disabled due to a chronic neuromuscular disorder was held using telephone conferencing. The goal of this cognitive therapy group was to assist clients in maintaining their self-image and to encourage emotional adjustment to the disability (Evans, Smith, Werkhoven, Fox, & Pritzl, 1986). In addition to positive outcomes for members of the group (with decreased loneliness being a significant result of participation), these researchers appreciated the opportunity to observe the way the members interacted with peers, providing important assessment information. More recently, Hopps, Pépin, and Boisvert (2003) evaluated the effectiveness of a cognitive behavior group for people with physical disabilities. The group met via interrelay chat, which is a synchronous text-based computer communication platform. The intervention was based on a skills training manual for people with physical disabilities and consisted of 12 two-hour sessions. Results showed significant improvements in loneliness, acceptance of disability, and a reduction of social difficulties, and gains were maintained at follow-up 4 months later. Furthermore, only one participant did not complete the course of treatment. Hopps et al. pointed out that their participants had to be able to use computers, including the keyboard, and to read, so they may not be representative of all people with physical disabilities.[1] Nevertheless, the effectiveness of the intervention is encouraging.

A group intervention for clients with mild to moderate IDs who were experiencing anger problems that led to aggressive episodes (Rose, West, & Clifford, 2000) was evaluated and found to reduce aggressive expressions of anger and depression, with gains maintained at 6- and 12-month follow-ups. Inclusion criteria were the ability to understand simple directions, the ability to sit with the group facilitator for a 20-min intake interview, and the availability of a staff member who would

---

[1] Computers can now be equipped with voice-recognition software, increasing access to this type of group for persons with disabilities.

accompany the client to the group. All group members were willing to attend and wanted to reduce their aggressive behavior. The group consisted of 16 two-hour sessions. Sessions included role plays and video feedback, and members were taught thought-stopping techniques, relaxation, and positive self-statements. The staff member who attended the sessions with the client was able to provide additional information to the group leaders and also to remind the member of his or her skills when he or she was outside of the group.

These examples provide evidence that group counseling is an effective treatment for people with a wide range of disabilities. As has been noted earlier, the benefits of group work may be even more salient for those with disabilities, given the high rates of isolation that are associated with disabilities.

PSYCHOEDUCATIONAL GROUPS

Psychoeducational groups are primarily used to convey, or teach, information. Therefore, these groups can be larger than counseling or therapy groups and are generally more structured than are other types of groups (Huebner, 2004; Marshak & Seligman, 1993). However, it is important to recognize that support groups, SHGs, and counseling groups also have educational components (Huebner, 2004); the difference is primarily one of degree, in that the stated purpose of psychoeducational groups is to provide information and education about a particular disability. Member interactions are not the focus but can be useful in helping members personalize the material. For example, in a group for persons with SCIs, information about bowel and bladder control might be upsetting to members and might generate questions about how to best manage bowel and bladder functions, as well as the embarrassment that might accompany the occasional "accident." Other group members' sharing of their own experience, and validating the fears, can make this type of group therapeutic as well as informative.

FAMILY GROUPS

The family members of persons with a disability are affected in many ways by their relative's condition, and groups comprising multiple families with common situations may be provided as an adjunct to the treatment of the person with the disability. These groups generally provide a combination of information and support, but the leader must be skilled at managing the interactions, which can be complicated by the number of participants and their different family roles. Leaders must decide on the number of families to include, whether siblings (if young children) should be included with adults or in separate groups, and how to structure the sessions.

GROUP THERAPY

Group therapy is typically a long-term treatment for deep-seated problems and differs from group counseling primarily in the intensity of the problems and the duration of the treatment. Group therapists utilize a variety of therapeutic approaches in their groups. We cover only a few here, but many other approaches might be appropriate and may need some adaptations to suit the particular clientele of a given group.

Theoretical Approaches

Group practitioners often use a particular theoretical orientation when they lead groups; these approaches are more or less suitable for groups with members who have a disability, depending on the nature of the issue that brings them to group. We expand on the insights provided by Huebner (2004) in the following sections.

Psychodynamic Approach

Psychodynamic approaches are grounded in theories that give significant weight to early childhood experiences. In varying degrees, they attend to unconscious processes that may affect the observed behaviors and troubles of clients. Concepts often utilized in groups are the reenactment of early family relationships, which may be triggered by transference experiences (responding to someone in the present on the basis of early experiences with similar figures). The group setting provides multiple transference opportunities. Clients are helped to understand these experiences by using interpretations provided by the therapist, and sometimes by other members. For this theoretical perspective to be appropriate, group members need to be capable of insight, which is considered important for growth. Catharsis, or the release of powerful emotions, can be elicited through reexperiencing early trauma, and members need to have sufficient ego strength and stability to tolerate such experiences.

A member with a disability who expects to be rejected (because he was rejected in early childhood and has internalized that expectation) and finds instead understanding and support may be able to make significant progress in the group setting. Similar revelations about the origins of unwelcome emotional reactions in the present may free the individual to move forward.

Psychodynamic groups tend to be less structured than groups that are based on other theoretical orientations. As with individual therapy, with free association and dream analysis as primary techniques, the therapist is likely to be more psychologically removed from the members to encourage transference reactions. Both of these features can be unsettling to some clients, and it is essential to assess the suitability of this approach before referring someone with disabilities to a psychodynamic group.

Psychodynamic groups might be better suited to persons with disabilities who have long-standing complex mental health problems that require long-term and in-depth treatment. In many cases, the group members will also receive concurrent individual therapy. But for the client whose disability was recently acquired and who is struggling with accepting him- or herself as a person with disabilities, this approach might be less useful.

Humanistic Approaches

Several theoretical perspectives are grouped under this category and share some common principles. Person-centered, Gestalt, and existential frameworks all believe that humans have innate potential for growth and fulfillment and help clients move toward self-actualization by focusing on the present (also known as the "here and now"), attending to nonverbal expression, and encouraging clients to accept responsibility for their own choices. All of these approaches also promote increased awareness on the part of clients.

Huebner (2004) believed that the acceptance that prevails in these groups may allow individuals to experience and work through their feelings about the disability (e.g., grief and anger) and realize that these are not pathological but frequent reactions to having or acquiring a disability. Techniques vary in these groups, which may change as various issues emerge. Role playing may be used; empty-chair techniques, rounds, and other techniques are used to help members actively engage in the process. The general outcome that may be the goal for groups from this perspective might be for clients to accept that they are responsible for their emotions and actions and that the disability is part of their identity and not necessarily the defining attribute.

Cognitive Behavior Approaches

Cognitive behavior therapy is widely used in rehabilitation settings because of the focus on the present and on presenting problems rather than on underlying personality dynamics. Included in this group of theories are rational emotive behavior therapy, cognitive therapy, cognitive behavior therapy, and solution-focused therapy. An important component of these approaches is to identify and dispute maladaptive cognitions; in a group setting, members learn to do this by assisting others. Common cognitions that are addressed in groups with persons with disabilities include such thoughts as "I cannot live with this disability" or "Other people should give me a break because I have a disability." These approaches utilize didactic or educational strategies to teach the basics of the theory in the hope that members will develop skills to assist others in the group while helping themselves. Because these groups tend to be more structured than are other approaches, there may be homework, reading material, and instruction in techniques such as progressive relaxation, deep breathing, time management, and activities of daily living, depending on the composition of the group. Groups that are more behaviorally focused may be more appropriate for clients with cognitive disabilities; reinforcement may be used in the form of tokens or other rewards for using targeted behaviors. It is important to note, however, that even though behaviorally oriented groups might be the approach of choice for cognitive and IDs, all members can benefit from the connection with one another that comes with interaction and sharing of ideas. Although overreliance on "talking therapies" is not advised, these members experience the same emotional responses as anyone to the stressors of living with a disability and profit from feeling supported and understood to the same degree as anyone else.

KEY TERMS

Counseling groups: Counseling groups include support as a function but also focus on interpersonal communication, problem solving, increasing self-awareness, and feedback as important functions.

Online groups: The Internet allows groups to exist in cyberspace using a variety of platforms, using discussion boards, chat rooms, video chatting, and software such as Skype and Google+ Hangouts to meet.

Psychoeducational groups: The primary purpose of these groups is the imparting of information. They differ from classes in both size and amount of interaction. That is, after information is presented, members are encouraged to discuss how this information affects them and to share their reactions and concerns with other group members.

Self-help groups: SHGs are formed to provide mutual aid among members and have no professional leader.

Support groups: The primary purpose of these groups is to give and receive emotional support. Behavior change, practical information, and other goals are secondary.

Therapy groups: Therapy groups are typically long-term commitments to explore underlying issues that are affecting the members. The goals involve making major changes in personality.

Theoretical orientation: In the field of counseling, there are a number of schools of thought about how people change, the causes of current problems, techniques for counselors to use, and strategies to improve clients' well-being. Each is called a theoretical orientation.

RECOMMENDATIONS FOR PRACTICE

1. Reflect on your own theoretical orientation. Will you need to adapt your approach for the group with persons with disabilities?
2. Do not prohibit clients in your groups from participating in self-help or online groups. Do encourage them to share what they are learning in those settings.
3. Develop a directory of SHGs in your area that seem to be beneficial to clients so you can provide guidance to members who are thinking of joining an additional group.
4. Reflect on your own beliefs and concerns about online groups. Read widely, and engage with counselors who conduct groups online.
5. Consult with professional associations if you are considering offering a group online. Be sure you understand security and privacy considerations, the choices of formats, and the advantages and disadvantages for clients with disabilities.

chapter 4
DIVERSITY ISSUES

Lia D. Falco[1]

Other chapters in this book focus on aspects of group work that may affect persons with disabilities, including group composition, types of groups, and types of disability. However, individuals with disabilities are a diverse population, and disability is only one dimension of identity that shapes the human experience. In addition to their disability status, persons with a disability may also belong to one or more cultural groups. Rather than considering disability alone as a form of diversity, this chapter examines how multiple forms of diversity such as race, ethnicity, gender, age, religion, and sexual orientation affect the lives of people with disabilities. Although many people with disabilities might disagree with or be uncomfortable being considered part of a minority group, they are often overlooked, disenfranchised, and stigmatized in American culture. For this reason, this chapter considers diversity issues through a "minority lens" by discussing the

---

[1]Lia D. Falco, PhD, is an assistant professor in the Department of Disability and Psychoeducational Studies at the University of Arizona in Tucson, Arizona.

ways in which multiple minority statuses may affect the identity and experiences of individuals with disabilities and, in turn, how these different statuses may inform group work for the individual, the group, and the facilitator.

DISABILITY AND MULTIPLE MINORITY STATUS

To say that a category such as race and gender is socially constructed is not to say that the category has no significance in our world.

—Crenshaw (1991, p. 1296)

Although the social model of disability sees the issue of disability as a construction of society and environment, and not a "problem" that lies within individuals, it may not fully capture the lived experiences of people with disabilities. For group facilitators, it is crucial to consider the intersection of multiple identity statuses in a real-world context, including the ways in which multiple identity statuses affect people with disabilities. *Minority* is a term that is regularly used in the disability and counseling literature to understand the experience of disability, but it is often ill-defined and misunderstood. The need to explore the meaning of minority status is especially important in light of increasing recognition of the importance of diversity issues in counseling interactions and provision of services.

Minority status is different from racial, ethnic, and cultural membership, but it overlaps with each of these constructs in certain contexts (Mpofu & Conyers, 2004). From a representational theory perspective, minority status refers to limited access to resources and privileges (such as economic opportunity) and not just to numeric representation within society. For example, women comprise the larger proportion of the population in most societies but are generally considered minorities because of the economic and social oppression that many experience. Within this perspective, minority status is defined by three core elements: restrictions in economic opportunity, communicative self-representation, and preferred lifestyle. On the basis of these criteria, people with disabilities can be considered a minority. For example, work contributions and skills of persons with disabilities are often undervalued (Yelin, 1991), and job- and employment-related discrimination against persons with disabilities continues in spite of the passage of the ADA (Chima, 1998). Person-first language ("person with a disability") represents an effort by the disability community to assert communicative self-representation (Bailey, 1991), but media and the public often use language that is rejected or unacceptable to people with disabilities. Although much progress has been made, many people with disabilities continue to have limited access to basic social amenities. All of these factors underscore the minority status of individuals with disabilities.

Disability in and of itself does not necessarily result in automatic identification with minority status, but using a representational theory perspective can be helpful in understanding how the experience of disability might vary by context and overlap with other statuses to shape one's identity. Among people with disabilities, there is tremendous diversity in characteristics such as gender, age, socioeconomic status, race, religion, and sexual orientation. Each of these characteristics influences personal identity (Reeve, 2000); however, disability status among racial, ethnic, gender, or cultural minorities can result in multiple minority statuses, because the negative social or economic effects may be compounded or experienced concurrently (Stuart, 1993). Before we can understand how an individual's multiple minority status is related to group work, we must first consider how multiple statuses intersect with disability to shape one's identity development. The following section is intended to provide the reader with a framework for understanding how multiple identities or multiple minority statuses can affect people with disabilities differently than their nondisabled counterparts, thus creating additional layers of context for group work.

Intersectionality

Disability as it intersects with race, class, gender, and other statuses creates a complex multiplicity of identities. Some have argued that social movements that focus on a single identity (the feminist, Black Power, LGBT rights, and disability rights movements) either conflate or ignore intragroup differences. This may lead to an unnecessary organization of differences into a hierarchy such that some gain prominence over others. For example, consider a person who is poor, Black, and disabled and a person who is Black, wealthy, and gay. For both, is race the stable register of minority status? Perhaps not. Some differences may coalesce to create a more abject form of inequity (poor, Black, disabled), and others might reinforce both invisibility and privilege within the same minority community (Black, wealthy, gay; Erevelles & Minear, 2010). Rather than thinking about multiple identities as intersecting with a common "master" category such as race, it is helpful to consider the different ways that social categories are intertwined and how they affect individuals within the broader historical and societal contexts.

The concept of intersectionality provides a way to understand the lived experiences of individuals with multiple minority statuses. It may be impossible to generate all the potential social categories that exist within all individuals, but we can use our understanding of intersectionality to examine multiple differences. Intersectionality situates the notion of "simultaneous oppression" as an experience of a majority of disabled people, because the majority is not a homogeneous group of disabled, White, heterosexual, middle-class young men. That is, they are likely to experience multiple forms of discrimination if they identify with more than one marginalized group. As group facilitators working with clients with disabilities, we must not assume that disability is their only concern. There is a unique experience at the intersection of individuals' identities, and efforts to isolate the influence of any one social identity fail to capture how membership in multiple identity groups can affect how people are perceived, how they are treated, and how they experience relationships and different life roles (Berger & Guidroz, 2009; Crenshaw, 1989, 1991).

Another way to think about the concepts of multiple minority status and intersectionality is to consider privilege and how it may moderate the experience of disability. Class privilege may offset or dilute discrimination or oppression both economically and socially (Vernon, 1999), if a person with a disability has access to financial resources to pay for transportation or a home health care worker, for example. Wealth gives one greater control over one's environment, thus potentially mitigating the effects of institutional discrimination in a society that largely ignores the needs of people with disabilities. Additionally, other privileges such as having White skin color, being male, being heterosexual, and being young create qualitative differences among individuals according to the number of societal norms one conforms to or deviates from. Social class, as well as the nature and severity of a person's disability—along with his or her ethnicity, gender, sexual orientation, and age—can amplify or attenuate the experience of disability. Individuals with disabilities from racial/ethnic minority groups, older people, poor or working-class people, gay men, and lesbians all experience oppression uniquely, collectively, or concurrently, depending on the setting and context (Vernon, 1999).

To discuss diversity issues as they relate to disability and group work, this chapter guides the reader to connect the concepts of multiple minority statuses and intersectionality to better understand the lived experiences of persons with disabilities. In reality, when asked "Who are you?" most people would not respond with a single identity. Rather, an individual's sense of self can be based on many groups with which he or she identifies, and people can be defined simultaneously by their race, ethnicity, class, gender, sexual orientation, religion, and other aspects of their identities (Jones, 2009). Therefore, from a group work perspective, we must operate from the stance that the experiences of people within cultural groups are distinctive according to the extent to which they are members of other marginalized or privileged populations and according to how salient one's disability is to one's identity. In other words, a gay Latino man who is disabled might not be more or less oppressed than is his straight, Latino, disabled counterpart; his experiences are uniquely shaped by his multiple identities and unique from those of his counterparts. It is critical to consider the perspective of disabled individuals and whether, and how, other identities may be more or less important aspects of their lives. For facilitators doing group work, it is important that they be able to respond to the needs of these clients and have some understanding of the complexity of identity development, especially considering levels of identification with (or rejection of) minority status (Mpofu & Conyers, 2004).

CULTURAL DIFFERENCES REGARDING DISABILITY

Cultural factors such as family roles, communication patterns, affective styles, values regarding personal control, individualism, and religion each contribute to a person's desire and ability to engage effectively in group counseling. Attitudes toward disability vary by culture and have profound effects on individual experiences of social acceptance. To be effective, facilitators must consider how disability is understood within different cultural groups.

Important cultural differences exist in beliefs about the nature, cause, and treatment of disability. Some cultural groups such as Mexican American, Chinese American, Arab, and Jewish communities tend to view disability as a normal, albeit unique, part of human development (Garcia, Mendez-Perez, & Ortiz, 2000; Mardiros, 1989; McCallion & Janicki, 1997; Reiter, Mar'i, & Rosenberg, 1986) but may perceive disability as fated or destined because of the will of a higher power. Studies have also indicated a variety of cultural explanations for disability that range from medical to metaphysical (Danesco, 2006). Furthermore, cultural groups vary according to how much or how little they view disability as a disease or illness that requires treatment and the extent to which a disability is "curable" (under the control of the individual or family) or "fated" (beyond the control of the individual). These cultural differences are likely to affect how individuals react to their own disability, including the level of psychological distress that they experience as a result of having a disability.

Culture also informs the attitudes, beliefs, and behaviors (i.e., stereotypes) exhibited by and toward individuals with disabilities. Individuals with disabilities might have many common experiences, but racism or other forms of discrimination may change the meaning or intensify the experience of having a disability. With this chapter's focus on intersectionality, it is critical to consider how stereotyping and discrimination can affect individuals with multiple minority statuses. Challenge yourself to think of your own attitudes regarding an old Black man in a wheelchair or a Hispanic lesbian woman with bipolar disorder.

Diversity has historically been examined as differences between racial/ethnic and other minority groups (between-groups differences). Recently, we have begun to recognize the myriad within-group identifications, and as our awareness expands, we continue to acknowledge the complexity and meaning of culture and multiple minority statuses. Stereotyped notions of various minority groups can lead to the denial of the diversity within those groups (Nettles & Balter, 2012). The stigma associated with belonging to one or more minority groups can also lead to the denial of these aspects of identity. Although there is abundant literature on the characteristics of specific minority groups, there is a dearth of information for practitioners who may work with individuals who identify with more than one marginalized group. Group facilitators may feel ill-equipped to address the needs of individuals with multiple minority statuses, and even those with strong multicultural counseling skills may not have had many opportunities to apply their skills in their work with individuals with multiple minority statuses. The purpose of the remaining sections of this chapter is to discuss the implications for practice of working with clients who identify with more than one marginalized group.

MULTIPLE IDENTITIES AND MENTAL HEALTH

Unfortunately, many individuals with multiple minority identities are likely to face serious stressors with the potential to affect their mental health. Very little research exists regarding the psychological impact of multiple minority statuses, but it is thought that individuals who struggle with multiple forms of discrimination may feel more socially isolated as they struggle to belong to any one group with which they identify. Ethnic minorities with disabilities, who struggle with discrimination on two fronts, may find it more difficult to overcome negative stereotypes for either of their minority statuses (Block, Balcazar, & Keys, 2001) and receive needed social support, although this experience may be less true for people who have a less visible disability.

As people accumulate marginalized statuses, they might experience compounded "minority stresses" that put them at greater risk for mental health and substance abuse disorders (Cochran, Mays, Alegria, Ortega, & Takeuchi, 2007). For example, negative mental health outcomes, such as increased anxiety and depression, are more pronounced for gay racial minorities than for their White (European American) counterparts (Balsam, Lehavot, Beadnell, & Circo, 2010). Trauma might also put some individuals at greater risk for mental health diagnoses, such as posttraumatic stress disorder (PTSD). Furthermore, individuals with multiple minority statuses are also more likely to be overdiagnosed with mental disorders and are at greater risk of not receiving needed treatment (Agency for Healthcare Research and Quality, 2010). Conversely, multiple minority statuses can also serve as the underpinning of psychological resilience if the individual developed in a relatively safe environment with access to social support and opportunities (Greene, 2003). The degree to which certain forms of discrimination were temporary or flexible during the individual's life may also be a factor in resilience (Jones, 1997).

MULTIPLE IDENTITIES AND GROUP WORK

Group counseling is different from individual counseling in that it occurs in a group setting with one or two facilitators who facilitate the process. Unlike individual counseling, the group itself serves as the agent of change, and interpersonal and group dynamics are in constant interplay in group counseling (Corey, 2016). In group counseling, the facilitator not only hears about the individuals' presenting concerns but sees them play out in the group setting, because people tend to function within the group as they do in relationships and the world outside of the group.

Although the American Counseling Association (ACA) has recognized the need to address the mental health concerns of members of marginalized groups, the organization has yet to incorporate specific best-practice guidelines for multicultural competence in working with individuals with multiple minority identities. One concern about the inclusion of other diverse identities with regard to multicultural counseling competencies is the potential to avoid the discomfort of addressing racism or other "-isms" (Sue & Sue, 2015). However, failure to consider multiple identities in counseling practice is arguably as harmful as ignoring ethnic/racial or other discrete forms of identity altogether. For more information regarding multicultural counseling competencies, including client worldview, the reader can refer to the recently published *Multicultural and Social Justice Counseling Competencies* (Ratts et al., 2015).

When we consider all the various aspects of identity—including race/ethnicity, sex, sexual orientation, disability, and so on—we see that identities intersect within the broader cultural context to create multiple, complex structures of privilege and disadvantage within marginalized groups. Racial/ethnic minorities, gay and lesbian people, older people, people with disabilities, and so on, who are marginalized within their ethnic/racial group, may experience their ethnicity and group membership distinctly differently than their groups' more privileged members. Individuals with multiple identities may experience simultaneous oppression, and questions about those experiences may never be explored if we do not consider attending to all aspects of clients' identities.

An understanding of multiple minority identities is vitally important to effective group counseling. For group facilitators and members, viewing identity development through a multiple minority lens necessitates a more complete understanding of within-group differences. The ability to attend to these differences creates a greater potential to bring about therapeutic change in minority and multiple minority, as well as majority, individuals (Nettles, 2012). Group counseling is a unique modality that uses the "between" interactions to foster "within" or intrapersonal growth and wellness. Individuals with multiple minority identities are often faced with the need to work on psychological tasks related to aspects of the self and relationships to other minorities and the majority culture as well. Thus, group work can provide a powerful way for clients to experience the therapeutic benefits of working on these tasks simultaneously through their interactions with the facilitator and other group members. For the group facilitator, a major responsibility lies in creating a sense of cohesiveness within the group while fostering integration of multiple minority identities that may exist within each member and between each member and the facilitator (Nettles, 2012). Ideally, the group should represent a place where the group members feel their identities are fully accepted and validated by the facilitator.

Group members should be able to experience and benefit from all aspects of the group, including "cultural transference" to the facilitator and other group members (Bonovitz, 2005). For example, histories associated with poverty may include unique cultural experiences, some of which could be interpreted pathologically. To the extent that these histories involve minority cultural issues, a cultural interpretation may be more appropriate. In group counseling, the ability to frame cultural issues as they surface in group interactions, and to balance the focus on psychological and cultural aspects of human functioning, can be considered an important aspect of multicultural competence (Nettles, 2012). Other key elements of multicultural competence include awareness of issues related to discrimination, oppression, and privilege, including the ability to accept others' worldviews (Sue & Sue, 2015). Effective group facilitators must also be able to develop a sense of within-group as well as between-groups comfort for the group members that goes beyond simply feeling competent to work with individuals from a group different from their own (Nettles, 2012).

SUMMARY

In practice, facilitators are likely to engage with clients with disabilities from diverse cultural backgrounds, many of whom will have multiple minority identities. Diversity in cultural and minority group membership, within and between group members, and between group members and group facilitators requires facilitators to pay particular attention to how these differences might play out during group counseling. Effective group facilitators have an ethical obligation to help group members work on fully integrating aspects of the self while also working on psychological tasks associated with integrating aspects of multiple minority group membership. Only by fully accepting and validating all facets of group members' identities can group members experience the therapeutic benefits of group counseling.

KEY TERMS

Class: a person's economic position within a society.

Communicative self-representation: the right to self-identify or to refer to oneself in self-chosen or preferred terms.

Diversity: individuals representing more than one national origin, race, ethnicity, religion, socioeconomic stratum, sexual orientation, and so forth.

Ethnicity: a social group that shares a common and distinctive culture, religion, language, or the like.

Intersectionality: the study of intersections between forms or systems of oppression, domination, or discrimination.

Marginalization: social disadvantage; relegation to an unimportant or powerless position in society.

Minority: a culturally, ethnically, or racially distinct group that coexists with but is subordinate to a more dominant group in a society.

Privilege: the sociological concept that some groups of people have advantages in relation to other groups.

Race: as a social construct, a group of people who share similar and distinct physical characteristics.

Sexual orientation: a person's sexual identity in relation to the gender to which they are attracted.

Stigma: extreme disapproval (by others in society) of individuals who differ from cultural norms.

RECOMMENDATIONS FOR PRACTICE

1. Develop awareness of your own cultural identity, including aspects of privilege that may affect your ability to work effectively with diverse clients.
2. Consult with other professionals who differ from you in cultural and minority identifications. When appropriate, cofacilitate groups with such individuals.
3. Maintain ongoing consultation and professional development related to group work that is oriented toward multicultural competence.

4. If a group member has a visible disability, other members may assume that is the salient aspect of her or his identity. Such assumptions should be challenged so that each member is free to identify in the way most important to him or her. The facilitator must allow all members to define who they are and how they choose to engage in the group.

5. In a group for persons with disabilities, or with specific disabilities, other components of identity also must be valued and explored as appropriate. For some members, the way in which persons with disabilities are regarded in their cultural group may present more challenges than the disability itself. Those who are LGBT with a disability may struggle on several fronts. These issues are grist for the group mill.

6. In a group to raise awareness of disability issues, an activity around multiple identities would be very beneficial. See Chapter 14 for ideas.

chapter 5
GROUP COMPOSITION

In their meta-analysis of the group psychotherapy literature, Burlingame, Fuhriman, and Mosier (2003) commented on the importance of group composition for the effectiveness of treatment. Groups are extremely complex entities with great potential to help clients, but they must be assembled with care to create optimal dynamics for growth.

THE FACILITATOR

Rhoda Olkin (1999) is a psychologist who also has a disability (postpolio syndrome). She wrestled with the question of whether a nondisabled person can be an effective therapist for persons with disabilities. She concluded that the extant research did not provide a clear answer to that question. She offered her own views on the debate and suggested that clinicians need to engage in serious reflection to identify their own biases with respect to disability. She noted that persons with disabilities are not immune to having negative biases and, in fact, may have internalized many of the negative valuations that they have encountered regarding their disability. Olkin believed that one cannot be an effective counselor for persons with disabilities unless one recognizes and embraces the social minority model of disability, described in Chapters 1 and 2 of this book. Furthermore, she argued that awareness of how language conveys attitudes and values toward disabilities is essential in those who treat persons with disabilities.

Reeve (2000) pointed out that counselors are people who live in our society and, as such, are subject to developing negative attitudes about disabilities. She believed that particular training is necessary to ensure that counselors who work with clients with disabilities are aware of their own biases and work to correct them.

Therefore, before we embark on a discussion of the composition of group membership, we touch briefly on the question of characteristics of the group leader in groups in which at least one member has a disability. The literature offers very little guidance on this issue, although a few empirical studies are relevant. This issue is not unique to groups with persons with disabilities, however, and we draw from our clinical experience to address the characteristics of an effective group leader for groups with persons with disabilities.

An early study (Strohmer & Biggs, 1983) found that the ratings of effectiveness and attractiveness of counselors by a sample of 40 persons with mobility disabilities did not differ by the disability status (disabled or nondisabled) of the counselor. Similar results were reported by Haley and Dowd (1988), who found that the counselor's disability status (deaf or hearing) was not associated with the participants' (106 deaf adolescents) willingness to see the counselor or their perceptions of the counselor's empathy and social influence. What did make a difference on these variables was the counselor's ability to communicate using sign language or an interpreter. This suggests that the salient factor was the ability to communicate, not the counselor's hearing status per se. A third analogue study investigated the influence of counselor self-disclosure about his or her disability on nondisabled college student participants' assessments of the counselors' expertness, trustworthiness, and attractiveness. The disabled counselors received equivalent or more positive ratings on all variables. Rated most highly on attractiveness were counselors with a nonvisible disability who disclosed their disability. There were no differences in participants' willingness to see the counselors portrayed in the stimulus videos.

Anecdotal reports from persons with disabilities who have participated in groups with nondisabled counselors suggest that although nondisabled counselors can be effective facilitators of groups of persons with disabilities, their knowledge of disabilities (including the specific disabilities of group members) and their use of appropriate language are critical in how they are perceived by members. TS recalled that the counselor who facilitated the high school group she attended was nondisabled and did not appear to understand the disability perspective. There is jargon, or slang, used by some subgroups within the disability community that was unknown to the counselor. She also used outdated language (e.g., handicapped), which suggested to members that she was insensitive. The counselor also did not seem to expect that although all students in the group had disabilities, they were different in many important ways.

Perhaps more important than disability status is the facilitator's openness to learn from group members and an acknowledgment of their limitations, noted TS. It is also essential that group facilitators, regardless of disability status, realize that even individuals with the same disability have very varied experiences; one must never assume or imply that one knows the experience of a member because one knows the disability.

STRUCTURAL ASPECTS

Size

Although not strictly an issue of composition, components of group structure may need attention when the group is for, or includes, people with disabilities. One such feature is the size of the group. Although psychoeducational groups are often larger than are counseling or therapy groups, when clients with disabilities are the members, that rule of thumb may need to be discarded. For example, in Chapter 2, we discussed the importance of health maintenance among persons with a variety of disabilities. Although this topic could be presented in a dyadic manner, and handouts used to list additional resources, this would not be the best approach with a group for persons with disabilities. The barriers they face are significant, and these may need to be discussed and processed in some depth to make the concepts more relevant. There may be more questions that would be less likely to be asked in a larger group, and the need to acknowledge the substantial challenges (including low income, transportation and accessibility problems, lack of support, etc.) cannot be overstated. In addition, members of the group might not be aware of their rights under the ADA and Section 504 of the Rehabilitation Act of 1973 (34 C.F.R. Part 104), which was the first legislation to guarantee rights of persons with disabilities; instruction and practice in self-advocacy may be very important in such groups. All of this requires a smaller group than would traditionally be considered appropriate for a psychoeducational group.

TM, a counselor mentioned elsewhere in this book, conducts counseling and support groups for persons with mixed disabilities. There might be persons with various physical disabilities and others with major depression or schizoaffective disorder in the same group. Helping members find commonalities across their disabilities is a critical task in such groups, and keeping the size of the group manageable (maximum of six members) is essential. Furthermore, when one also takes into account that some clients have multiple disabilities, and others bring histories of trauma and abuse along with their disabilities, TM is acutely aware of the sensitivity and reactivity that can permeate the group; having too many members, with all the many possible interaction patterns, can make it too overwhelming to note and process all of those issues.

Setting

Setting is an important consideration for several reasons. First, any group that includes a person with a disability (and referring to our mention of universal design earlier in this book, any group) needs to be accessible for members. That means the room needs to be accessible to transportation and parking, and in the physical setup of the room, but also private and free of distraction. For example, persons with hearing impairments or difficulties in attention and concentration may be unable to focus on the conversation in the room if there are distractions coming from the hallway, sounds from forced air systems, and other sources (e.g., a telephone ringing in the room).

Given that many group members have not always been treated respectfully in agencies or public facilities, a pleasant and welcoming atmosphere accomplishes a great deal toward creating a positive climate. Designating a room that does not have a shared function and that has plants, comfortable seating, soothing colors, and other homey touches makes a statement about the nature of the place and the group. Although it is not always possible to have a dedicated space for groups, it should be a goal, and when not available, every effort should be made to make the room as pleasant as possible. In addition, physical obstacles (for persons with mobility impairments) should be moved before the arrival of the group. Enough space to allow for seating in a circular arrangement is also necessary. Although economics and other constraints may make these recommendations difficult to incorporate, counselors are advocates for the clients and should continually make the case for the importance of the setting for group development.

Length and Duration

The appropriate length and duration of a group is a complicated decision. The facilitator needs to consider the goals and membership of the group and the capacity of the group. For example, for groups with persons with attentional disabilities, shorter group sessions would be most beneficial. A group for persons with visual impairments who have high intellectual abilities might profit from longer sessions to allow for deeper exploration and processing. To some degree, the larger the group, the longer the sessions need to be to ensure that all members have an opportunity to participate. However, longer groups might be difficult for some individuals with chronic pain or orthopedic disabilities. The type of group (psychoeducational, counseling, therapy) will also influence this decision, because therapy groups and some counseling groups will likely require longer sessions to accommodate the complex work to be done.

Duration of a group might be limited by external constraints and the presence or not of a waiting list, for example. A counselor may be the only one offering groups in a particular setting, and having groups of long duration keeps other members from participating. One solution is an open group, in which members enter and leave at various points according to their individual needs. Open groups are common in hospitals and rehabilitation centers, where individuals who have recently sustained disabilities are being admitted and discharged on a rolling basis. TM indicates that though that is the format dictated by the external requirements at her agency, she finds that the entries and exits slow the progress of the group, so that when new members join, the group development may regress to earlier levels of trust and sharing. In my own clinical experience, the open group format turned out to provide excellent opportunities for members to reassess their goals, share their progress to date, and practice newly acquired social skills.

Homogeneous or Heterogeneous Groups

One of the most important decisions the group counselor must make is whether to have a homogeneous or a heterogeneous group. This is true for any group, but for groups whose members include persons with disabilities, it may be even more critical to make the right decision. People with disabilities are the largest minority group in the United States (Brabender, Fallon, & Smolar, 2004), yet they often experience marginalization from the mainstream culture. It is important that they are not further mistreated in group counseling. The composition of the group has a significant impact on the experiences of members, so the decision about homogeneity or heterogeneity is an important one that must be made prior to the beginning of the group.

When we speak of homogeneity in a group, we typically refer to a group whose members share a specific presenting problem. However, Adler (1995) pointed out that there are a number of characteristics on which groups can be homogeneous other than the presenting problem. For example, grouping can be based on age, sex, culture or ethnicity, race, or disability and on such characteristics as ego strength, even motivation to change. However, Adler was adamant that regardless of other similarities or differences, members must share the goals of the group if the group is to be therapeutic. This means that the facilitator must be very explicit about those goals and even about the therapeutic techniques that are likely to be used so that the potential member and the counselor can be certain that he or she is aligned with the goals. This discussion should occur in the screening interview.

There is a widely held view that a group whose members share the same problem will become cohesive more quickly than would a heterogeneous group. Unger (1989) observed that these groups tend to have better attendance, less conflict, and quicker results. Lieberman, Wizlenberg, Golant, and DiMinno (2005) cited previous research in support of the position that homogeneity in groups is associated with higher levels of cohesiveness and satisfaction with the group experience. A woman who participated in several group experiences for persons with disabilities as a teenager and young adult confirmed this bit of conventional wisdom. In those groups, she reported, the members had much to discuss about their experiences of being marginalized and treated as a curiosity by nondisabled persons, and they welcomed the opportunity to talk about these events with others who they believed would easily identify with their frustrations.

Homogeneity is particularly important for relatively short-term groups. Lieberman et al. (2005) tested their hypothesis that this would be the case for an online 20-week support group for people with Parkinson's disease with goals of reducing feelings of loss of hope, loss of control, and unwanted aloneness. In their study, the researchers studied online groups, because all interactions were preserved and could be analyzed as text. Their experimental groups were homogeneous for time since diagnosis; there were three control groups that were heterogeneous on that factor. As was expected, they found that participants in the homogeneous groups were more attracted and committed to their groups than were those in the heterogeneous groups. They also found that this cohesion developed within the first 5 weeks of the groups. In addition, those in the homogeneous groups showed significantly greater improvement in depression and severity of Parkinson's symptoms than did those in the other groups, but there was no difference between the two compositions for a quality-of-life measure.

Another study investigated group composition on the basis of homogeneity of a personality variable: quality of object relations (QOR; Piper, Ogrodniczuk, Joyce, Weidman, & Rosie, 2007). QOR refers to a trait that encompasses the individual's tendency to establish certain kinds of relationships with others. One's QOR can be primitive, searching, controlling, triangular, or mature. All of the 110 outpatient participants in the 18 groups shared the problem of complicated bereavement. The groups met for 90 minutes weekly for 12 weeks and were either interpretive (psychodynamic) or supportive, following manualized guides. Groups were either homogeneous for QOR or heterogeneous for that trait. Findings did not support the hypothesis that homogeneous groups would result in better outcomes. Regardless of the type of therapy or the individual QOR rating, groups that had a higher proportion of members with mature QOR had better outcomes on general symptoms and grief symptoms for everyone in the group. They also discovered that members with high QOR had better outcomes in the interpretive groups and that members with lower QOR scores did better in supportive groups.

This raises another consideration for the group leader: Are homogeneous groups better for some approaches to counseling and heterogeneous ones for other approaches? Clearly, for psychoanalytic approaches, heterogeneity is essential (Wolf, 1999) because that provides more opportunities for recapitulation of the primary transference objects and situation. From this theoretical perspective, a homogeneous group leads to an unspoken expectation of conformity and denies the members the challenge that comes from interactions with those who represent very different aspects and types.

In discussing group composition for members with chronic mental illness, Stone (1996) proposed that the diagnosis is less important than is the individual's level of functioning. He gave the example of a group for patients with schizophrenia who could have difficulty interacting with others. He believed that they would fare better in a group heterogeneous for diagnosis. We discuss this in some detail in Chapter 9 when we talk about groups for persons with psychiatric disabilities. In addition, the more restrictive the criteria for inclusion, the more difficult it will be to find a sufficient number of members to constitute a viable group. Stone believed that a wide age range is not problematic, but cautioned that a very large imbalance (mostly elderly individuals with one young adult, or vice versa) is contraindicated, whereas a range of several decades can provide opportunities for therapeutic engagement.

Brabender et al. (2004) believed that groups that are homogeneous for a presenting problem can unintentionally ignore important diversity in the group that affects the group's functioning. They embrace the addressing framework that was originally proposed by Hays (1996). Although the model does not include every conceivable aspect of diversity, it uses the letters of the word *addressing* as an acronym to think about clinically relevant factors on which group composition might be built: *a*ge, *d*evelopmental or acquired *d*isability, *r*eligion and spiritual orientation, *e*thnicity, *s*ocioeconomic status, *s*exual orientation, *i*ndigenous heritage, *n*ational origin, and *g*ender. The lesson is that disability is only one of many characteristics of an individual, and automatically assuming that it is the most salient, or even the defining, characteristic is insensitive at best. Counselors facilitating groups with persons with disabilities need to understand the meaning of the disability to the member in order to make good decisions about group composition.

We look now at the advantages and disadvantages of the heterogeneous and homogeneous groups for each of the types of groups from Merchant's (2013) framework. If a group is for a specific disability (e.g., persons with SCIs), does that make it homogeneous? To answer the question, we first need to know the goal of the group. Table 5.1 presents an overview of ways in which groups can be composed and the advantages and disadvantages of homogeneity on a given variable.

TABLE 5.1

Considerations Regarding Group Homogeneity

Group Goal	Population	Homogeneous for ...	Advantage	Disadvantage
Increased adjustment to disability	Individuals with specific disability	Onset (congenital vs. acquired)	Need to explain condition to others is reduced; friendships may develop.	May obscure common issues; may assume disability is primary defining attribute.
		Time since onset	Cohesion is likely to develop quickly.	Progression of disability varies across individuals.
		Degree of impairment	Tendency toward unfavorable comparison is reduced.	May lead to belief that improvement is unlikely, loss of hope, or both.
		Age	Issues are likely to be generational; impact of disability varies across life span.	May minimize contributions that could be made by older/younger members.[a]
		Gender	Some issues (e.g., sexual assault) might be easier to discuss in single-sex group.	
To increase understanding of disabilities in nondisabled people	General public; students; future educators; mental health professionals	Desire to increase sensitivity to persons with disabilities	Provide opportunity to dispel stereotypes, talk openly about myths, exchange information, etc.	If a number of disabilities are represented, logistical issues may be challenging (e.g., accommodating for wheelchair, interpreter). Facilitator must be very alert to reactions and responses of members and to ensure all members have opportunity to participate.

(Continued)

73

TABLE 5.1 (*Continued*)

Considerations Regarding Group Homogeneity

Group Goal	Population	Homogeneous for …	Advantage	Disadvantage
To increase support and developing coping strategies for presenting problem (e.g., divorce, loss of job)	General population	Identified problem	All members share same concern; cohesion develops rapidly; many therapeutic factors evident. Therapist models appropriate language and communication etiquette.	The effect of the disability on the problem may be ignored. The meaning of the disability and its relation to the presenting problem may be overlooked.
		Age/gender	Members may feel more easily understood; impact of some problems varies by gender (e.g., women tend to suffer greater economic impact after divorce; the loss of a spouse may be more traumatic at age 40 than at age 80).	The opportunity to learn from the other group is absent; members who are similar on many variables do not have opportunity to see progress in others who are further along in the healing.

[a]Heterogeneous grouping that results in a majority of members in one age group could minimize the contributions of those in the minority age group.

To make decisions about the composition of the group, the counselor must have considerable knowledge about the potential members. It is necessary to include questions in the interview regarding disability, even if none is apparent, because there are numerous disabilities that are not visible.

Heterogeneous groups offer possibilities for growth that may not be present in homogeneous groups (Unger, 1989). For example, one way that members profit in a group is by learning from other members who are different from them. One member may observe another member coping with a difficulty in a way that he or she had not considered and decide to emulate that model. The number of kinds of interactions and transferences are greater, and members can receive feedback about how others respond to them. This can be very powerful when those other members do not share the same problem. However, conflict is more likely to emerge in a heterogeneous group; conflict can be positive and growth enhancing, but it also has the potential to be damaging to the group process if not managed carefully. Probably the most important consideration for heterogeneity is the similarity to the world outside of a group. If the goal of the group is, for example, to improve daily functioning or to assist with work-related challenges, then having a membership that is as diverse as the real-world context will provide the best opportunity to test one's skills. Perhaps some members with disabilities are coping well with the impairments but are frustrated with the struggle to fit in with nondisabled persons. Again, the group that is heterogeneous for type of disability or on all variables is most likely to provide learning opportunities.

Although heterogeneous groups have many advantages, as has been shown above, there are some kinds of disabilities that are best treated in homogeneous groups. These include groups for members with IDs, some cognitive disabilities, and communication disabilities. For intellectual and cognitive disabilities, the process may move more slowly than in other groups, which is appropriate for those members but might be frustrating to other members. To avoid possible scapegoating of the member and to ensure that the member has the opportunity to profit from a meaningful group designed to meet his or her needs—including perhaps shorter sessions, more frequent summaries of content, and more explicit modeling by the therapist—it may be best if those clients are served in homogeneous groups.

For clients with communication disabilities, there are several possibilities. If they are able to communicate effectively using a keyboard, online groups might be very appropriate, either synchronous or asynchronous. If keyboarding is not possible, the facilitator may need to explore having a group for persons with similar difficulties and make adaptations to the slower pace of interaction. The facilitator would need to be respectful of members and allow them to communicate in whatever manner and at whatever speed is necessary. For example, the facilitator must avoid finishing sentences or supplying words for the client (Olkin, 1999). However, particularly when speech is slurred or articulation difficulties are present, the facilitator may need to use skills such as paraphrasing to a greater degree to ensure that the member's communication is correctly heard by all members of the group. When assistive devices are available—speech boards, speech synthesizers—and comfortable for clients, they should be supported. The point is that the client should determine the most comfortable way to communicate in the group, and the facilitator must model patience and respect. This is likely to happen most smoothly in a homogeneous group.

Unger (1989) suggested that when members suffer from embarrassment about their problem or feel isolated, a homogeneous group might provide the best outcomes, because they can realize that others share their predicament. This might be an important consideration in deciding whether a group that is homogeneous by disability is indicated.

SUMMARY

In this chapter, we have discussed the many factors that must be considered when deciding on group composition and on which leader is appropriate for a given group. We have suggested that there is no formula or decision tree that will cover all the circumstances of a group, so the skilled leader, armed with the information from this chapter, must make an educated decision on the basis of the available information. It is important that the ethical mandate to "do no harm" be foremost in planning; thoughtful screening interviews are imperative to ensure that all members are appropriate for the group and to provide the facilitator with needed information about disabilities present in the members. Counselors are obligated to ensure that the group experiences in which clients participate provide opportunities for growth and healing.

KEY TERMS

Composition: the characteristics of the members of the group.

Facilitator: counselor who plans and conducts a group.

Heterogeneous: groups in which members differ on a particular characteristic.

Homogeneous: groups in which members are alike on a particular characteristic.

Structure: the arrangements that must be decided prior to beginning the group.

RECOMMENDATIONS FOR PRACTICE

1. Once the type of group has been decided, the facilitator should conduct screening interviews with members to determine salient information and appropriateness for the planned group.
2. Given the information obtained in the interview, make a decision regarding the homogeneity or heterogeneity of the group. Table 5.1 in this chapter can help in making that decision.
3. The structural characteristics can be determined once the facilitator knows the disabilities and needs of members.
4. Depending on the number of members, facilitators might wish to conduct outreach to local agencies, physicians, and other sources of referrals to recruit an optimal number of members.
5. Consider working with a cofacilitator if that is possible. Ensure that a potential cofacilitator has the appropriate knowledge, attitudes, and skills.
6. Prepare an informed consent document to present to those who will be in the group. A good model for this document can be found here: http://therapychanges.com/wp-content/uploads/2015/09/ConsentTreatment_2015_TC.pdf. This one is quite detailed and complete.
7. If this is a psychoeducational group, plan the schedule of topics and activities in advance but allow for flexibility as the group develops. Arrange for any speakers and prepare handouts in accessible formats.

chapter 6
ETHICAL CONSIDERATIONS

This chapter reviews a number of ethical considerations, many of which are useful in thinking about working with diverse groups, but which may be particularly important for facilitators in working with people with disabilities. Several professional guidelines exist to guide group facilitators in working with people with disabilities, including the 2014 *ACA Code of Ethics* (ACA, 2014), the Commission on Rehabilitation Counselor Certification's (CRCCs; 2009) *Code of Professional Ethics for Rehabilitation Counselors*, the Association for Specialists in Group Work's (ASGW's) *Best Practice Guidelines* (Thomas & Pender, 2008), and the ASGW *Multicultural and Social Justice Competence Principles for Group Workers* (Singh, Merchant, Skudrzyk, & Ingene, 2012).

GROUP COMPOSITION:
CHOOSING INCLUSION VERSUS EXCLUSION

There are many reasons for adopting a bias that favors inclusion of members with disabilities versus exclusion. First and foremost is the consideration that disability is a characteristic that is part of the natural human condition. People who have disabilities are much more similar to those without disabilities than they are different from them in their wants, needs, and desires, and facilitators and group members alike will quickly learn this while also benefitting from learning firsthand about the experiences associated with having a disability. Despite any discomfort on the facilitator's and members' parts, it is also important to remember that people with disabilities have the same right to access all of the advantages of groups in addressing their issues as anyone else. Counselors can do significant harm by turning away individuals seeking help solely on the basis of a disability. The implicit message is "You're not good enough" or "You make me uncomfortable and I don't want to be around you." Remember, in some cases, the stress of managing similar implicit messages on a day-to-day basis may be part of what brought the individual to the counselor for help. To receive the message from the helper is doubly traumatizing.

In addition to the moral harm argument for favoring inclusion versus exclusion, to deliberately deny access solely on the basis of a disability is discriminatory and expressly prohibited by the ACA *Code of Ethics*. The ACA *Code of Ethics* (ACA, 2014) defines *discrimination* in the glossary as "the prejudicial treatment of an individual or group based on their actual or perceived membership in a particular group, class, or category" (p. 20) and specifically states in Standard C.5 that

> counselors do not condone or engage in discrimination against prospective or current clients, students, employees, supervisees, or research participants based on age, culture, disability, ethnicity, race, religion/spirituality, gender, gender identity, sexual orientation, marital/partnership status, language preference, socioeconomic status, immigration status, or any basis proscribed by law. (p. 9)

Although the injunction against discrimination has been present in the ACA *Code* through a number of revisions, the list of the bases on which discrimination is prohibited has grown with each revision. Prior to the 2014 *Code* revision, this standard applied only to clients, assumed by most to be individuals with whom a counseling relationship had been established. By adding the phrase "current or prospective clients," the authors of the 2014 *Code* clearly intended to give the message that denying access to counseling on any of the listed bases, including the presence of a disability, is unethical, and to do so would constitute a breach of ethics.

There are also legal, as well as ethical, reasons to seek inclusion. Recognizing the historic discrimination and exclusion of individuals with disabilities from participation in many of the rights and privileges available to others, the authors of the ADA, in Title III, required specific actions to ensure that public accommodations are accessible and that discrimination is not a factor in lack of access. Public accommodations include counseling organizations, hospitals, private practices, rehabilitation agencies, and other venues in which counselors might provide group counseling services. Denying access to membership in a group on the basis of considerations such as physical accessibility or needs that are reasonably easily accommodated is illegal.

Some facilitators might feel that their relative inexperience with a particular disability or with people with disabilities generally creates competency concerns and may feel that a referral to someone who is more knowledgeable about working with disabilities is called for on ethical grounds (Mason, 2007). After all, both ACA and CRCC, in their respective codes of ethics, address the need for counselors to be competent. There are multiple problems with this perspective. First of all, the ACA *Code of Ethics* is clear that "whereas multicultural counseling competency is required across all counseling specialties, counselors gain knowledge, personal awareness, sensitivity, dispositions, and skills pertinent to being a culturally competent counselor in working with a diverse client population" (ACA, 2014, p. 8, Standard C.2.a.), accompanied by the caveat that "while developing skills in new specialty areas, counselors take steps to ensure the competence of their work and protect others from possible harm" (p. 8, Standard C.2.b.). Such steps in this case might include doing some reading and research; discussing the issue with the client and determining whether or not he or she is comfortable with helping you to understand his or her life view and pertinent aspects of disability culture; or consulting with a rehabilitation counselor skilled in working with this client population. The ASGW *Multicultural and Social Justice Competence Principles for Group Workers* (Singh et al., 2012) are clear that group facilitators are expected to develop competencies in three domains when working with diverse populations: (1) awareness of self and group members, (2) strategies and skills (group worker planning, group worker performing and processing), and (3) social justice advocacy.

Having argued for adopting a bias for inclusion, it must be said that counselors also have obligations to engage in a screening process prior to selection for group membership (ACA, 2014; Thomas & Pender, 2008), and sound reasons do exist for screening out individuals. Both the ACA *Code of Ethics* and the CRCC *Code of Professional Ethics* state that the screening process should result, to the extent possible, in the selection of members "whose needs and goals are compatible with the goals of the group, who will not impede the group process, and whose well-being will not be jeopardized by the group experience" (ACA, 2014, p. 6, Standard A.9.a.; CRCC, 2009, p. 6). The presence of a disability, in and of itself, should never be considered the basis for being screened out, but there may be very legitimate and important reasons connected to an individual's disability that constitute a legitimate reason for noninclusion in a given group. Erford (2011) discussed two potential pitfalls of group therapy with individuals with disabilities. He noted that research conducted by Kissane et al. (1997) found that members who dropped out of treatment reported that the group therapy was simply too anxiety provoking. Furthermore, Spiegel et al. (1999) found that when members of the group interact with other members who have experienced advances in their disease or who do not appear to be adjusting well, there is the potential for a great deal of distress. It is important to note that this is not always the case. Just as people who are newly diagnosed differ in the amount of information that they can and wish to take in at first, some individuals want and need to get a complete picture of what kinds of complications they might expect. If an individual is likely to be overwhelmed by confronting the future, or if there is not a full understanding of the risks attendant to the emotional impact of such interactions, the situation could result in harm to the client and harm to the group at large. Consequently, facilitators should discuss this possibility with prospective members who have progressive disabilities or for whom the likelihood of serious complications is high, when other members' disabilities are further progressed or they are experiencing great difficulties in adjustment. An additional consideration is mentioned by Greer (2002), who noted that various theoretical approaches may be more appropriate with some individuals than with others. For example, he noted that cognitive models may be more appropriate for patients recently diagnosed with a chronic illness and that supportive–expressive types of therapy that incorporate discussion about existential concerns may be more useful for persons with advanced illnesses. Although this may be a consideration in an ideal world in which multiple groups using different theoretical approaches are readily available, it is probably more realistic to opt for inclusion, assuming that the risk of harm for all is minimal, and incorporating aspects of both approaches. Finally, as discussed elsewhere in this book, various issues related to working with individuals with psychiatric or cognitive disabilities may result in exclusion, based on the potential for scapegoating, aggressive behaviors, or the need for changes in group structure and process to accommodate problems in attending, concentrating, or other cognitive issues.

INFORMED CONSENT

The importance of ensuring that the decision to engage in a group is made only with fully informed consent is critically important for all members of a group. Section A.7.b of the ASGW *Best Practice Guidelines* reads,

> Group Workers facilitate informed consent. They communicate information in ways that are both developmentally and culturally appropriate. Group Workers provide in oral and written form to prospective members (when appropriate to group type): the professional disclosure statement; group purpose and goals; group participation expectations including voluntary and involuntary membership; role expectations of members and leader(s); policies related to entering and exiting the group; policies governing substance use; policies and procedures governing mandated groups (where relevant); documentation requirements; disclosure of information to others; implications of out-of-group contact or involvement among members; procedures for consultation between group leader(s) and group member(s); fees and time parameters; and potential impacts of group participation. (Thomas & Pender, 2008, p. 114)

Furthermore, they add in §A.7.c that "Group Workers obtain the appropriate consent/assent forms for work with minors and other dependent group members" (p. 114). The key consideration here in working with group members with cognitive or intellectual disabilities is the injunction to communicate the specified information "in ways that *are both developmentally and culturally appropriate* [italics added]" (p. 114). Achieving fully informed consent is always challenging (Shaw, Chan, & Lam, 2004) but is especially challenging when working with someone with limitations in cognition or intellect. The CRCC *Code of Professional Ethics* goes even further to ensure that informed consent is adequate, requiring that the oral and written review occur "in a manner that best accommodates any of their limitations" (CRCC, 2009, p. 3, Standard A.3.a.). The CRCC *Code* also adds that "rehabilitation counselors recognize that disclosure of all of these issues may need to be reiterated or expanded upon throughout the counseling relationship" (CRCC, 2009, p. 4, Standard A.3.a.). Obviously, counselors should carefully explain all of the above in writing and orally, with both the written material and the discussion occurring in clear and simple language, matched to the reading level and cognitive abilities of the client. Shaw and Tarvydas (2001) recommended several strategies for ensuring comprehension that may prove useful with these individuals, including the use of short, highly readable forms; using short sentences, simple vocabulary, and straightforward concepts; using forms as a vehicle for discussion; questioning clients about their understanding of the form; and encouraging clients to take forms home to read in a less stressful atmosphere, with follow-up at the next meeting. Adams and Boyd (2010) noted the difficulties in assessing an individual's capacity to give informed consent and that understanding can fluctuate on the basis of the complexity, degree of cognitive impairment, emotional circumstances and the relative risks and benefits. They observed that people with IDs have a tendency to agree with any questions put to them, so that asking "Do you understand?" is likely to be met with an enthusiastic nod, whether or not there is any understanding present. Adams and Boyd recommended using "either/or" instead of "yes/no" questions, using simple grammar and simply constructed questions, and asking for examples to assess understanding. Additionally, both the ACA *Code* and the CRCC *Code* include several additional items that must be disclosed and understood by prospective clients, including the nature of potential risks and benefits of services. Potential group members should be advised that other members are likely to be curious about their disability or needed accommodations and should discuss any potential feelings of embarrassment, as well as preferred ways of addressing any anxiety those feelings may evoke.

CONFIDENTIALITY AND SOCIALIZING

The difficulties in ensuring confidentiality in group settings are well known (M. S. Corey, Corey, & Corey, 2013; Gladding, 2015; Johnson & Johnson, 2008). Group members, unbound by codes of ethics and licensure boards, have no professional obligation to ensure confidentiality. Most group experts recommend that the facilitator take such steps as explaining the reasons for and the importance of confidentiality, providing examples of what might go wrong if confidentiality is violated by fellow group members, discussing what to do if confidentiality is violated, and informing all members that confidentiality cannot be guaranteed. For some individuals with disabilities, maintaining confidentiality may prove especially challenging. For example, individuals with TBI or other cognitive disabilities may forget the facilitator's injunctions because of short-term memory impairment. Additionally, there is a greater risk in groups for some people with disabilities of outside-the-group socialization. Individuals with IDs who live in group homes or individuals attending groups in hospitals or rehabilitation centers may find it more challenging to keep what happens in the group in the group, because they may interact on a daily basis, not only with group members but also with individuals who are staff or friends, or with individuals who are known by everyone in the group. Group conflict can easily spill outside of the group, creating threats to confidentiality and to the cohesiveness of the group.

In these situations, it is particularly important to review the reasons for and importance of maintaining confidentiality, as is described above. Facilitators may wish to make it a practice to review and seek renewal of the group's commitment to confidentiality at the close of every group. Staff in residential treatment centers may be alerted to the need to be watchful for potential breaches and to step in with reminders to take any unfinished business back into the group. An additional issue of concern for individuals with disabilities is ensuring that during the informed consent process, potential exceptions to facilitator confidentiality are discussed and understood.

A particular area of concern in this regard is related to the increased risk of abuse among people with disabilities. Embry and Grossman (2006) noted that children with disabilities are 1.7 times more likely to be abused. Some of the disabilities that have been identified as making people especially vulnerable to abuse include developmental disabilities, intellectual impairments, physical impairments, behavior problems, and chronic health problems (Tutty & Giurgiu, 2010). Being female or older elevates the risk still higher (Teaster, n.d.). Perpetrators are often family members, personal care attendants, and staff (Young, Nosek, Chapping, & Rintala, 1998). Most states have mandatory reporting laws for vulnerable adults that in most cases include people with disabilities, although definitions, processes, and procedures vary from state to state. Group facilitators working with individuals with disabilities will want to be well acquainted with the laws in their jurisdictions and ensure that this important exception to confidentiality is noted.

A final note on confidentiality involves the occasional presence in the group of interpreters or personal care attendants. Interpreters who are certified or are associate members of the Registry of Interpreters for the Deaf adhere to a strict code of ethics that requires them to keep all of the content that they interpret confidential. Although most interpreters will understand that their obligation to confidentiality applies to communications by the other, hearing members of the group as well, it is possible that relatively inexperienced interpreters or interpreters who work only in specific types of situations with limited exposure to groups may benefit from a reminder by the group facilitator that the need to keep all group communications (including those of members for whom the interpreter is not interpreting) confidential applies to everyone present, inclusive of the interpreter. This should occur in advance, because the interpreter will need to focus all attention on his or her interpreting responsibilities during the group. For noncertified individuals or for personal care attendants, there may be little awareness of the need for confidentiality, and the group facilitator should ensure that the importance of confidentiality is impressed upon them.

ONLINE GROUPS

The use of online groups by people with disabilities has expanded greatly in recent years. For many people with disabilities who live in rural areas or have difficulties obtaining accessible and dependable transportation, SHGs can be made available simply by pressing the computer's on switch. These groups are also attractive to caregivers, whose ability to attend an in-person group is limited by caregiving responsibilities. Most of these groups are peer facilitated and fall into the category of SHGs. Finn (1999) described SHGs as being based on "principles of empowerment, inclusion, nonhierarchical decision making, shared responsibility, and a holistic approach to people's cultural, economic and social needs" (p. 220). He discussed several advantages of online self-help groups, including reduced barriers of time, distance, and social status; increased freedom to participate and discuss highly personal issues because of the greater degree of anonymity; the ability to respond and communicate at speeds that accommodate slower response times due to either physical or IDs; and for those who choose not to actively participate, the opportunity for vicarious learning to take place by lurking.

Although these are undeniably great advantages and may help explain the recent dramatic increase in the numbers of such groups, there are also some cautions, many of which have implications for ethical practice. Although some groups are monitored to prevent negative, hostile, or malicious posts, many are not. Because electronic communications are usually anonymous, and because this form of communication lacks the full range of social cues that normally constrain behavior, online communication may be disinhibited and perceived as inconsiderate, rude, or insulting (Avery, 1998; Walther, 1996). Additionally, members may receive misinformation and act on it, only later checking back in to find the information corrected by other members. Finally, this form of group support has been criticized as excluding those who lack access and computer skills, raising social justice concerns. Although most groups are peer facilitated, a particular difficulty may arise for participants who are counselors or other mental health professionals, but who also participate in these groups and may have disabilities themselves. Boundary issues and confusion about their role can become problematic. In such cases, the participant should clearly define his or her role.

Increasing numbers of counselors have also ventured into the world of electronic groups (e-groups) and provide group therapy in an online format. In recent revision of the ACA *Code of Ethics*, issues regarding the provision of counseling using electronic/digital technologies were infused throughout, and a new section titled "Distance Counseling, Technology, and Social Media" was created (Section H). This section includes information to guide counselors in such areas as informed consent and disclosure (§H.2.a.), confidentiality (§H.2.b.), acknowledging limitations on confidentiality (§H.2.c.), the need to ensure confidentiality of information (§H.2.d.), the need to verify the identity of the client (§H.3.), benefits and limitations of using technology applications (§H.4a.), maintaining professional boundaries (§H.4.b.), ensuring that clients are able to use technology appropriately (§H.4.c.), determining the effectiveness and suitability of distance counseling services (§H.4.d.), access to pertinent applications (§H.4.e.), the need to explain differences in communication when using electronic communications and how to prevent and address potential misunderstandings (§H.4.f.), issues surrounding records and web maintenance (§H.5.), and the use of social media (§H.6.). Although not necessarily referring specifically to group counseling or to counseling people with disabilities, it is critically important for counselors who engage in e-group counseling or other online group processes with individuals with disabilities to be fully familiar with and to comply with these standards, given the particular advantages and disadvantages of online groups for people with disabilities, as is discussed above.

SUMMARY

In conclusion, group counseling approaches have great advantages and can potentially be very beneficial for people with disabilities, but with great advantage comes great responsibility. Awareness of ethical guidelines and resources are critical to the ethical practice of group counseling with people with disabilities.

KEY TERMS

Bias: a prejudice for or against one side of a continuum or duality, a preconceived idea of the correct course of action.

Cognitive model: an approach to counseling that views thoughts as the root of problems.

Informed consent: the process of providing full and complete information about a treatment so that the client can decide whether or not to participate. When the client agrees, he or she must have the capacity to understand the information provided.

Intellectual disabilities: impairment in the ability to process and understand information; cognitive abilities that are significantly below average and significantly affect function.

Supportive–expressive counseling: an approach that focuses on supporting the client in his or her struggles and encouraging the expression of emotions.

RECOMMENDATIONS FOR PRACTICE

1. Review the professional guidelines to ensure that you are fully informed of ethical considerations.
2. Seek consultation with colleagues when you are concerned about an existing or potential ethical dilemma.
3. To address the ethical expectation of competence, seek consultation, reading, or both to learn about a group member's disability. Consultation may be with the client.
4. Prepare a thorough and accurate informed consent document (see the "Recommendations for Practice" in Chapter 5 for

sources of sample documents). Emphasize that confidentiality is expected of the member and indicate when confidentiality must be broken by facilitators.

5. Advise potential members with a disability that other members may be curious about their disability.

6. Attend carefully to—and prepare group members for—the importance of confidentiality. This will be especially challenging in settings (residential, hospital, school) in which members have contact with each other outside of the group context. Provide members with examples of situations in which keeping confidentiality may be difficult or awkward, and demonstrate ways to deal with such situations.

7. If you choose to conduct groups online, get professional advice regarding the platforms available, security and privacy measures, and other technical issues. Do not neglect screening and informed consent, and obtain accurate contact information for each member to ensure that his or her identity is as presented. Members can use only first names in the group to preserve privacy.

chapter 7
TRAINING CONSIDERATIONS

So far, we have been building a foundation of information about group work with persons with disabilities. Before we turn to specific disabilities in Part II, we conclude Part I with training considerations for facilitators of such groups. In Chapter 1, we introduced Merchant's (2013) model and applied it to groups with persons with disabilities. The first section of Chapter 7 is on the type of group designed to increase the awareness of group members about issues of diversity as they relate to persons with disabilities. We then examine legal considerations, general etiquette, and the responsibilities of the group practitioner when working with persons with disabilities.

RAISING AWARENESS

We believe the best way to become comfortable around persons with disabilities is to be around persons with disabilities. Graduate students in rehabilitation counseling programs often enter the field because of personal experience; they may have a disability themselves or have a family member or close friend with a disability. Even those individuals with personal experience have to be careful not to assume that because they have a disability, or know about a disability, they know all about disabilities or about all people with disabilities. We stress that each individual with a disability is a unique individual with a unique set of symptoms, attitudes, experiences, and other characteristics. Also, it is important to keep in mind that having a disability does not prevent a person from holding negative attitudes toward disability (Olkin, 1999). Given the negative attitudes toward persons with disabilities with which we are all surrounded, it is understandable that some of those might be internalized.

Awareness Group

One way to understand one's own attitudes and knowledge of disabilities is through reading pertinent literature, taking classes, watching good videos, and so forth. But given that we promote group work as a mechanism for personal growth, it appears fitting to utilize a group as a vehicle to increase self-awareness of counselors and to develop understanding of persons with disabilities. Given that these groups are most likely to occur in university settings as a requirement for counselors in training, we assume a time-limited group (semester long) with a closed membership (students in a counseling class). We hope that facilitators, current or future, who are reading this book, however, will consider conducting groups such as these in kindergarten through Grade 12 schools and community settings to allow a broad section of the population to benefit.

So, if we want to plan a group counseling experience, how might we go about it? One possible goal for such a group is to increase awareness of self as an emerging counseling professional and, in particular, to examine one's attitudes and understanding of how one relates to persons who are different from oneself. Those differences will include disability, by design, but no doubt other differences will emerge (see Chapter 4 of this book). Let us consider a 12-week group that meets weekly for 90 minutes. To reach the goal, participants will engage in activities designed to help participants learn how they are perceived by others, while also getting to know others in a personal way. We propose a group comprising members with and without disabilities. All members will be recruited from the counseling program, but if additional members with disabilities are needed, disability centers on campus might be able to assist the facilitators in finding graduate students with disabilities who would benefit from such a group.

We begin by conducting a screening interview with prospective members, even if we know we will not screen out anyone if it is a class experience. This reminds facilitators and members of the dual purposes of the pregroup screening: deselecting any potential members who are floridly psychotic, who are actively abusing substances, or who are not fluent in English and providing informed consent. Informed consent includes information to ensure that members understand the purposes of the group, the role of facilitators, and their role as members. Facilitators should gather information about any accommodations that members might need—such as an American Sign Language (ASL) interpreter, wheelchair access to the group location, or a therapy dog—so that the facilitators can make any adaptations needed and be ready to prepare other members for any specific situation (e.g., if a therapy dog will accompany a member, other members must ignore the animal no matter how cute it is). Potential members should understand that active engagement with the group is expected. Facilitators provide time for them to ask questions and begin to determine a personal goal that is consistent with the group goal. This interview is critical to setting up a positive expectation for the group.

One way to achieve the goal of increased awareness of both disabilities and how one thinks and relates to disabilities is to facilitate a here-and-now process-oriented interpersonal group á la Yalom (1995). This means that the facilitators must keep the focus in the present and on the group as a whole and its members. In our experience, counseling students rarely have any previous experience as a group member, so there is often some initial anxiety about the group. That is a great place to start. How are members feeling about being in the group? What is their hope for this experience? What are their fears? What could make the group a valuable experience? What does each member bring to the group? How are they feeling about the other members of the group? What do they hope other members will understand about them? Who are they curious about? Who in the group is most like them? Who is most different from them? It is helpful for facilitators to be active without being directive. That is, there is ample material in the group for the group. The facilitators need to help the members focus their energies in productive ways and explore their reactions to each other.

There are many activities in such compilations as *Group Workers Share Their Favorite Multicultural Activities: A Guide to Diversity-Competent Choosing, Planning, Conducting, and Processing* (Salazar,

2009) and *Experiential Activities for Teaching Multicultural Competence in Counseling* (Pope, Pangelinan, & Coker, 2011) that would be appropriate for such a group, although, sadly, exercises will have to be adapted because neither otherwise-excellent volume includes a section on disabilities. The facilitators are urged to use exercises only when they are a way to illuminate a dynamic or process present in the group. That is, the facilitators should not let the exercises drive the group. Rather, the issues that emerge from within the group may benefit from exercises that enhance and clarify a process that is already there. If exercises are used, it is essential that ample time be allowed for processing the experience, making meaning for members.

For a more structured psychoeducational group, again we propose a group that includes both persons with disabilities and persons without disabilities. An excellent outline of such a group (it is described as a workshop, but with processing and interaction, it can easily become a plan for a psychoeducational group) is found at http://www.projectvision.net/map/trainers/workshop. html. The goals are to "increase participant awareness of disability issues and disability culture, offer a basic understanding of the barriers preventing people with disabilities from full participation in society, and encourage participants with disabilities to share their knowledge and help educate others" (para. 1). The activities described are meaningful, interactive, and engaging, and many are done in subgroups and brought back to the group as a whole. To convert this workshop to a psychoeducational group format, the primary enhancement would be the processing of the personal and interpersonal reactions to the activities. For such a group, it would be ideal to have members with a variety of disabilities, both visible and invisible, so the facilitator might want to invite non–class members to participate to ensure that there is a good representation of disabilities.

This particular workshop is noteworthy for its focus on disability culture rather than focusing only on medical aspects or deficits. The nature of the activities is such that all members, with or without disabilities, can learn and grow. Project Vision's website has useful tips for facilitators, including one that is important to highlight here. In a psychoeducational group about disabilities, it is not unusual for someone to disclose either painful personal material or deeply felt reactions to the content of the group. The facilitator needs to be prepared to assist both the discloser and the rest of the group.

Acknowledging the trust in the group that allowed the disclosure, thanking the person for his or her honesty, and checking with the rest of the group to see how they are feeling and whether they can verbalize that are all important leader functions in that situation. In addition, the facilitator might ask the discloser what he or she would like from the group, having shared what she or he did. Sometimes people want to know how others are reacting to the shared material; other times, they will say just having someone listen was already helpful. The facilitator needs to be sure to take sufficient time to process this event, even if it means omitting an activity.

Simulations

The reader will note, we hope, that in the previous sections we did not mention using simulations in the proposed groups. Simulations are tools for learning that are effective in many situations: Pilots learn to fly using computerized simulations, and surgeons similarly practice their techniques on simulated patients who cannot be harmed by mistakes. Law students participate in mock trials. Simulations allow people to have an experience that they are unable (or unready) to access in vivo. Allowing novice pilots to "fly" large planes without risking passenger safety is an excellent way to learn. Surgeons can better learn from a procedural mistake on a virtual patient than on a living one. This type of learning is popular and widely used in a wide variety of settings. Thus, some might suggest that an effective way for able-bodied individuals to understand persons with disabilities is to participate in simulations in which one temporarily and artificially experiences some kind of disability, such as spending a day in a wheelchair, or with a blindfold, or wearing earplugs. Groups to raise awareness of disabilities might use such activities thinking that they will help able-bodied members empathize with members with disabilities (Olson, 2014). Is this a good idea?

Behler (1993) believed that simulations of disabilities are effective in raising participants' awareness of their own inaccurate beliefs about disabilities, and he described the various ways that he used these activities in his own classes. As a person who is completely blind, Behler is invested in helping his students develop more enlightened values related to disability, and he attempted to address the objections to simulations that many others express. Behler acknowledged that the simulations tend to emphasize the physical aspects of the disability and that the cultural and societal aspects may be overlooked. He believed that can be remedied with instruction. He also recommended that the simulations be followed by testimonies from persons who have successfully adapted to a disability, either via films or readings, or most effectively through guests in the setting who can share their personal perspective. He believed, on the basis of written and verbal feedback from his students, that simulation had been a valuable activity.

The use of simulations designed to increase participants' understanding of other cultural groups has not been effectively evaluated, so one is taking a risk that unintended outcomes may appear. For example, a widely used cultural sensitivity game, BAFA, is intended to improve intercultural understanding, but an unexpected result was increased ethnocentrism in participants (Burgstahler & Doe, 2004). Unintended outcomes are only one of the reasons we recommend that simulations not be used. French (1992) was one of the first to examine the use of these activities for disability awareness training, and she concluded that not only were simulations not helpful, they were harmful. More recently, Silverman, Gwinn, and Van Boven (2015) came to the same conclusion. They pointed out that what the simulations of disabilities really do is provide the experience of becoming disabled rather than being disabled. That is, the person who is blind for the day, for example, has not received any mobility training, cannot read Braille, and so is likely to focus on all the things he or she cannot do. They do not see the ways in which a blind person is quite competent and how she or he utilizes skills and adaptations. Those who use a wheelchair in a simulation may think about how difficult it is to get where they want to go, or those who have limbs immobilized are likely to think about how challenging it is to do basic things (Burgstahler & Doe, 2004). A brief encounter with the physical manifestations of a disability is not the same as having a congenital disability, or even an acquired disability with which one has learned to cope effectively.

Ladau (2014) told of an able-bodied person who became so frustrated when using a wheelchair in a simulation that she confessed that she just picked it up and went around barriers. Those who participate in simulations of disabilities often think that they would be helpless and incompetent if they had the disability, which leads them to think of persons with that disability with pity. On the basis of their own limited experience, they believe that someone with that disability is less capable of being employed or living independently. That is, simulating disabilities results in more negative attitudes and opinions about disabilities than positive ones.

Ladau (2014) stressed that disability is not just a physical condition, it is an identity and a culture. She believed that the simulations focus on the physical aspects that obscure the experiences of discrimination, the repeated experience of negative attitudes on the part of others, or environmental barriers (e.g., cars parked across the ramp access to sidewalks). Simulations also do not provide experiences of the accomplishments and achievements of a person with disabilities. Ladau used a potent analogy: We would likely be much offended if, in a multicultural setting, students were asked to simulate being Black by wearing blackface for a few hours or a day. We would think that is outrageous and totally inappropriate. And yet we think that simulating disabilities is a way to understand the experience of persons with a disability.

One important concern about simulations is that there are no valid and reliable measures to assess the impact of simulations (Burgstahler & Doe, 2004). Nevertheless, Burgstahler and Doe (2004) believed that simulations can be worthwhile if done carefully. They recommended that objectives be clear and given to participants when explaining the activity. That is, they should know why they are being asked to do this and what they hope to gain from participating. No one should be forced to participate. The experience should be designed in such a way that participants recognize the barriers experienced by someone with the disability but also see ways that barriers can be overcome. They described two simulations (one for blindness and the other for deafness/hard of hearing) that they believe are likely to produce positive outcomes. They strongly suggested that any simulation be designed and facilitated by persons with disabilities who should also be clear that the experiences of each person with a disability are different so that the simulation is not intended to represent a typical experience. They went on to say that those who participate in simulations should be encouraged to share their attitudes and beliefs, even if they are negative, so that they can educate everyone about common misconceptions or negative attitudes that may be quite common. This also gives the facilitators and other members an opportunity to examine how those beliefs and attitudes change after the simulation. That has important implications for how the members will apply the experience to their lives.

LEGISLATION

Americans With Disabilities Act

We include this section simply as a reminder to group facilitators that they must abide by the provisions of all relevant legislation. We do not review these laws in detail but rather provide an overview of the most important provisions. As counselors, group facilitators are subject to these laws and can be held accountable if they are not in compliance.

To reiterate, the ADA of 1990 defines a person with a disability as someone who has a physical or mental impairment that limits at least one major life activity, who has a record of such an impairment, or who is regarded as having an impairment. Amendments to the ADA, passed in 2008, clarified that disability was to be interpreted broadly and includes disabling conditions regardless of whether there are medications or corrective devices that could ameliorate the effects of the impairment. Any organization or agency that provides services (such as counseling) to the general public must be in compliance with provisions of the law. For group facilitators, the law should come to mind when a person with a disability (or a group for persons with disabilities) seeks services. The law states that one cannot discriminate against a person with disabilities but goes further to say that an agency or counseling center must modify practices or procedures to ensure nondiscrimination. For example, the law requires that architectural barriers be removed (e.g., stairs replaced by ramps or elevators) and that the counselor is responsible for providing auxiliary services (such as interpreters or handouts with enlarged type) to work effectively with clients who have a disability.

Consider the location where you might hold your group. First, a person with a disability should be able to access the location from public transportation, parking (marked for handicapped parking), or sidewalks. That means that there must be cuts in the sidewalk so that a person can get from the bus stop to the sidewalk and then to your location. Interior spaces also need to be accessible, including bathrooms and sufficient turning ratios for wheelchairs, ramps, and elevators. If making adjustments to your location is too costly, you are obligated to provide services via alternative means. There are guidelines for what constitutes an undue burden for the counselor in terms of making modifications. For group facilitators that might involve renting space from another practice that is accessible, offering online groups, or reserving a space in a public building. You are also obligated to allow service animals (dogs or other animals) when they are used by a client with a disability. Any materials you provide (brochures, forms, etc.) must be available in a format accessible to a person who is blind or someone with limited vision. In addition, the facilitator should inquire about what assistive communication would work best for the client. In a group, it is important that if the person has communication difficulties, you and the client determine how he or she might best communicate not only with the facilitator but also with the entire group. Websites also need to be accessible to people with disabilities. It is important to note that the counselor may not charge the client for the cost of any necessary auxiliary services.

The facilitator should know that a client who believes his or her rights have been violated can request an investigation by the U.S. Department of Justice. Investigations are conducted by the office of the Attorney General. Counselors who facilitate groups for or with persons with disabilities are thus legally and ethically bound to follow these laws. The ADA includes sections (referred to as "titles" in the law) that address nondiscrimination in employment, state and local government services, telecommunications, and other miscellaneous areas. Group facilitators who are also employers or who are employed by state and local governmental agencies may particularly want to learn more about the other titles of the ADA.

Many states also have state disability nondiscrimination laws that may go beyond the ADA in some areas. Group facilitators should be familiar with the laws in their jurisdiction and ensure that they are complying with all elements of all laws that apply to them.

Section 504 of the Rehabilitation Act

Prior to the passage of the ADA, Section 504 of the Rehabilitation Act of 1973 (34 C.F.R. Part 104) provided some protections against discrimination on the basis of disability. It applied to organizations that receive any financial assistance from the federal government, including many mental health centers or social service organizations. The definition of disabilities is almost identical to that used in the ADA (see the preceding section), as modified by the 2008 amendments to the ADA. Included in covered disabilities are AIDS, cancer, blindness and deafness, heart disease, mental illness, diabetes, and alcoholism and former drug addiction (current drug use may not be covered).

The law requires that an employer must take reasonable steps to accommodate the disabilities when the person can perform the job with these accommodations. Section 504 prohibits an organization from denying access to a person with a disability because of physical or structural barriers. Group facilitators should familiarize themselves with the provisions of these laws and not assume that their agency or employer will take care of compliance. They are obligated to speak up and refer to the law if they are unable to conduct a group for persons with disabilities because of noncompliance in their workplace. Remember that counselors are advocates for clients, and tolerating a work setting that does not allow equal participation of persons with disabilities is not consistent with the role of a counselor or with his or her ethical and legal responsibilities.

GENERAL ETIQUETTE

Facilitators of groups with persons with disabilities must know, abide by, and model etiquette for interacting with persons with disabilities. In an initial session when norms are being established, principles of etiquette should be addressed. The facilitators might use handouts of one of the useful lists of etiquette or ask the group to develop a list and add to it as they become aware of more items. There is an excellent video called "The Commandments of Disability" (Bernard, 2014) that we recommend be viewed at the initial group meeting. A slightly longer version is available for purchase.

We summarize the key points here:

1. Speak directly to the person with whom you are communicating, not to the interpreter or assistant. That means looking at the person while you are speaking and also when you are listening to the interpreter or assistant.
2. Offer to shake hands with a person with a disability. Use whatever hand works best. If the person is unable to reciprocate, he or she will probably tell you.
3. When communicating with a person who is blind, be sure to tell that person who you are. In a group, this is particularly important, because it will be difficult to tell people apart by voices until considerable time has elapsed. Also let the person know whether you are leaving the vicinity. He or she may not otherwise realize that you have gone.
4. If you think the person might like help, ask him or her and wait for the response before taking any action.
5. Treat persons with disabilities as the adults they are (unless you are working with children with disabilities). There is a tendency to talk down to them, use childlike intonations, and so on, which is very demeaning.

6. Persons who use wheelchairs consider them to be an extension of their bodies. Do not lean on the chair or otherwise use it for your own needs. And never pat anyone (including persons who use a wheelchair) on the shoulder or head. It is a violation of their personal space.

7. If the person with a disability has difficulty speaking, be patient. Wait for him or her to finish before you respond. When possible, ask questions that can be answered briefly or nonverbally.

8. Try to be at eye level with people with whom you are speaking, whether they are using a wheelchair or are otherwise below eye level.

9. Many deaf people cannot read lips. If you wish to speak to someone who is deaf, tap that person lightly or wave your hand. If someone does read lips, be sure to face him or her, and do not put your hands close to your mouth during the conversation. When talking, do not try to overenunciate or shout. People who read lips may be thrown off if you are not speaking naturally.

10. Do not worry if you use a word related to an ability the person lacks. It is okay to say "I'm running off now" to someone who uses a wheelchair, to say "see you later" to a blind person, and so on. They are accustomed to hearing these figures of speech and generally do not take offense.

Although these guidelines are the most common, there are other behaviors to keep in mind.

1. Do not speak in a loud voice to a person with a disability. He or she will let you know if you need to increase the volume.

2. If you do make a mistake, apologize, and remember for the next time.

3. If the person has an assistive device, it is his or her property, and no matter how curious you might be, do not ask to handle it or try it out.

4. Do not press people to tell you about their disability. It may come up naturally in conversation, but it is not your place to interrogate someone to satisfy your own curiosity.

5. Do not make assumptions about what a person can do or cannot do. For example, many people who use wheelchairs are able to transfer to a regular chair without assistance. And some are competitive athletes.

6. If you are giving directions to a person who is blind, be specific, using left, right, forward, or back, or describe locations using the numbers on a clock.
7. If you are out somewhere with a person who is blind, be sure to read aloud any signs or notices that are important. If you are out for a meal, ask whether the person would like you to describe what is on the plate and in what position.
8. Never engage with an assistance animal. When they are on the job, their focus should be on their work, not on you.
9. Do not pretend you understand something that you do not. Ask the person to repeat, or correct your information.
10. When speaking to someone with cognitive or intellectual disabilities, try to use concrete words without being overly simplistic.
11. Be patient if you are asked to repeat something. Short-term memory loss may make it difficult for a person with certain disabilities to retain information after one hearing.
12. Do not interpret being distracted or needing to move around as rudeness. Similarly, forgetfulness or lack of follow-through may not mean a lack of motivation. These are symptoms of some disabilities. When meeting with the potential member for pregroup screening, it is essential to gather information about the needs of each client so that accommodations can be provided.

RESPONSIBILITIES OF FACILITATORS

Facilitators are required to abide by all relevant ethical guidelines, including those specifically for group work (http://www.asgw.org/). They need to be competent in both group leadership and disabilities. This is a tall order, and one that we have addressed in this chapter. We have suggested several types of groups that might be effective in helping counselors-in-training or others to increase their knowledge, examine their attitudes, and develop skills for conducting groups with persons with disabilities.

Facilitators must also model the characteristics and behaviors that they wish to impart. They need to be mindful of the "Ten Commandments" and use their best clinical judgment when the groups include persons with psychiatric disabilities or intellectual disabilities. Facilitators must be aware of the pertinent legislation and, as counselors, must be advocates for their clients, sometimes helping group members understand the laws and their rights. They must also be familiar with resources (online, print, and human) that can provide information and assistance to clients and should have that information available to pass along to clients. Finally, we hope that those who facilitate groups for persons with disabilities will become advocates for inclusion of persons with disabilities in all domains of society.

KEY TERMS

Acquired disability: A disability with onset that occurs after birth. Such disabilities may be the result of disease or injury.

Awareness: We use this to describe a conscious focus on disability issues, knowledge of disabilities, or interest in one's own attitudes toward disabilities.

Congenital disability: a disability present at birth.

Ethnocentrism: the process of seeing the world through the lens of one's own culture; evaluating other cultures by using one's culture as the standard.

Etiquette: a code that describes polite behavior in society; accepted ways of behaving.

Exercises: These are planned, structured activities designed to help group members increase self-understanding, relate to others, improve communication, and so on. They are the means to accomplish a particular objective and not themselves the objective.

Simulation: acting out or mimicking a disability for a defined period of time, ostensibly to learn about the disability via first-hand experience.

Undue burden: a significant difficulty or expense that would occur if a business (or individual practitioner) were to be forced to redesign or retrofit or adapt a facility to make it accessible to persons with disabilities.

RECOMMENDATIONS FOR PRACTICE

1. Become an advocate for training in the area of disability, regardless of your counseling specialty.
2. Read some of the books listed in Chapter 14, particularly those that are first-person accounts of life with a disability.
3. Find out whether disability awareness groups are offered in your area, and sign up to participate.
4. Attend a disability support group. Call ahead, because many are open to anyone, but some are not.

5. Reflect on the issue of simulations, and take a stand if you are asked to participate in an activity that involves the simulation of a disability.

6. Be sure to practice disability etiquette in your life and your practice. You may want to create a flyer with key points for your office that can be used to remind group members of expected behaviors.

7. Watch the video mentioned in the section "General Etiquette"; encourage your program to purchase the full version. If you are an educator or trainer, use it in a required class so that all students have an opportunity to see and discuss it.

8. Review the ADA and Section 504 provisions to assess your practice and make changes as needed. Learn the specifics of undue burden to decide whether the required changes are feasible for your situation. Periodically review relevant state legislation.

9. Most important, make a conscious effort to be more inclusive by attending events sponsored by disability organizations or programs and by volunteering for agencies or programs that will put you in contact with persons with disabilities.

10. Consult with a rehabilitation counselor if you have questions or need more information about legal issues, etiquette issues, or other questions related to disability.

part II

SPECIFIC
DISABILITIES

chapter 8
SENSORY DISABILITIES

Visual impairment and blindness, and hard of hearing and deafness, are not singular disabilities. That is, in both general categories there are variations of type and degree of impairment that affect many aspects of the lives of people with these disabilities and that will have an effect on how they participate in and benefit from group counseling and therapy. In this chapter, we provide basic information about these two categories of disability to ensure that the reader has a general understanding of terms and conditions and then discuss strategies for working with groups that include members with sensory disabilities.

LOSS OF VISION AND BLINDNESS

There were 60,393 U.S. children under 21 years of age who were legally blind in 2012, according to data supplied by states. Among Americans ages 16–75+, 6,670,300 persons had a visual disability (National Federation of the Blind, 2016). Rates were slightly higher among women than among men; among racial/ethnic groups, rates were around 2% for Whites, Hispanics, and "other" races; almost

3% for Blacks/African Americans; almost 4% for American Indian/ Alaskan Natives; and 1.2% for Asian Americans. Of working-age adults with significant loss of vision, 37.7% were employed (Erickson, Lee, & von Schrader, 2014).

Vision is the sense through which we detect light, shape, size, texture, and color and objects that are close, distant, or in the periphery. *Blindness* is a level of vision loss that actually has legal status. It is defined by the U.S. Social Security Administration as "best corrected visual acuity of 20/200 or less in the better eye; or a visual field limitation such that the widest diameter of the visual field, in the better eye, subtends [creates] an angle no greater than 20 degrees" (Hellem, 2015). *Visual impairment* refers to diminished ability to see (less than 20/60) that is not possible to correct with known treatment or lenses. It may be caused by disease or trauma and may be present at birth or acquired because of injury or a degenerative condition. *Visual acuity*, sometimes called central vision, is what most people think of as simply the ability to see clearly. When expressed as a ratio, it shows the distance at which a person can see an object of 5 minutes of arc (5/21,600 of a circle). A person with 20/20 vision can see that object at 20 feet from the target, whereas a person with 20/200 vision could see at 20 feet what a person with 20/20 vision sees at 200 feet. The measure of visual acuity is made with the best corrective lens available. *Visual field* describes the area that a person can see when looking ahead; this includes peripheral and central vision. Some types of visual impairment retain central vision while peripheral vision is gone, and vice versa.

In addition to near-sightedness, far-sightedness, and astigmatism, which are common conditions usually corrected by eyeglasses or contact lenses, there are other types of visual conditions that result in congenital impairments. These include strabismus (each eye looks in a different direction, and they do not focus simultaneously), cataracts (cloudy lens; can be congenital or acquired), retinopathy of prematurity (when the retina has not completely developed before a premature birth), retinitis pigmentosa (an inherited disease in which the retina is slowly destroyed, and blindness results), colobama (part of the eye's structure is missing), optic nerve hypoplasia (affects the optic nerve and causes problems in depth perception, light sensitivity, and visual acuity), and cortical visual impairment (the result of damage to the visual parts of the brain, not the eye) (Center for Parent Information and Resources, 2015).

In adults, the most common cause of blindness is age-related macular degeneration, which accounts for 54% of all blindness in White persons. For Blacks, the most common causes are cataracts and open-angle glaucoma, with the latter being the most common cause among Hispanics. Diabetic retinopathy also is a cause of vision loss (National Eye Institute, 2004) and affects about 80% of persons who have had diabetes for 10 years or more.

Sometimes, people with partial sight (i.e., very low vision) experience considerable anxiety due to fears about their prognosis (Falvo, 2014). It may not be clear whether they will have further loss of vision, or what the rate of loss might be. As vision deteriorates, the person may need more assistance from others, which may affect relationships. In addition, some of these individuals may cling to the idea of having some vision and be particularly reluctant to give up important activities, such as driving. They may also be unwilling to receive mobility or orientation training in an effort to minimize their impairment. In some cases, these decisions put them and others at risk. This is one group of people who may derive particular benefit from participating in a group with others with visual impairments. In that setting, they can receive support and understanding and benefit from the ways that others in the group have adapted to the loss and handled the uncertainty.

WA, a counselor who became blind as an adult, facilitates groups for persons with vision loss or blindness. She believes that she brings an enhanced understanding to the group because she has lived in the sighted world and then became blind. She would not say that a sighted person could not lead such a group, but she believes it would be much more difficult to help members engage on a deeper level. WA believes in the power of groups and has observed many clients who make enormous progress. She treats living with blindness as a problem that can be solved and believes that life will go on. In her case, she completed all her postsecondary education after becoming blind, so she serves as a role model for members. She believes that members find camaraderie in the group and that they derive strength from each other.

In groups for blind and visually impaired members, goals might include teaching coping skills in a supportive environment, building self-esteem and confidence in the new identity, and validating and reinforcing the person's strengths. To accomplish this, careful screening is essential. Any personality clashes or other conflicts should be addressed as they would be in any group; the facilitator needs to recognize that although members may have a disability, that does not mean that they are emotionally fragile or that inappropriate behavior should be ignored.

WA also facilitates grief and loss groups in the community, which may have a member with blindness or another disability. In that setting, she finds it best to acknowledge the disability but not to focus on it. In her screening interview, she always asks what challenges the client might anticipate so that they can discuss them in advance. In her experience, these can be readily managed. WA finds it helpful to allow the person to enter the meeting space ahead of time to get a sense of what is there and how the room is arranged.

She believes that the sense of belonging and the inclusive nature of the group allow the blind participant to be a valuable member. In this context, some sighted members initially feel anxious about unintentionally saying or doing something wrong. They fear that using the word *see* will upset the blind member, and so on. WA encourages (and models) asking the group directly if one is uncertain but also prepares the group by teaching some basic etiquette. She reminds members to identify themselves when they speak, because the blind person will need some time before being able to recognize voices. It is also polite to announce when you are entering and leaving, so that the blind member knows who is there. Members need to be careful of the space by not inadvertently placing barriers in the likely path in and out of the room. If the blind person has an assistive animal, it should be ignored. This is sometimes challenging for sighted persons when the animals are cute, but it is necessary.

Groups for Children and Adolescents

KT facilitates groups for school-aged youth in a state school for the blind and deaf. Although she is sighted, she finds that is not an obstacle to her role. She believes that students understand (and she reminds them) that she is not there to pretend to know what blindness is but to help them think about things in a new way. She also demonstrates her sensitivity in small ways, such as not moving things in the room without telling them and not saying "come here" but saying "move four feet to your left." She always identifies herself to the group when she speaks and reminds all members to do so as well. If she senses that a member needs guiding, she does not assume that she is correct but asks, "Would you like to take my elbow?" As the facilitator, she pays close attention to how the group is responding and is certain to describe any nonverbal communication that is useful for the members to know.

Groups for youth in the context of a state school have many things in common with groups in other settings, but they also have unique elements. As with many youth, the members are concerned with transitions, graduation, how to fit in, friendships, healthy relationships, and so forth. But because the young people in the school have a wide range of vision loss, some issues emerge that are significant for this population. For example, those who have lost their vision after school age may experience anger at their circumstances and feel upset when they know their sighted peers are excited about getting driver's licenses. This subgroup may experience grief over the loss of vision and may resist learning to read Braille or use a cane, because they are not yet accepting this new part of their identity. She sometimes takes these students on night hikes so that they can see the importance of their skills.

The students in KT's groups are concerned about how the general public thinks about blind people, worry about being stereotyped, and have more mundane (but not unimportant) concerns—such as how to eat in public without making a mess, how to think about "eye contact"—that they hear so much about. They have to learn to look toward the person speaking and to keep their heads up, which can be practiced in groups and reinforced by the sighted counselor. An additional behavior that the facilitator may have to teach is to resist the impulse to poke their eyes. KT says that some youth do this because they can get the sensation sighted people do when they do the same thing, such as seeing stars. That is appealing to them because it is a "visual" experience, but when it becomes habitual, it can cause physical damage. The facilitator cannot give subtle visual cues with this population, so she has to devise ways to gently remind the students to stop without drawing unwanted attention to them. Finally, the group leader needs to be aware of how silence is interpreted in a group comprising blind and visually impaired members, children or adult. These participants cannot survey the group to look for nonverbal clues about the meaning of the silence, and they may need a verbal intervention by the facilitator, in which the facilitator of a sighted group might allow the silence to continue and use it therapeutically. Some activities that are useful in groups for young people will not be possible in groups for this population (trust falls, mirroring, line-up games, and other activities), so the facilitator will have to be both mindful and creative when designing exercises for the group.

Those who became blind after starting school have some basic concept of how things are in the world, which is unavailable to those with congenital blindness. If they had sight for a time, they typically get the idea of how streets are arranged, for example, but this is a basic concept that is inaccessible for many with congenital blindness. This requires the facilitator to be aware of this challenge and to teach those concepts, perhaps in an individual setting. In addition to supplemental individual counseling, the facilitator should make sure that clients are aware of useful resources that provide access to information and advice. The web sites of the American Federation of the Blind (http://www.afb.org/default.aspx) and the National Federation of the Blind (https://nfb.org/) are excellent sites to recommend.

DEAF AND HARD OF HEARING

Approximately 1 in 1,000 U.S. newborns have a hearing loss (Mehra, Eavey, & Keamy, 2009). The rate of at least mild hearing impairment in childhood is between 1.9% (self-report) and 3.1% (audiometric data). Hispanic children have higher rates of hearing loss than do other groups, as do lower income children. Genetic factors explain about 23% of hearing loss. Ninety percent of deaf infants are born to hearing parents. The rate of hearing loss increases with age in childhood, as is true for the adult population. For adults, a study using audiometric data found that approximately 29 million adults had a hearing loss in the frequencies that detect human speech. Although this is 16.1% of the overall population, only 8.5% of those ages 20–29 years had a hearing impairment, indicating that hearing loss is more likely as people age. Men were 5 times as likely to have a hearing loss as were women, and the odds were 70% lower in Black people. Hearing impairments were found at younger ages among those who smoked, who were exposed to loud noise, and who had cardiovascular risks (Agrawal, Platz, & Niparko, 2008).

There are three types of hearing loss: Conductive hearing loss is caused by problems within the ear; sensorineural hearing loss is the result of problems in the nerves of the inner ear; and mixed hearing loss refers to a condition in which problems of both types are present. Each of these types has multiple causes, including structural abnormalities, infections, trauma, allergies, and other diseases. There are surgical procedures that can correct some of the problems. In many cases, hearing can be improved with hearing aids, although this may not work for people with severe and profound losses of the sensorineural type, who might be assisted by cochlear implants. These are surgically implanted devices with both under the skin and visible components that allow the persons to hear sounds and understand some speech. The use of this procedure, which can be done in infancy, has increased in recent years (Hearing Loss Association of America, n.d.).

Hearing loss is often categorized as mild, moderate, severe, and profound (Card & Schmider, 1995). Those with mild to moderate losses are more successful in groups with some accommodations. They may use hearing aids or personal microphones, and the setting should be well illuminated, with little or no ambient noise, and the person should be encouraged to take the seat that allows the best hearing. Those with severe or profound hearing loss are most likely to communicate using ASL. Some persons who are deaf are able to lip-read, which requires the speaker to face the listener and not place visual barriers in front of the mouth. These clients will often require an ASL interpreter, discussed in more depth later in this chapter.

Those who are deaf and use sign language (ASL, in the United States), who often were educated at schools for the deaf, who associate primarily with other deaf people, and who attend deaf cultural events are considered Deaf (with a capital *D*). Those who are deaf or hard of hearing but were educated in schools for the general population, who may not know sign language, and who associate with a mixed group of deaf and hearing people, are deaf (with a small *d*) in terms of their hearing loss but are not part of the Deaf culture. Among persons with hearing loss, there may be some tension between the two groups.

Those in Deaf culture consider themselves part of an ethnic and linguistic minority group and believe that Deaf should be listed on census forms along with other racial and ethnic minorities. Culture involves shared language, history, customs, and behavioral norms; a sense of belonging to the cultural group; an artistic tradition; and social structures (Whyte, Aubrecht, McCullough, Lewis, & Thompson-Ochoa, 2013), all of which apply to Deaf culture. From this perspective, the use of the lowercase-*d deaf* reflects a medical diagnosis and audiological status, and the term *hearing impaired* is offensive because it implies that hearing is better ("hard of hearing" is the preferred term). Whyte et al. (2013, all of whom are Deaf counselors) pointed out that hearing children of Deaf adults often identify as Deaf themselves and are active in the Deaf community. However, deaf people raised in hearing families may be isolated from Deaf culture and community, may not use ASL, and may be well suited for group counseling to receive support from others who share that experience and struggle.

This perspective (Deaf as culture, not disability) has generated several deaf identity development models, generally based on models for other minorities. For example, the Minority Deaf Identity Developmental Framework (Small & Cripps, 2012) parallels the Cross (1971) model of Black Identity Development (preencounter, encounter, emersion, internalization, and internalization/commitment). As applied to deaf persons, the preencounter stage refers primarily to children of hearing parents who have not yet had experience with Deaf culture or community and who hold the assumption that the hearing world is superior.

There are a number of other models that have been proposed to describe the process of identity development; we provide an overview of two of them here. The first was developed by Glickman (1996) and includes four stages, which are somewhat sequential: The first stage is hearing, in which the individual's reference group is the hearing population; the view of deafness is one of pathology; the view of the deaf community is uninformed and stereotypical; and the emotional tone is despair and depression (because one recognizes that one cannot be a full member of the hearing world). The next stage is marginal, in which the person shifts back and forth from a Hearing identity to a Deaf identity but still regards deafness as pathological, vacillates between viewing the Deaf community as good and as bad, and feels considerable confusion and conflict. In the immersion stage, the person aligns with the Deaf community, now views deafness as cultural, and takes a positive view of the Deaf community, feeling at times angry and at other times enamored of all things Deaf. In the final stage, bicultural, Deaf is the reference group although the person can interact in the hearing world, the view of deafness is cultural, and the perspective on the Deaf community is positive, resulting in self-acceptance and pride in being Deaf (Leigh, 2009). Other theorists have observed differences in these stages between children whose parents are Deaf and those who are hearing, and between those whose deafness is congenital and those in whom it was acquired. The reader is referred to the book by Leigh (2009) for a more detailed discussion of these points.

Another model is that of Deaf acculturation, which has four similar stages (hearing acculturated, marginal, deaf acculturated, and bicultural) and considers five aspects of acculturation in determining the stage of development of a given individual: cultural identification, cultural involvement, cultural preferences, language competence (speech using the voice, ASL), and cultural knowledge (Leigh, 2009).

The stage of identity development is a critical piece of information for group facilitators to know; a group comprising children who are all in the preencounter stage may not provide the greatest opportunity for growth, whereas a group with members in various stages is likely to be more powerful. Simply thinking Deaf versus deaf may not provide sufficiently nuanced information. Among adults, there are benefits and disadvantages to having both congenital and acquired hearing loss represented in the group; the facilitator should consider the goal of the group when deciding what is best (Card & Schmider, 1995).

Whyte et al. (2013) and many other deaf people are emphatic in their belief that a counselor who provides services (including groups) to Deaf people should be Deaf as well. This presents a problem in rural or isolated areas where there may not be a Deaf counselor; Whyte et al. insist that a referral to an agency that offers videophone counseling, which provides the ability to see the hands and facial expressions of the other participants, is preferable to a hearing counselor providing live services. We believe that this decision should be made with the client and should consider the best interest of the client. We discuss other options below, including hearing facilitators who are fluent in ASL.

In groups of all Deaf members, it is likely that the facilitator will be Deaf or fluent in ASL. Nevertheless, there are some practices that should be used, such as keeping the size of the group small (four to six people, maximum), because following ASL with too many speakers is challenging, and one's eyes become tired. Even with adults, the duration of groups should be shorter to avoid fatigue; it might be more productive to meet several times per week for shorter sessions (30 minutes) than to have sessions of 60 to 90 minutes.

Group facilitators, when screening members for the group, must also consider the preferred mode of communication of the deaf person. Some deaf persons were educated in systems that emphasize vocalization; they may lip-read and not know ASL. To accommodate such persons in a group, it will be important to have no visual obstacles and to encourage everyone to look at the person when speaking.

In a group with a single deaf person, an interpreter may be the best option if the facilitator is hearing and the preferred mode of communication for the deaf person is ASL. Most deaf or hard-of-hearing persons are accustomed to having interpreters present in a variety of settings (schools, public events), and using an interpreter in a group can be quite effective. Whyte et al. (2013) recommended that counselors always use a nationally certified interpreter who is experienced at working in counseling situations. Confidentiality is particularly important to Deaf persons, whose community is small, making the risk of disclosure very high. Interpreters who work in group or individual counseling need to understand the absolute and unwavering need for confidentiality and also must be prepared to hear about difficult and disturbing topics, such as abuse. It is also best practice to have the same interpreter (or interpreters) for the life of the group.

In a group with a deaf participant and an interpreter, the facilitator must make clear to the group that the interpreter has a specific function and is not part of the group. They need to know that the person has been informed about confidentiality and that he or she will honor that commitment. Members should be directed to look at and address the deaf participant directly and to expect pauses sometimes if the ASL is lengthier than the English phrase. Seating the interpreter next to the facilitator makes this easier to accomplish. The facilitator should model all behaviors so that the group members can learn from observing him or her. In addition, it is appropriate to remind the group that when several people speak at once, it is impossible for the interpreter to sign accurately, and so speaking one at a time is essential.

In addition, some differences in ASL and English can be handled using scaling techniques. In ASL, several words with related meanings may have the same sign. Whyte et al. (2013) gave the example of the words *mad, angry, furious, livid,* and *enraged,* which might have the same sign. Asking the client to describe his or her anger on a scale from 1 to 10 (with 1 being only a tiny bit angry and 10 being the angriest you have ever been) would reveal more about the member's emotional state. The facilitator should be careful not to presume that he or she knows the client's experience (this should be the case for all clients, disabled or able bodied) and point out when others are doing so. The counselor should also recognize that if people are talking in front of a deaf person and no one is signing the conversation to them, it is understandable if they feel that people may be talking about them.

AT, a Deaf counselor, pointed out that the small size and close relationships of many in the Deaf community make participating in a group very risky. Many would not want to be noticed even going to a counseling facility for fear that everyone would learn about it. AT suggests that for this reason, online counseling groups can be a boon for many Deaf persons; they typically prefer to remain anonymous, so a chat format is ideal. AT participated in a group with hearing persons that was held in a counseling center in Second Life (an online virtual world). Members chose avatars that resembled their physical selves to a greater or lesser degree, so anonymity was preserved. Although Second Life can be used with speech, chat is also available and avoids many of the problems with multiple microphones (feedback, screeching). Using online groups also allows Deaf persons to participate in groups on relevant themes without necessarily disclosing that they are deaf. For some, that provides an opportunity to relate to people who do not see hearing status as a defining feature and to engage in dialogue with others on the basis of their common interests and concerns. Others may feel that hearing persons will not understand how many issues are complicated by deafness and will seek an online group composed of other deaf persons.

It is worth pointing out here that AT facilitated a group of hearing persons, using an interpreter. It was interesting to hear from members who said they soon forgot about the interpreter (who was the same for all sessions) and liked the pauses that naturally occurred while the interpreter signed to AT. They said it gave them time to collect their thoughts, and they felt the pace of conversation was calmer.

Groups for Children and Adolescents

Most children who are hard of hearing are educated in mainstream classrooms and use assistive technology. This means they may not know many (or any) other youth their age who are also hard of hearing. Madell (2015) believed that groups are especially useful for these young people because it gives them an opportunity to discuss their concerns with others who understand. Generally, it is best to group children by preferred communication method, although most students who are educated in mainstream classrooms have speech.

In most ways, these groups involve the same dynamics and processes that are found in other groups. The content is what may differ. For example, children will share their problems that are related to the hearing loss and work together to find solutions. A child who feels uncomfortable swimming with hearing friends because he must take off his hearing aids in the water and then cannot hear might be advised to explain this to his swimming friends and work out a plan together. Another topic that comes up, particularly with teens, is the resistance to using assistive technology. In their desire to fit in with peers at school, who are all hearing, they may decide they do not need to wear their hearing aids. Madell (2015) suggested demonstration and discussion of the kinds of things that the student will be unable to hear so that they realize that much of soft conversation will be missed. Finally, bullying and victimization are both more prevalent among youth with disabilities, and group time spent on this topic can be very productive.

In mainstream schools, if children who are hard of hearing receive special services (e.g., speech therapy), they may miss out on activities that their peers get to do, and they may want to vent about their frustrations. They will likely receive support from others in the group. If this is an issue for the children, the group facilitator might want to advocate that special services be scheduled at times that do not bring attention to the student's disability and do not require that he or she miss out on enjoyable activities with peers.

Children and adolescents who use hearing aids are visibly different from peers at a time when fitting in with the peer group is extremely important. Sometimes these children become shy and reserved and thus have fewer opportunities to practice social skills. The group is an excellent laboratory in which to learn and practice effective communication. Madell (2015) used a child peer relationship scale to raise awareness and stimulate sharing about the social impact of being hard of hearing. Children can talk openly with peers about problems they have and receive feedback and suggestions to manage situations that they encounter. She also recommended the toolbox and My World game available at http://idainstitute.com/newsroom/news/blog/show/living-well-for-teens-and-my-world-tools-presented-at-eaa/.

In summary, a group for Deaf persons with the goal of adjusting to their disability is inappropriate because they perceive themselves as a minority cultural group rather than as disabled (which has connotations of deficit and the medical model). Thus, such a group is likely to focus on other common concerns but be homogeneous on the basis of communication preferences. However, for people who have recently lost their hearing, particularly in adulthood, the process of deaf identity development may be just beginning, and the support and understanding of a group of others who have lost hearing as an adult can be invaluable. Children have different needs and issues, whether they are educated in schools for the deaf or mainstream schools, and especially for children who do not have other hard-of-hearing children in their classes or schools, group counseling can be a very powerful influence during these developmental periods.

Parent Groups

Finally, for both vision and hearing disabilities, parents can benefit tremendously from both educational and support groups. Parents need accurate information and often value the chance to share their parenting concerns with others in similar situations. Parents need a safe place to share their feelings about having and raising a child with sensory disabilities without fear or judgment. Issues such as protection versus overprotection, changing developmental needs of children as they grow, and social needs of children are likely to be important topics.

SUMMARY

Group counseling can be a useful treatment component for clients with sensory disabilities. Persons who acquire these disabilities can benefit from education and support around adaptations and skills to live with the disability, and groups are a very effective milieu for those who have these goals. In other situations, persons who are deaf or hearing impaired or blind or vision impaired will join groups for other issues, and the facilitator needs to be prepared with appropriate knowledge, understanding, and skills to ensure the optimal experience for all participants. We included this chapter to provide that background to facilitators.

Some Deaf clients, however, consider themselves not as disabled but as cultural minorities who sometimes encounter prejudice, oppression, and aggression from the majority culture. Attending to these cultural issues is critical to providing appropriate services for this population.

It is important for facilitators to be mindful that clients who are blind and deaf may have other issues: Substance abuse, eating disorders, mood disorders, serious mental illness, and so on are not reserved for the able bodied. The sensory disability may affect the group, but it should not overshadow other pressing concerns for which the client is seeking help.

KEY TERMS

American Sign Language (ASL): the sign language used in the United States. It involves hand signs and movements of the face and torso. Grammar and syntax are not parallel to English grammar.

Assistive technology: any device or product that allows a person with disabilities to increase or maintain their ability to function or to accomplish tasks that could not be done or would be extremely difficult to do without the technology.

Cochlear implants: a small device that provides a type of sound to a person who is deaf or extremely hard of hearing. It includes a microphone, a speech processer, a transmitter and receiver/ stimulator, and an electrode array that picks up the signals and sends them to the auditory nerve. It does not provide normal hearing but gives the person a type of sound. It has been approved for use in very young children since 2000. The implant is a surgical procedure and is followed by intensive therapy to learn to use the sounds.

Hearing aids: devices that amplify sound for someone who is deaf or hard of hearing and are worn externally.

Identity development: the process of defining one's stable, enduring constellation of personality, beliefs, attitudes, and way of relating to the world. Although this occurs throughout life, adolescence is thought to be the developmental stage in which this is most salient.

Interpreter: Because the two languages (e.g., ASL and English) are not directly equivalent, the sign language interpreter engages in conveying the meaning of a message that captures the nuances of the communication. Interpreters earn certification.

Orientation and mobility training: learning how to know where you are in space and in the environment and how to move safely from one place to another.

RECOMMENDATIONS FOR PRACTICE

1. If you regularly employ the services of an ASL interpreter (or a service that sends an interpreter), request that the same interpreter be available throughout the group. If fatigue is an issue and two interpreters will be used, the same suggestion

applies. That way you can build a relationship, and they can become accustomed to the style and pace of communication in the group. They can learn any phrases or expressions that are used frequently and can more seamlessly engage in the task.

2. Use the suggestions in this and previous chapters to adapt your setting to a member who is blind or who has very low vision. The arrangement of your meeting place should be the same for each meeting; any changes should be explained to the member who is blind before he or she enters. Get in the habit of verbalizing meaningful nonverbal communication so that the member has the same input as others in the group.

3. If you will work with Deaf or blind clients, it would be helpful to spend some time immersed in a setting in which those clients are at home. When Sheri Bauman first began working with a school for the Deaf, she was a bit nonplussed when no one made eye contact when she gave a presentation. Of course, everyone was looking at the interpreter, but she was accustomed to gauging the audience response by their eye contact and facial expressions, and it took time to adjust. She also learned that it is fatiguing to watch an interpreter for lengthy periods and that more breaks are needed. When talking with hearing persons in the presence of a Deaf person in that setting, the bilingual party would always sign the conversation so others would know what was being discussed. In the same scenario with hearing people, others in the room can gauge whether the conversation relates to them by listening; signing the conversation gives the Deaf person that information.

chapter 9
PSYCHIATRIC DISABILITIES

In this chapter, we focus on persons with serious and chronic mental illness. There are a number of disorders that come under this general umbrella (schizophrenia, bipolar disorder, schizoaffective disorder, mood disorders, Asperger's disorder); what they have in common is the presence of persistent psychiatric symptoms that are severe enough that the person is unable to function in his or her environment. These symptoms often include distortions of reality, such as hallucinations (auditory, visual, or both) or delusions (false beliefs). The often odd behavior of the person with serious mental illness (SMI) may disturb others as well as themselves. These conditions are typically of long duration, sometimes lifelong, and are usually treated with pharmacotherapy as the primary intervention.

Although modern advances in pharmacology have provided an array of medication treatment options, many of these have significant side effects—such as muscle spasms, tardive dyskinesia (involuntary repetitive movements, including excessive blinking, grimacing, tongue movements, lip movements, and abnormal postures that may be permanent), difficulty with urination, weight gain, and restlessness or decreased energy—that are so unpleasant that some patients will not adhere to the medication regimen. SMI often leads to social isolation and loneliness (and sometimes to homelessness) and to estrangement from family. In addition, the stigmatization of those with mental illness ("crazies," "nutcases") often contributes to an already vulnerable self-esteem and fear of getting help.

Group counseling and therapy have been used in a variety of settings (inpatient, outpatient, community settings) with persons with psychiatric disabilities and have been effective primarily in increasing social skills. Marshak (1990) summarized the extant research and concluded that group therapy was superior to individual therapy in 80% of studies when they were compared and that treatment focusing on improving social skills in a group setting showed more favorable outcomes than did insight-oriented approaches. In addition, clients who received group treatment were more likely to avoid hospitalization.

We first discuss group work with persons with serious/chronic mental illness and then turn to the specific disorders of posttraumatic stress disorder (PTSD) and substance abuse.

SERIOUS MENTAL ILLNESS

Definitions

Although this section is not intended to replace a course in mental disorders, we provide brief descriptions (based on the *DSM–5*) so that the reader can understand what clients with these disorders bring to the group context and the challenges that might be faced by the facilitator.

Schizophrenia affects approximately 1.1% of the adult population in the United States (National Institute of Mental Health, n.d.). It is a mental disorder characterized by the presence of both positive and negative symptoms, including thinking disturbances. These symptoms interfere with the individual's functioning in work, interpersonal relationships, or self-care and must be present for at least 6 months for the person to qualify for the clinical diagnosis. Positive symptoms include delusions (false beliefs that persist despite evidence that disproves them) and hallucinations (perceptions—sounds, sights, touch—that are experienced without external stimuli). When one has a hallucination, the subjective experience is the same as that of any other perception, except that one cannot control it (e.g., by looking away, putting fingers in ears). Disorganized thinking is also present and is noticeable when the person rapidly changes topics when speaking with no apparent connection between topics or, in extreme cases, when speech is an incomprehensible "word salad." Motor behavior may be unusual, from catatonic (lack of response to the outside world), to rigid postures, to agitated purposeless movement. Negative symptoms include minimal emotional expression—absence of facial expression, tone of voice, gestures, and so on, which usually accompany speech and convey the emotional tone—and a lack of motivation for any activity. This may be expressed in the inability to appreciate ordinarily pleasurable activities, reduction in speech production, and lack of interest in others. According to schizophrenia.com, 10 years postdiagnosis, 25% of people completely recover, 25% are much improved and functioning independently, 25% are somewhat improved but still require extensive support, 15% are unimproved and hospitalized, and 10% are dead (often from suicide). This means that there is hope for improvement, and group facilitators should see their work as contributing to the more positive outcomes.

Delusional Disorder is diagnosed if hallucinations are absent or minimal and when functioning is adequate in major life areas. The prevalence of delusional disorder is lower than that of schizophrenia and is estimated to be about .025% to .03% of the population (Eifert, n.d.). Among those diagnosed, 33%–50% will eventually be in complete remission, 30%–40% will continue to have symptoms over time, and 10% will have fewer delusional symptoms while retaining some irrational beliefs.

Schizoaffective disorder is characterized by the presence of a depressive or manic mood episode along with hallucinations. It is difficult to diagnose, and it has been estimated that 2%–30% of persons in treatment for psychiatric disorders may qualify for this diagnosis.

We include personality disorders (PDs) within SMI because of the enduring patterns that cause impairment in functioning. One estimate of prevalence puts the rate at about 9% of U.S. adults in 2007 (National Institute of Mental Health, 2007). PDs emerge in late adolescence or early adulthood and are stable patterns of perceptions and behaviors that are very different from those of other people in the cultural context. They often co-occur with other mental disorders. The PDs most likely to be seen in groups for SMI include schizotypal PD, which is a pattern that involves extreme discomfort in close relationships, eccentric behavior, and cognitive or perceptual distortions. Borderline PD is seen when interpersonal relationships are chronically unstable, with erratic emotionality and notable impulsivity. Narcissistic PD describes someone with an extreme belief in his or her own self-importance, fantasies about success, power, and so on, who needs admiration from others and believes it is his or her due, lacks empathy, takes advantage of others, and believes in his or her exceptional gifts.

Depression involves a mood that is notably different from previous functioning and that may include depressed mood (sad, hopeless), anhedonia (loss of interest in previously enjoyed activities), a change of body weight due to increased or decreased appetite, sleep disturbances, lack of energy, feelings of worthlessness, and motor activity that is either agitated or noticeably retarded. Symptoms must be present for at least 2 weeks for a clinical diagnosis to be made. It is one of the most common mental disorders and in 2014 was reported to occur in almost 7% of U.S. adults in the previous year (National Institute of Mental Health, 2007).

There are numerous anxiety disorders, which all exhibit excessive fear and worry that cause subjective distress and interfere with one's functioning. The National Institute of Mental Health (2014) estimated that in a given year, about 18% of adults will qualify for this diagnosis, with 4.1% of the population having a severe case. Data show that less than 37% of persons with this disorder receive treatment.

GROUP WORK WITH SMI CLIENTS

SMI involves ongoing challenges with many tasks of daily life. Group therapy and group counseling have been effective in helping clients manage their illness and their lives. Marshak (1990) proposed that supportive group psychotherapy is the approach specifically developed to assist this population after deinstitutionalization became policy, with the goal of improving ego functioning. Group therapy works to help clients with SMI build relationships with the facilitator and members of the group, to learn adaptive behaviors, and to strengthen defense mechanisms that are protection against decompensation (in contrast to psychodynamic groups in which confronting, and sometimes dismantling, those defenses is often a goal).

Bedell, Hunter, and Corrigan (1997) described characteristics of effective treatment that are relevant for group facilitators. First, it is important that the facilitators maintain a positive view of the clients. Although many clients will have lifelong illnesses, others will recover, and still others will improve significantly over time. If the facilitator has a pessimistic view of the course of the disorder, it is likely to negatively influence her or his behavior in the group. Second, the approaches that have been found to be most effective are those that focus on learning and skill development. The facilitator needs to recognize that and utilize those approaches in his or her groups, regardless of overall theoretical orientation. Third, clear, specific, and objective goals for both the group and the members are helpful. When the client has not met the goals that he or she has set (with the assistance of the facilitator and the group), the goals or approach must be modified. The client should not be considered a failure. Finally, the facilitator should consider resources in the community that can bolster the work being done in the group and consider holding groups for families of persons with SMI.

The programs with the best outcomes for this population have been those that include interpersonal communication skills, problem-solving skills, and social skill training (Bedell et al., 1997). These types of training are ideal for group counseling/therapy. Bedell and colleagues (1997) thought it effective to offer time-limited groups for a particular set of skills. The client can continue to participate in groups focused on additional sets of skills at any time. The group should include both didactic and experiential components, so that the skills can be practiced within the safety of the group setting. Clients will then attempt to apply the skills in their life outside the group and report on their successes. If they face obstacles, the group can help them review the skills and get additional practice with feedback.

One Clinician's Perspective

We share some insights provided by TGK, a therapist who conducted groups for clients with SMI for a number of years. Although his overall theoretical orientation is psychodynamic, he worked somewhat differently with this clientele. In his opinion, most of the clients, regardless of specific diagnosis, had narcissistic disturbances, or insults to the integrity of the self. In adults, those with narcissistic disturbances are likely to display both grandiose thinking and depressive symptoms, often alternating between the two (Stringer & Molnos, n.d.). Many feel considerable shame about having a mental illness, and they struggle to feel as though they are as good as others in the group; ensuring that all members have their share of "air time" can be critical to avoid a member feeling as though he or she is not as good or not as well liked as the other members.

According to TGK, in groups for this population there is a need for more structure than in an insight-oriented group. Activities and exercises are very helpful and ensure that members feel that they are successful participants. The activities reduce members' anxiety about how and when they are expected to contribute by providing a format for disclosure.

Some practical considerations follow: TGK had mixed-diagnosis groups for several reasons. One, there may not be enough people with SMI in the community seeking group treatment of any specific diagnosis at the same time. Second, given the emotional volatility of this group, members come and go, and having a reasonable number of members (six to seven) for a group is easier to accomplish with mixed diagnoses. Because members would leave (sometimes to be hospitalized, or to go jail, or to terminate), new members were added periodically. When a new member would be ready to join the group, TGK would prepare the members for several weeks before the new person's first session. They would discuss what the member was like, how they would introduce themselves, what they wanted the new person to tell them, and so on. Because the members had a chance to adjust to the idea of a new member in advance, the addition typically was not disruptive. In fact, it was helpful to have continuing members tell the new member their goals, and so on, because it reminded all members of the purpose of the group. Exits were usually unanticipated, so a formal good-bye did not become part of the group's rituals.

One dynamic that TGK observed in this group was that the members appeared to take the lowest functioning member under its collective wing. Rather than being annoyed by active symptoms, the group seemed to derive benefits from their perceived altruism, so that the entire group profited from their efforts on behalf of the struggling member. Another dynamic was the result of a member who kept secrets about himself. One of the members in TGK's group had been charged with possession of child pornography on his computer several years before he joined the group, but he was unwilling to tell the group, fearing that he would be rejected. When he was arrested for violating the terms of his probation, the rest of the group was extremely angry and upset. One of the members, a woman with a history of sexual abuse, was so distressed that she reported the facilitators to an insurance company. Although the insurance company was not the appropriate agency for a complaint, her behavior illustrates how disturbing the revelation was.

TGK now believes that if the therapist is aware of a potentially important secret, he or she must help the member to disclose it to the group early on to avoid feelings of betrayal in other members. Another pattern that can be disruptive to the group is the member who personalizes comments made in the group but says nothing about the hurt feelings until he or she explodes in an intense angry outburst that takes everyone by surprise. The facilitator needs to be extremely attentive to detect such building emotion and help the member express it early on rather than allowing it to build.

Finally, TGK notes that unlike most therapy groups in which contact outside the group is discouraged or prohibited, such contact is encouraged in his groups for SMI clients. In fact, every year he organizes potluck meals for the group around significant holidays, with group members collaborating on arranging the table and so on. The group members eventually became cohesive enough to meet for meals or other activities outside of group time. The shared meals became a much-anticipated event that the members looked forward to and enjoyed. TGK believes that this is an important step toward increasing social and interpersonal communication skills, a major goal for the group.

TGK always worked with a cofacilitator when conducting groups for the population with SMI and found that having a female cofacilitator seemed to be the best configuration in the mixed-gender groups that he led. There is so much to attend to in these groups that the second facilitator makes a significant difference, and the opportunity to process the group afterward gives facilitators a chance to reflect and if necessary revise their approach or strategize how to handle a particular situation or client.

Therapist Characteristics

TGK believes that several characteristics are necessary in someone who facilitates a group with SMI clients. These include exposure to a variety of diagnoses; the experienced clinician will be better able to recognize when a client is experiencing hallucinations or delusions, will not be disturbed by the labile affect that is likely to be present in some members, and will be able to sense when anger is building. In his opinion, working in an inpatient setting is invaluable experience to prepare for this kind of work. That setting shows the counselor what the person with these disorders looks like when he or she is out of control, resulting in increased empathy and understanding. The inpatient setting also provides skills for helping clients manage their fears and for identifying moments when a client may need to step away from the group for a brief period to calm down (and for managing such situations logistically). In addition to knowledge and skills, a person who is solid and not easily rattled, and with a sense of humor, is ideal for facilitating groups for clients with SMI.

TGK's view is largely consistent with the characteristics of effective group facilitators for groups of SMI clients, which is summarized by Marshak (1990). Marshak noted the importance of the facilitator being willing to take a very active role in the group, including teaching appropriate social behaviors. She recommended that the facilitator be willing to acknowledge any small gains made by clients and to realize that the gains are likely to be incremental rather than monumental. Marshak also noted that it is essential to have the ability to tolerate or even enjoy the sometime bizarre behavior or verbalizations of the clients and the perceptiveness to recognize and interpret nonverbal clues to the client's internal experience.

Specific Strategies

Now we turn to more general recommendations. The recommendations in this section come primarily from Stone (1996), Marshak (1990), and Kanas (1996). We begin with appropriate goals for groups for SMI clients. Of course, an overriding goal is to keep clients in the community and avoid hospitalizations. Group members may find common ground in their disappointment with previous treatment and their difficulties with medication. Despite this commonality, the facilitator must ensure that the group does not support a client discontinuing medication or treatment without consulting prescribing medical personnel. Marshak (1990) noted that in her experience, groups will not support discontinuing treatment or medication, and she believed that this is particularly effective because the member recognizes that the others in the group do understand his or her frustrations.

Another appropriate and important goal is acquiring new social skills. The group provides a safe place to learn and practice skills that are useful outside the group as clients struggle to form and maintain interpersonal relationships. As groups progress, they may find that helping each other solve problems is a valuable function. There are many problems of daily living that members encounter, and being able to seek assistance from the group is a beneficial opportunity. However, it is recommended that the facilitator teach and coach the group in problem solving so that they learn a process in addition to finding a solution.

It is important to limit participation, particularly in an outpatient setting, to clients who are not actively psychotic, in a manic episode, or displaying highly paranoid delusions. They are unable to participate in a meaningful way, and their presence is likely to disrupt the group. As noted above, clients in groups for SMI are often highly anxious about the group, particularly as it is just starting. The presence of clients in an acute psychotic state is likely to exacerbate those fears. Among other fears, they may be concerned about losing control themselves and concerned about what would happen if others in the group lose control. Those who have delusions that their thoughts are being broadcast or that thoughts are being inserted into their minds may fear that this will happen in the group. Others may fear that they will be rejected or humiliated in the group as they have been in other settings. Marshak suggested that these fears are likely to subside, although not entirely disappear, as the group continues to meet and develop cohesion. When anxiety builds, it may be appropriate to take short breaks (coffee, anyone?) or divert the group's attention to a less fear-provoking topic.

We wish to emphasize that one of the most effective ways to manage anxiety in these groups is to have a high degree of structure and use carefully selected exercises and activities. When clients realize that the facilitator will provide structure, their anxiety decreases because the unknown is diminished. That structure should include clear expectations of member behavior, and these should be communicated to members in their screening interview and reiterated with the group at its first meeting. It is also useful in the first session to talk about what topics will be discussed in the group so that group members realize that the facilitator understands their needs. Related to structure is the need to intervene promptly when a group member's communication is unclear, when a member needs encouragement, or when a topic is clearly causing anxiety. All of these facilitator actions keep the group on task and assure the members that they are safe.

The symptoms of SMI may include difficulties with communication. Marshak (1990) recommended that the facilitator intervene without focusing on the client's difficulty but rather by saying, "I'm not sure I am following you," or something to that effect, which does not label the client's speech as jumbled or incomprehensible. If the facilitator chooses to paraphrase, again, tentative language is helpful: "I want to be sure I get this right. What you are saying is . . . ," thus providing the client with an opportunity to rephrase. When client speech is pressured and disconnected, the facilitator can try slowing his or her own speech, and if that does not work, it may be necessary to interrupt the client until he or she is able to slow down. For those clients whose speech is already very slow, the facilitator needs to ensure that the client has ample time to respond before someone else takes the floor. The facilitator might say, "We'd like to hear what you have to say, John, but first we want to give Jane a chance to share." Overall, frequent summaries are helpful, and the facilitator must be very active in cutting off those who take too much of the group's time while encouraging more reticent clients to share.

When delusional clients persist in professing their delusional beliefs, the facilitator is likely to have the most impact by helping the client examine the evidence for and against the belief. This is typically more effective than simply confronting the client with the illogic of the belief, although people with fixed delusions are unlikely to respond to this approach. In those cases, it may be more useful to focus on the reactions they receive from others when they talk about their delusions. The facilitator can help them examine whether they prefer the reactions they get when talking about their delusions or when keeping them to themselves, and group members will be very helpful in sharing their reactions. Unlike TGK's observation that his group coalesced to take care of a low-functioning member, Marshak (1990) cautioned that a member whose florid symptoms are worsening may cause group members to withdraw, because they are reminded of the possibility that their own symptoms could worsen.

Facilitators should be aware that Recovery International (http://www.recoveryinternational.org/) is an organization dedicated to assisting people with mental health problems to live functionally in the community. The organization offers SHG meetings, in person or via telephone or chat, and provides materials that enable a new member to understand the concepts on which the program is based, which are based on the work of Alexander Low. The program is a structured cognitive behavior approach that is facilitated by trained volunteer leaders who have benefited from the program themselves. Professional counselors may not lead these groups but should consider familiarizing themselves with the program should a referral be indicated.

THEORETICAL PERSPECTIVES

Kanas (1996) reviewed the theoretical approaches that have been the basis for inpatient groups for individuals with SMI. Because these theories could apply to other settings for groups, we briefly summarize Kanas's observations and then present his integrative model, which some readers might want to adopt in their own work. The educative approach focuses on the management of symptoms and problems in daily living that are related to the disorder. Members are taught strategies to cope with hallucinations and delusions and to handle related problems. In groups based on this approach, there is considerable teaching, practicing, role-playing, and frequently homework. The focus is not on historical events or intrapsychic exploration but on here-and-now concerns. One of the topics covered is medication, because clients in the group might be noncompliant with prescribed pharmaceutical treatment. Kanas suggested that with clear information about the biological substrates of the mental illnesses and the way that the medication works, members are more likely to be compliant. In this model, the therapist takes the expert role, and the relationships among members are not emphasized.

In the psychodynamic approach, the emphasis is on seeking insight into the origins of the illness, believed to be in early childhood (Kanas, 1996). The practitioners who use this perspective believe that the group becomes the "mother figure," who is responsive to the members' needs and thus functions to reparent the wounded ego. This approach encourages exploration of unconscious material and transferences in the group, and the supportive environment allows the client to risk doing this difficult work. Group members are engaged in confronting each other's defenses and assisting each member in revisiting the psychic traumas of childhood so that they can be free to function without these burdens. This approach has been criticized for being reminiscent of the discredited "schizophrenogenic mother" theory that held that the origins of psychosis were the mother's inadequate parenting.

The interpersonal approach focuses on improving the social world of members by emphasizing interactions in the present in the group and by using the group as a laboratory for developing more effective skills. In such groups, exercises to encourage interaction among members are used, and members are encouraged to observe when interactions generate unpleasant reactions so that they can help members learn more appropriate ways to communicate. As we have stated several times, these groups should be carefully structured to keep anxiety at bay, and the facilitator should be active and engaged in the process.

Kanas (1996) described the structure for inpatient groups for people with schizophrenia developed by Yalom (1995), which includes an orientation, warm-up, exercises (the bulk of group time), and review of the session. The warm-up activities should be brief and nonthreatening, setting up the relaxed and supportive atmosphere for the session. The exercises are designed to elicit some self-disclosure and to encourage member interaction. Games are sometimes used toward these ends. When anxiety is high, sometimes dyads or triads are used to decrease the number of members with whom the client interacts. In the review segment, members help the facilitator summarize the session, and time is allotted to provide positive feedback to clients who were engaged in some way during the session.

It is obvious that each of these approaches alone is insufficient to address the many and complex needs of the population with SMI. Each has advantages that are important, but in some cases the disadvantages leave much territory uncovered. Thus, Kanas (1996) designed a group format that integrates the three approaches, which he calls an *integrative* approach. For these groups, there are two major goals: to help members cope with their psychotic symptoms and to help members improve their relationships with others. For the first goal, medication generally reduces or eliminates the symptoms, but they persist in some cases. The first step is to help clients see that these experiences are part of the illness and that they interfere with their lives. The members of the group can provide reality testing (they do not hear the voices) and help the symptomatic member develop coping strategies by sharing the methods that they have found to be effective. For the second goal, members can share interpersonal problems that they are having, and while they are discussing the problems, all members are using interpersonal skills in a safe environment and with the oversight of the facilitator.

For this integrative group, Kanas (1996) recommended that groups in the community meet once or twice a week for an hour each session and that they be closed to new members to allow trust and cohesion to develop. The groups typically have a set life of 12 weeks, but members who wish to continue are encouraged to join another group after one concludes. Optimal membership is 8–10 members, with two facilitators. That assumes that with some members missing, each session will have about six to eight members present. Confidentiality is important in these groups, as it is in all groups. Because many of the members will have multiple providers, it is helpful to be very specific about what kind of records the facilitators keep, who has access to those records, and under what circumstances. Kanas also believed that although the two-facilitator model is best, regular and consistent meeting times are most important, so that if one facilitator must be absent, it is advisable for the group to meet rather than cancel or reschedule.

Because of the type of disorders present in an SMI group, the role of the facilitator is perhaps different than in other groups. The facilitator must be highly active and directive to keep members focused on the goals. The facilitator must use clear and concrete (nonclinical) language. Kanas (1996) referred to psychotic breaks as "nervous breakdowns" when speaking to the group. Because of the thinking and attentional problems members may have, the facilitator should be sure to repeat important information often. Members may need reminders to look at the person to whom they are speaking, for example, and to address others in the first person. In these groups, it is also acceptable for the facilitator to give advice or state his or her opinions when the purpose of such intervention is to benefit the member and group. Of course, the main role of the facilitator is still to encourage members to relate to one another and to learn from each other, and the facilitator should help members seek advice from each other. Chronic and severe mental illness is associated with problems in finding places to live, in finding jobs, in managing money, and in numerous other tasks with which other members will be familiar. Additional suggestions for group facilitators may be found in the chapter on cognitive disabilities, because they are useful for any disability that involves impaired cognition, including some psychiatric disabilities.

Group workers are mindful of the importance of the first and last sessions in the life of a group. In groups for SMI, this is especially true. In the first session, everyone begins by just stating their names. The facilitators then describe the goals of the group and the norms that will be followed. This is a good time for the facilitators to promote the positive impact of the group and share their optimism that improvement is likely. Then all members share their most salient problems related to their disorder and what their hopes and expectations are for the group. As the problems are shared, the facilitator selects one to begin the format that will be followed in subsequent sessions.

Kanas (1996) structured sessions in a particular sequence: Early in the session, a topic related to the group goals is identified. Sometimes the facilitator will need to help focus the topic, but ideally it will come from the members. Once the topic has been identified, all members are encouraged to discuss how the topic relates to them; if this does not happen, the facilitator can initiate a structured go-around. Once everyone has commented, the focus shifts to coping strategies.

POSTTRAUMATIC STRESS DISORDER

PTSD was recognized as a mental disorder only as recently as 1980, when it was added to the *Diagnostic and Statistical Manual of Mental Disorders* (3rd ed.; American Psychiatric Association, 1980). In the *DSM–5*, PTSD is no longer grouped with anxiety disorders. It is placed in a section on trauma- and stress-related disorders. The diagnosis of PTSD requires that the individual be exposed to actual or threatened death, serious injury, or sexual violation in one of the following ways: having direct experience of the event, witnessing the event in vivo, learning that the event occurred to someone to whom the person was close, or experiencing repeated exposure to the negative details of the event. This must lead to distress or impairment in functioning, and it is diagnosed only when the symptoms are still present a month after the traumatic event. Symptoms of the disorder are reexperiencing the event (flashbacks, dreams, intrusive thoughts), avoidance (of associated situations), negative cognitions and mood, and arousal (self-destructive behavior, sleep disturbance, hypervigilance). The lifetime prevalence of PTSD in U.S. adults is 7.8%. The rate is twice as high in women as in men. It is important to remember that many people experience traumatic events without developing PTSD. The most common traumatic events are witnessing a death or severe injury, being involved in a fire or natural disaster, being involved in a life-threatening accident, and being in combat. It is notable that among Vietnam veterans, 30.9% of men and 26.9% of women had PTSD during their lifetime.

Group therapy for PTSD is widely used, so it is puzzling that the research is not conclusive about the benefits. Research on group counseling and therapy is difficult to conduct, analyses are complex, and large-enough samples are difficult to obtain. Ruzek

(2003) noted that absence of definitive research on group work for PTSD, and almost a decade later, other researchers (Sloan, Bovin, & Schnurr, 2012) reiterated that there is a paucity of robust studies on this important form of treatment. Sloan et al. (2012) conducted an extensive review of the literature, which included several meta-analyses, and cautiously concluded that group treatment for PTSD is effective but not as effective as individual treatment. Moreover, none of the studies have established that a particular approach is more effective than another.

Group treatment for PTSD is widely used because the rationale makes intuitive and clinical sense. People with PTSD are often isolated and alienated from others (Ruzek, 2003; Shea, McDevitt-Murphy, Ready, & Schnurr, 2008), and groups provide an opportunity to learn the universality of their trauma responses while building a sense of safety and trust in others. Social support is a therapeutic aspect of treatment; trauma survivors often think others cannot understand their experience and feelings, which leads to isolation and the sense that they are different in essential ways from others. They may be embarrassed or feel shame about the traumatic event or about their inability to get over it, feel guilty, and worry about negative reactions from others. Survivors of trauma often avoid any reminders of the traumatic incident, which further reduces their social engagement and exacerbates their loneliness and isolation. By relating with others in the group around a shared trauma, the isolation often diminishes, and over time, the positive relationships with others in the group may transfer to those outside the group.

Wolfsdorf and Zlotnick (2001) determined that affect dysregulation (the inability to manage strong emotions) is frequently seen in clients with PTSD with a history of childhood sexual abuse and may be present even without this history. This feature can be quite disruptive to people's lives and can also make treatment difficult. Wolfsdorf and Zlotnick's approach is recommended in conjunction with individual treatment, during which they believe that exposure therapy is more appropriately conducted. The affect management group is based on cognitive behavior therapy, with a focus on the present time and immediate concerns. An important goal is cognitive restructuring of maladaptive thinking patterns such as overgeneralization, all-or-nothing thinking, and emotional reasoning. A second goal is to improve the ability to handle distress. This is accomplished through direct teaching of skills in a safe environment in which skills can be practiced and in which triggering situations can be prepared for. Individuals also observe and learn from other members how to utilize the skills. The team theorizes that in the environment in which sexual abuse took place, the child may not have ever developed necessary coping skills, so direct teaching is necessary. Their model includes 15 sessions, each 90 minutes long and focused on a specific skill (e.g., distraction skills, self-soothing skills, anger management skills), with a structured format: review of homework, didactic component on new skill, rehearsing skills, and assignment of homework. To test their approach, Wolfsdorf and Zlotnick randomly assigned 48 women to either their affect management group or a wait-list control group. All participants also received individual therapy and medication. Findings indicated that those in the affect management group had significantly fewer PTSD symptoms and also showed improvement in depression and dissociation.

It is important to note that many individuals with PTSD have experienced more than one trauma. In some treatment approaches, the emphasis is on improving self-esteem and interpersonal relationships, which are often compromised by trauma. However, Lubin, Loris, Burt, and Johnson (1998) were interested in reducing the primary symptoms of PTSD. They delivered an interactive 16-session psychoeducational group with 29 women (five groups) who reported multiple forms of victimization and who had been diagnosed with long-standing PTSD. Assessments were administered at baseline, at 1-month intervals during the program, at termination, and at 6-month follow-up. Significant improvement was detected on PTSD symptoms of reexperiencing, avoidance, and hyperarousal at termination and at 6-month follow-up. Although there was no control or comparison group, the improvements are noteworthy, and the program appears worthy of further investigation.

In addition to the lack of strong empirical support for groups for PTSD in general, there is also disagreement about which of the approaches results in the best outcomes for members. In general, the two major treatment perspectives are those that focus on the trauma and those that focus on present-related concerns (such as coping skills, managing symptoms, etc.).[1] We provide an overview of the most commonly used theories on which specific programs are based and then provide examples of specific trauma groups that have been implemented. We conclude with general recommendations for facilitators who are considering providing such groups.

---

[1]A useful table summarizing the differences in these two types of groups can be found in Module 4 of *An Overview of Evidence-Based Group Approaches to Trauma with Adults* (Foy, Unger, & Wattenberg, 2004).

All groups for PTSD include an educational component. Members learn about PTSD and its symptoms, which shows them that their experiences are common among those who have experienced a trauma. The educational material also helps them see that their symptoms are somewhat predictable, and thus are less anxiety provoking. It is important that the education be delivered in such a way that members are actively engaged in discussion of the material, are considering how it relates to their experience, and are considering how their present coping strategies (especially if they are using substances) are working to manage the symptoms. Group members should also learn about their likely progression in treatment so that their expectations are realistic. In some groups, this didactic portion includes information about effective coping strategies, and if so, there should be time to practice with feedback from group members.

Some groups, often called supportive, focus on the role of nonjudgmental support and empathy for trauma survivors and incorporate strategies to increase self-esteem and strengthen interpersonal connections within the group. In this type of group, the traumatic memories are avoided, and defense mechanisms against those memories are enhanced.

Other groups emphasize the development of coping skills. They incorporate education but spend more time on demonstration and on practice with feedback and coaching, and practice is repeated numerous times. In such groups, members receive homework that typically involves self-monitoring records and practice in their usual settings. They can then report back to the group on how well they are doing, practice again, and so on. Some of the coping skills that are typically taught are problem solving, managing distress from trauma-related thoughts, recognition of triggers that are associated with unwanted thoughts, relaxation, deep breathing, grounding, assertiveness, and seeking social support. When members actively participate in the treatment, including the homework, improvement is likely to occur fairly soon.

Trauma-focused groups, however, are based on the premise that integration of the traumatic experience is necessary to reduce symptoms and restore functioning. The present-focused groups emphasize the need to reduce the isolation of the members and provide skills (with practice and feedback) to address problems that they are currently having.

Trauma-focused groups can be further divided by the theoretical orientation that guides the practitioner. For example, some such groups are psychodynamic, focusing on bringing to consciousness the unconscious components of the trauma, whereas cognitively based groups apply desensitization, extinction, and cognitive reconstruction. Psychodynamic, interpersonal, and process-oriented groups all help members gain insight into their dysfunctional interpersonal patterns, and they help the members see how these patterns are connected to the trauma. These three approaches all emphasize the social impact of the trauma and focus on the here-and-now interpersonal interactions in the group as a vehicle to regaining trust and improving relationships. Cognitive behavior groups use behavioral skills training, cognitive skills restructuring, and imaginal trauma exposure. In these groups, symptoms often increase initially and then diminish as the desensitization takes effect.

According to Ruzek (2003), exposure and cognitive restructuring are the best-validated treatment strategies for PTSD. However, this effect has been found for individual treatment and has not yet been confirmed for the group format. When these strategies are used, several sessions are spent on education and coping skills prior to engaging in exposure, which is the main technique used. The structure of the group is explained, as is the rationale for exposure. Members need a clear understanding of what they will be doing and the level of commitment needed to see positive outcomes. Rules or norms are established to ensure that members feel safe. The repeated (in group and outside) exposure to the traumatic memories is believed to reduce symptoms of PTSD by reducing the level of anxiety experienced when the memory is present and can also correct faulty cognitions about the experience when a member recalls a detail that puts the incident in a different perspective.

Given the intensity of the emotional distress associated with the traumatic experience, it is not surprising that retention in treatment is a challenge when exposure is the primary technique used. A moving account of the challenges of exposure and treatment in general for combat-related trauma can be found at: http://mobile. nytimes.com/2015/09/20/us/marine-battalion-veterans-scarred-by-suicides-turn-to-one-another-for-help.html?referrer=&_r=0.

In the group, each member has a turn (or more than one) to describe in detail a single highly distressing memory of the trauma, and member is told to include all the sensory experiences that they can recall, their thoughts and emotions at the time. Usually, the member is not interrupted during this narrative, unless the member appears to be avoiding immersing him- or herself in the memory. In most groups, this account is recorded so that it can be used for the homework, which involves listening to the recording at least weekly and noting the levels of distress and the coping skills used.

Cognitive restructuring can be combined with exposure. This technique helps members reconsider some of the beliefs that they have about the incident and their role. Many clients with PTSD will have self-blaming attributions or negative evaluations of their response to the trauma. Part of cognitive restructuring involves educating the clients about how thoughts affect emotions and behavior and the importance of testing these cognitions for accuracy. When group members challenge another member's beliefs, it is extremely powerful because the member knows they are speaking with personal knowledge and deep understanding. Again, homework and practice is involved in this component so that the restructured thoughts about the trauma are incorporated into the person's automatic thinking.

Many of the programs described above are manualized. These manuals are scripted instructions for therapists to follow. However, we do not recommend that a novice facilitator conduct a PTSD group without extensive training and supervision and a thorough knowledge of PTSD. Certainly, to facilitate trauma-focused groups, one must be prepared for the level of intensity and emotionality that may occur and must be confident of her or his ability to provide the structured support required. We also strongly recommend that there be coleaders for groups for PTSD for the same reasons that we mentioned in the section on SMI. In PTSD groups, it is possible that a member will experience such intense anxiety that he or she will choose to leave the group room. With two facilitators, one can step out to ensure the safety of that person, to help moderate the anxiety, and if possible to assist the member in returning to the group. Facilitators must be alert to the possibility of vicarious traumatization, and the coleader model is most likely to bring that, and transference issues, to the attention of the facilitators.

Experts believe that there is sufficient evidence to advise facilitators on group composition. They suggest the following:

- Not to include only one member who differs from the rest of the members on a significant characteristic, such as gender or type of trauma.
- Not to include members who are actively psychotic, severely depressed, or severely cognitively impaired.
- Not to include someone who does not have a stable residence (who could become preoccupied with problems related to the living situation and be unable to commit to attend).

- Not to include someone who voices strong objection to group treatment.
- Not to include members who are currently abusing substances or who are paranoid or sociopathic.

These clients are unlikely to profit from treatment and may disrupt the process for other members. For example, one study found that in a group that contained one member with borderline personality disorder, the gains for the entire group were negatively affected (Shea et al., 2008).

A factor to consider when putting a group together is the recency of the trauma and the severity of symptoms. If a potential member has PTSD related to a trauma that occurred in the distant past, that person may not be appropriate for a trauma-focused group, because he or she may not be willing to revisit the trauma. Such clients, and those with extremely high levels of anxiety, are probably better suited to a supportive group or to one focused on coping skills. In addition, it makes sense to have homogeneity of trauma type (e.g., combat, motor vehicle accident, natural disaster, sexual assault) so that members know that they will be understood, and cohesion and trust will develop more quickly.

Types of PTSD Groups

Combat PTSD

PTSD groups for combat veterans are widely available. The U.S. Department of Veterans Affairs often provides these groups at its facilities, but many communities also have them in local areas. PTSD is a high-frequency problem among veterans, and with the recent wars in the Middle East, more returning soldiers are presenting with symptoms. One reason given for implementing group treatment programs is to increase efficiency and provide services to more members than could be done individually. In response to this need for treatment, Foy, Ruzek, Glynn, Riney, and Gusman (2002) developed a manualized treatment protocol (and member workbook) to use with this population. They implemented the trauma-focused type of therapy, which had been used extensively for individual therapy but was quite new to the group approach. They based their program on behaviorist principles of classical and operant conditioning. Although they emphasized the trauma exposure, they also included an interactional approach and considered how the individual characteristics of each member, the characteristics of the trauma, and the characteristics of the environment were involved in the development of PTSD. The goal of the group was to enhance quality of life for members by learning to manage the symptom increases that were likely to occur at various times in the person's life. Their program involved prolonged and repeated exposure to the traumatic memory and a relapse prevention segment. They devoted a third of each 2-hour session to working with one member's traumatic combat memory.

The Foy et al. (2002) group program is designed to meet for 30 sessions, and their article includes an outline of each session. There are three phases: introductory sessions, warzone focus sessions (Sessions 9–22), and relapse prevention and termination sessions. The introductory sessions are 90 minutes long. This carefully designed program begins with education about both PTSD and the treatment approach. Prior to introducing the exposure activity, the facilitators ensure that group rules and structure are well established, the members are becoming cohesive, coping skills have been taught, and members understand the rationale for and expectations from this type of treatment.

Also prior to the exposure sessions, members share premilitary autobiographies and military autobiographies to create a context for the trauma memories. For the trauma-focused sessions, members are asked to select a trauma scene that will be the focus of the work. It should be one that is particularly upsetting and related to symptoms and one that generates fear. The stories are told with details of feelings, thoughts, and emotions that members experienced at the time, and vivid images are encouraged; the narrative is recorded for later use in homework. Following the sharing of the memory, cognitive distortions are identified by facilitators and other members. As in other groups of this type, the members are instructed to listen to the recordings at least once a week and to note their level of distress and coping skills used to manage that distress. Each member will have two sessions devoted to this work. Subsequent sessions focus on topics to develop coping strategies and to engage in specific relapse prevention planning.

Sexual Violence

Exposure to sexual violence is experienced as highly traumatic and can result in PTSD. About 40% of women in the Democratic Republic of Congo have experienced sexual violence, and PTSD is a widespread problem. Bass et al. (2013) devised a way to provide therapy to this high-need population, many of whom had co-occurring depression and anxiety. The researchers translated measures of PTSD into local languages to select appropriate candidates for their groups. What is particularly notable in this situation is that because of a shortage of mental health professionals, the program was implemented by local psychological assistants, who were trained for 2 weeks by the team from the United States and provided with a detailed manual to follow. To study the effects of this program, Bass and colleagues randomly divided eligible women into two groups; one received the treatment, and the others were able to telephone a supportive counselor as needed. After screening and attrition, the remaining study participants were 157 women who were in the treatment group and 248 in the control group (with individual supportive services available). Each member had one individual session of 1 hour and eleven 2-hour sessions in groups of six to eight women. The treatment utilized a cognitive processing approach without exposure. The entire program was designed for illiterate participants and translated into four local languages and Swahili, which was spoken in some of the villages in which the program was conducted.

Their results were impressive. Those who received the therapy had significantly greater improvement from pre- to postassessment than did those in the individual support condition, with all effect sizes being very large. For example, at baseline, 70% of members in the treatment groups met criteria for likely depression or anxiety in addition to PTSD, and less than 10% did so after treatment. In the control condition, 83% met criteria at baseline, and 53% did so at the end of the treatment period. The same difference in gains was reflected on the PTSD measures. Although there were limitations to the study, the results suggest that group therapy can be useful in far less than optimal conditions and that, using approaches that do not involve exposure, specifically trained paraprofessionals can be effective facilitators.

PTSD Due to Motor Vehicle Accidents

A group was designed for survivors of traumatic motor vehicle accidents (MVAs). The developers chose a cognitive behavior perspective for a 14-session group facilitated by cotherapists (J. G. Beck & Coffey, 2005). A unique issue faced by this clientele is that members will often arrive to group in an anxious state because they need to drive or ride in a car to get to the treatment site. To give members a chance (and a tool) to reduce that anxiety, sessions begin with a brief mindfulness exercise to improve focus in the group. Members are also encouraged to use that technique while driving to ensure that they are not distracted by their fears or do not use unsafe practices in an attempt to be safe. Because of concerns about individual narratives of accidents causing heightened symptoms in other members, the exposure component is conducted via homework.

Many survivors of MVAs also suffer from chronic pain and may be taking medication (or self-medicating with alcohol and other drugs) or be unable to sit for the duration of the meeting. Facilitators accommodate those needs. Although there is a manual, facilitators select topics on the basis of the needs of the largest number of members. In the first session, as in other groups that we have discussed, some standard tasks are accomplished, and education about PTSD is provided. In this group, progressive muscle relaxation is taught at this time and reviewed in the next session. Early in the group, members write detailed descriptions of their MVA but do not share them with other members. One of the facilitators reads the narrative and provides feedback to the member to ensure that the description is sufficiently detailed. Members are taught a "subjective units of distress" rating procedure that they will use in subsequent work. The members are told that exposure should continue until this rating decreases by 50%. This approach also has members develop an avoidance hierarchy on which some of the sessions will focus. J. G. Beck and Coffey (2005) reported anecdotal and some quantitative measures of their five-member group. Four of five members reported improved symptoms by a 4-week postgroup follow-up assessment. This is clearly not an empirically supported treatment at this time, but their work helps facilitators conceptualize how groups for persons with PTSD following a MVA might be constructed.

PTSD in Survivors of Childhood Sexual Abuse

Finally, we look at results of a cognitive processing group for PTSD clients whose symptoms were related to childhood sexual abuse (Chard, 2005). Several assessments were administered to ascertain that potential members qualified for a PTSD diagnosis.

This population may have current problems not as salient as in other groups, including attachment and sexual intimacy issues. In Chard's (2005) study, participants were randomly assigned to the treatment or wait-list control groups. The treatment design was somewhat different from the ones described above, in that members received an additional 60-minute individual session for the first 9 weeks of the 17-week group (90-minute sessions). Chard described a developmental sequence of sessions that is reminiscent of the many PTSD groups, with particular foci at the initial meetings. There is homework each week (e.g., writing about the ways in which the abuse affected their views of the self and the world, writing a detailed account of the most traumatic incident of sexual abuse). Worksheets are completed to identify and challenge beliefs about the abuse, and other sessions focus on assertiveness, sexual intimacy, and social support.

All sessions were videotaped for supervision purposes. Those recordings were coded by an independent rater, who determined that the session protocol was followed 98% of the time. The treatment group had significantly larger improvement than did the control group, with large effect sizes. Posttreatment, 7% of the treatment group members met criteria for a diagnosis of PTSD, and 74% of the controls did. No participants reported increased symptoms. Gains following treatment were maintained at 3-month and 1-year follow-up assessments. Chard (2005) observed that drop-outs from the treatment groups tended to have higher initial scores on the PTSD measures, suggesting perhaps that the severity of symptoms be taken into account when making initial treatment decisions. Given the reliance on written assignments and handouts, this program might not be suitable for clients with reading difficulty or for those who speak a language other than English.

Groups With Child Victims of Sexual Abuse

Groups are also effective with children who have been sexually abused (Riva, 1990). For younger children, art and play therapy are typically the approaches used. Games and snacks might be incorporated because of the difficulty young children have sustaining attention on an activity for long periods. For older children and adolescents, groups provide a safe place for them to talk about either the trauma or the associated issues that have developed. Regarding the trauma, it is critical not to push a group member to share any information about it. Although some members will want to talk about their experience, others will not, and pushing or coercing them can feel like revictimization. Typical issues that arise in groups for children who have been sexually abused are the sense of isolation, guilt and shame (blaming themselves), anger (at the perpetrator, others who did not protect them, investigators), low self-esteem, sexuality, distrust of adults, and so forth.

The facilitators will have to determine the age range that they can accommodate in group members. Experts recommend an age span of no more than 2 years, because developmental differences might make it difficult to explain concepts and build cohesion in groups with wider age differences. Although girls are sexually victimized much more often than boys, boys are not immune. Although it is important at some point for children who have been victimized to be able to interact with people of both sexes, early in treatment, gender-specific groups are recommended. Some facilitators may want to have groups that are homogeneous for relationship with the perpetrator (known or unknown to the child prior to the abuse). The dynamics of being victimized by a trusted, known person in comparison with being sexually assaulted by a stranger are different, and mixing the two circumstances in a group could be problematic. Another possible grouping factor is time since the abuse. Children whose abuse has recently been discovered or reported may have to deal with the legal system and thus would require different support strategies than would children whose cases have been resolved.

Riva (1990) suggested that groups for sexually abused children should continue for several months at a minimum. She also weighed the advantages of open versus closed groups, pointing out that open groups can more easily accommodate children needing treatment, and with children at various stages of healing, both interpersonal learning and instillation of hope might more easily occur. Alternatively, trust is easier to build in a closed group. Coleadership is also recommended for these groups, and a male-and-female leadership team allows those who were victimized to learn to relate to someone who is not an abuser. The leaders also model healthy relationships, and the presence of both may simulate a safe and supportive family, which will be especially important to children whose families were damaged or destroyed by the abuse.

In summary, group treatments have been used with some success in treating a variety of persons with PTSD, although the empirical data are not yet definitive. Some groups include exposure as a primary method, whereas others eschew it. Neither approach has been found to be more efficacious than the other.

Group facilitators should keep in mind that many clients who have PTSD also have other disorders, so those must be taken into account in the planning. The most common comorbid disorders are depression, anxiety, and substance abuse, which are discussed in the next section. Because of the complexity of these groups, we strongly concur with the experts who encourage a coleadership model. We also recommend supervision for counselors facilitating such groups, to protect both clients and facilitators.

SUBSTANCE USE DISORDERS

In the *DSM–5*, the two categories of substance abuse and substance dependence were combined into a broader category, substance use disorder, which ranges from mild to severe. Each of 10 substances is now listed as a separate disorder (e.g., alcohol, cocaine), but the 11 diagnostic criteria are similar across those disorders. If a client has two or three symptoms, the disorder is classified as mild; four or five symptoms are considered moderate; and six or more qualifies as a severe disorder.

Groups are widely used in the treatment of substance use disorder. Best known is the SHG AA and its many offshoots, also known as 12-step groups. No research has been able to assess the effectiveness of these groups, but some mental health professionals require attendance at these groups as an adjunct to individual therapy. Some clients resist attending 12-step meetings for various reasons; clinicians should be aware of the wide range of approaches to substance use treatment (see Bauman, 2008, for a description), most of which are delivered in the group milieu. They should also be aware that some members will adamantly insist that the approach they use and believe in is the only effective approach, and the facilitator may need to ensure that dissenting opinions are respected.

Because there are many excellent books about group work for substance abusers, we do not take space here to review the general principles. We instead discuss issues that are often overlooked in discussions of groups for people with substance use disorder.

One issue that seems to arise in substance abuse groups more so than in other groups is whether the facilitator needs to be someone who has recovered from the disorder (see Center for Substance Abuse Treatment, 2005, p. 126). Some believe that to truly understand group members, facilitators need to have shared the experience of the members. Others believe that expertise in an area can be obtained in other ways (classes, reading, internships, mentoring, personal interactions with substance abusers) and that, in fact, there are two reasons to be cautious about relying on facilitators who are former substance abusers: (1) Sometimes, the facilitator finds him- or herself identifying so closely with members' experience that they use the group for their own therapy; (2) sometimes, persons who have recovered using a particular approach are narrowly focused on that approach and do not consider the needs of members; and (3) their ability to be objective about group members is compromised, and countertransference is likely. We believe that facilitators with expert knowledge about substance abuse and addiction who have solid training in group work are well-qualified to be group facilitators.

Another issue that facilitators of groups for persons with substance use disorders need to think about is working with mandated clients. Some individuals who have committed offenses in which drugs or alcohol was involved are diverted to treatment as an alternative to incarceration; others are mandated to treatment as a condition of release or believe they will increase their chances for a lighter sentence if they show they are in treatment when their case comes up. Mandated clients typically do not see a need to change their behavior and feel coerced to join a group. In the screening interview, it is helpful to point out to the prospective member that despite the external requirements to attend, both the client and the facilitator have choices. The purpose of the pregroup meeting is for both client and facilitator to decide whether this group is a good fit for the client. For example, when asked why he or she is interested in the group, if the client responds "I have to come. If I don't, I'll go back to jail," the counselor might respond, "So you've chosen to come to this group instead of going to jail." Another possible direction to take the interview in is to say something like, "Yes, it stinks to be forced to do something that doesn't seem necessary to you. But since that's the situation, what might be a way the group could be helpful to you?" Or, taking a tactic from the solution-focused toolkit, the counselor might respond with, "It sounds like your goal is to get this requirement out of your way (or get the judge to remove the requirement). How do you think you can do that?" Any of these lines of inquiry could begin to acknowledge the client's anger and frustration with being compelled to participate and raise the possibility that the group could be useful. The facilitator must make the best choice for the group; if it is clear that a particular client would not function well in the group, the facilitator should make that decision.

One approach has gained acceptance as a method to work with involuntary clients (and others as well). Motivational interviewing is a counseling approach that is designed to motivate change in individuals with addictive behaviors. The therapeutic approach is based on a theory of change that posits that change is not a single event but occurs via a series of stages. The first is precontemplation, in which individuals do not acknowledge that they have a problem and do not see any need to change. In the contemplation stage, the person recognizes that there is a problem but is not ready to change the behavior. The preparation stage is the one in which the client is ready to make a change and is beginning to explore options for doing so. The action stage is the one in which the client makes a serious and sustained effort to change. Once that has been accomplished, the maintenance stage is necessary to continue the new behaviors. As with many stage models, this does not always occur in a linear fashion, and clients move back and forth between stages. When clients relapse, they may retreat to precontemplation or enter the action stage with a determination to make a better plan.

Motivational interviewing reframes what has been termed *resistance* in the literature and refers to it as *ambivalence*. The goal is to help the client resolve the ambivalence and move toward the action phase of change. Resistance, then, is not seen as a problem that resides in the client but is an expected manifestation of the client's uncertainty about change. A team in Seattle, Washington, developed and pilot tested a group-based motivational approach for substance abusers and reported positive outcomes (Lincourt, Kuettel, & Bombardier, 2002). Their group was a six-session program that was completed prior to starting a long-term substance use disorder group. Clients were referred to the group if they were unable to articulate a goal for treatment during their intake process. In Session 1, members share their feelings about treatment and how their substance use resulted in the referral to the program. Lincourt et al. (2002) advised facilitators to use motivational strategies developed by Miller and Rollnick (1991) for early stages of group: Use open-ended questions, listen reflectively, summarize, affirm ("I appreciate that you came today despite your reservations about the program"), and, especially, elicit and reinforce self-motivational statements (statements about the need for change made by the client). In Session 2, the facilitators show a clip from a TV show in which a character faces a decision regarding his drinking, followed by a discussion of how the character reached his decision. Members then discuss difficult decisions that they have made in their lives and how they ultimately reached them. The last topic is how they would consider the advantages and disadvantages of change in their present situations.

In Session 3, the facilitators give a presentation on the stages of change model, and members determine which stage best describes their current situation. Then members discuss what motivates people to move forward or backward in the stages, using examples from their own lives. Prior to Session 4, this program uses a motivational interviewing strategy (feedback from assessments) in a unique way. Clients each meet with an individual counselor and complete a series of assessments of their current substance use. The counselor writes a summary that includes results of the assessments, the client's pattern of use of substances, negative consequences that they have experienced, and an assessment of current motivation. In Session 4, each member reads their feedback (omitting actual scores if they choose) to the group, and the group shares their reactions. In Session 5, the group engages in an exercise on decisional balance, coming up with a list of possible behaviors at this decision point. Then the group discusses the pluses and minuses of each option and shares their own experiences with past attempts to make changes in their substance use. Session 6 is a summary and evaluation, and group members share what they decided about substance use and whether they plan to continue in treatment.

Over a period of 2 years, 75 clients completed the motivation group and then standard treatment, and 92 attended only standard treatment. The two groups were initially equivalent on most demographic measures, but 57% of the motivation group were diagnosed with substance dependence (vs. substance abuse) in comparison with 76% in the standard treatment group. Results showed that more clients from the motivation group completed treatment (56%) than did those in the standard treatment group (32%). Those who participated in the motivation group also missed significantly fewer sessions. Although the study had limitations and the sample was not large, results are quite encouraging and suggest that for clients who are mandated to attend groups, this pregroup group could engage reluctant participants.

SUMMARY

In this chapter, we have provided an overview of group work with clients with SMI, PTSD, and substance use disorders. What is important to keep in mind is that many clients in these groups will have more than one disorder; substance use disorders are particularly likely to co-occur with the other two major topics covered in the chapter. The facilitators will need to make a determination of the extent to which the group can accommodate members with multiple disorders and, if so, how they might need to modify standard approaches to that situation. We recommend that substance use disorders be treated concurrently with other issues, but not in the same group. It might also be helpful to get the client's permission to consult with the facilitator of that group to assess the client's progress.

Finally, we wish to underscore the importance of adequate training and supervision in groups described in this chapter. For example, we mentioned motivational interviewing as a useful approach with clients with substance use disorder; although one can read about the approach, a training program is a highly recommended way to ensure that the facilitator has mastered the skills. This is true for all group work, but especially so for the groups that are the focus of this chapter, because clients are especially vulnerable.

KEY TERMS

Ambivalence: feeling torn between alternatives, at times being drawn to one side and at other times feeling inclined toward the other. This is often present in substance abusers who are thinking that quitting might be good but are reluctant to give up the perceived positive aspects of using.

Avoidant coping: related to avoidance behaviors (e.g., staying away from reminders of the traumatic experience, feeling emotionally numb) used to manage the anxiety associated with a traumatic experience.

Disinhibition: the absence of restraint or attention to social conventions.

Hyperarousal: excessive vigilance, so that the individual is easily startled, feels tense or agitated, and has difficulty sleeping.

Labile affect: excessive emotionality or emotional expression that is not consistent with the situation (laughing at a sad situation, sobbing over a trivial incident).

Negative symptoms: behaviors that people without these disorders do have that are absent, such as flat affect (not showing emotion in face or voice), lack of pleasure, reduced or absent speech. Some ignore basic hygiene.

Pharmacotherapy: using prescription medication to treat symptoms of psychiatric disorders.

Positive symptoms: behaviors that people without these disorders do not have, such as hallucinations (sensory experiences in the absence of actual stimuli—hearing voices, seeing things, smelling things, feeling things), delusions, thought disorders (inability to connect ideas logically), or movement disorders.

Reexperiencing: also called flashbacks; the individual experiences the trauma repeatedly, including physical reactions such as sweating, rapid heart rate, and so forth.

Resistance: usually describes a pattern in a client in which ideas and in fact the need for counseling are rejected. Resistance can be expressed overtly (saying "this is a waste of my time") or indirectly (being consistently late for, or missing, appointments). In many theories, resistance is seen as a client problem, whereas motivational interviewing considers it to be the counselor's problem.

RECOMMENDATIONS FOR PRACTICE

1. Conducting groups with persons with psychiatric disabilities requires knowledge and skill that exceeds that for many other groups. Therefore, in training, actively seek experience both with clients with SMI and groups within that population. Supervision is essential for developing competency.
2. Cofacilitation is strongly recommended. The dynamics in these groups can be extremely complex, and having a second facilitator in the group helps manage situations that may arise.
3. Become familiar with medications often prescribed to persons with psychiatric disorders. This will help you to respond to questions with accurate information but also to recognize when someone's medication (or noncompliance with medication regimen) may be causing behaviors.
4. Develop a consultation relationship with a psychiatrist with whom you can discuss medication and other serious issues.
5. If the client is under the care of an agency or is being mandated to treatment, be sure to understand what is expected of you in terms of reporting. It is also important to communicate those requirements to clients as part of informed consent.
6. It is impossible for a counselor to have personal experience with every disorder. However, reading some of the books or consulting websites listed in the Resources chapter of this book is necessary if one is to work with clients in that population. Although clients can be excellent informants, a more objective account or scientific explanation might be required.
7. Continuing education is essential, because new developments occur rapidly. Many professional organizations offer or advertise conferences or webinars for specific training; as a professional working with clients with SMI, it is imperative that you commit to participating in such events regularly to keep current with new developments.
8. If you think motivational interviewing would be an appropriate approach with your clientele, we strongly recommend that you attend one of the training workshops available.

chapter 10
COGNITIVE DISABILITIES

A *fairly wide array of* disabilities feature some degree of cognitive involvement, including psychiatric disabilities, TBI, stroke, IDs, autism, learning disabilities, Alzheimer's disease, and others. Although these disabilities each have unique features, they all have in common some type and some degree of limitation or difference in the way the brain functions. Below is a brief summary of the more prevalent types of disabilities that involve cognitive dysfunction. Although this list is not all-inclusive, it is hoped that the reader might extrapolate from the common experience of these individuals regarding cognition and consider the ways in which the group facilitator might make the group more accommodating to individuals with disabilities that involve a cognitive component. This chapter (1) briefly describes several common disabilities that include a cognitive component and (2) discusses considerations in adapting a group to the needs of individuals with cognitive disabilities.

INTELLECTUAL DISABILITIES

The term *intellectual disabilities* evolved out of an increasing discomfort with the term *mental retardation*, which was considered stigmatizing. It is often used interchangeably with the term *developmental disabilities*, although *developmental disabilities* includes a wider constellation of disabilities with or without a cognitive component that originate before adulthood, including autism and various types of neurological and neuromuscular disabilities.

IDs occur in 0.71% of the population (Boyle et al., 2011) and involve some combination of limitations in both intellectual and adaptive functioning. A diagnosis of ID often involves intelligence testing coupled with an assessment of social skills, problem solving, and ability to perform everyday life tasks. A diagnosis of ID requires that the disabilities be present prior to age 18 (American Psychiatric Association, 2013). ID may be caused by a variety of impairments, including genetic conditions such as Down syndrome, illnesses, or the introduction of toxic chemicals or conditions in utero (e.g., rubella, alcohol abuse, radiation, hypoxia) or in childhood (meningitis, lead poisoning, hypoxia due to drowning).

IDs are generally categorized as ranging from mild to moderate to severe, with varying prognoses for success in academic, social, and vocational functioning. Many individuals with IDs have co-occurring disabilities or health conditions that are the result of the underlying causal factor. Individuals with IDs may have varying degrees of both receptive and expressive language skills and underdeveloped social skills, and they may exhibit a kind of naiveté about the complexities of life that may be perceived as being overly trusting or simplistic. These behaviors may stem from the impairment itself, may result from a lack of exposure to real-life experiences, or both.

Historically, individuals with IDs have tended to be isolated from other children academically because of concerns that they could not function in "normal" classrooms, and expectations for their participation in common adult roles such as employment and parenthood were very low. Increasingly, however, children are included in integrated classrooms, and there has been a growing recognition that people with IDs may be limited as much by low expectations and limited opportunity as by their cognitive impairment. Children with IDs may also internalize the lack of acceptance and devaluation that results from such harmful behaviors as bullying, discrimination, and harsher discipline (Reiter & Lapidot-Lefler, 2007). Such threats to the self-concept may result in lowered self-esteem and depression. Individuals with IDs may also lack the communication skills to fully process information and to effectively express their needs and frustrations, sometimes leading to acting-out behaviors and further social isolation.

AUTISM SPECTRUM DISORDER (ASD)

Autism was once understood to be a discrete, severe brain disorder with a characteristic set of symptoms that included behavioral and social dysfunction. However, it is now viewed as a spectrum of symptoms, ranging from mild to more serious symptoms that include impairment in communications and social interactions and limited interest in play or typical childhood activities. Individuals who were previously diagnosed with Asperger's syndrome are now considered to be included in the higher functioning part of this spectrum. Individuals with ASD usually manifest with impairments in their social interaction and communication and appear to be unable to relate to and interact with others in their environment. Language delays are common, and children with autism tend to ignore social cues and react with avoidance, and sometimes anger, to physical touch. A child with ASD may exhibit both positive and negative symptomatology. Negative behavioral symptoms include a scarcity of emotional reactions and an absence of response to the presence of other people, in fact preferring objects to people. Individuals with autism may appear very passive. Conversely, many children with ASD exhibit hyperactive behavior, often displaying repetitive body behaviors, such as rocking, gesturing, head banging, or other self-injurious behavior. They may also engage in repetitive verbal behaviors, such as echolalia. This stereotypical and seemingly nonproductive behavior is often attributed to some type of dysregulation in response to stimulation. Indeed, many individuals with ASD exhibit extreme reactions to touch, sound, and pain. Individuals with ASD often exhibit difficulties in cognitive and sensory integration and may have a wide range of intellectual abilities.

TRAUMATIC BRAIN INJURY

Traumatic brain injury is an acquired injury to the brain caused by an external blow to the head or the penetration of brain tissue by an external object. It is differentiated from other types of acquired brain injuries in that it is not congenital, nor is it caused by a disease process, although some of the symptomatology may be similar to other types of brain injury. The leading causes of TBI are falls, MVAs, and assaults. The specific effects on function are related to the areas of the brain that sustain injury. In closed-head injury, the damage to the brain may be diffuse and widespread, due to the movement of the brain within the cranium, with subsequent scraping and injury to tissue at multiple sites. Additionally, there may be other associated trauma to the brain cells, including ripping and tearing of axonal tissue, disrupted blood flow, and subdural hematomas, or bleeds into the brain tissue. In penetrating wounds, the damage may be much more localized.

Brain injury can range from mild to severe. Mild head injury usually results from a concussion with a brief loss of consciousness and may include headache, disequilibrium, difficulty concentrating and sustaining attention, disorganization, and irritability, among others. Taken together, these symptoms are referred to as post-concussive syndrome. These symptoms tend to decline over time, but not uniformly, and the subtlety of the symptoms and lack of positive results on most medical tests may lead to perceptions of malingering and an overlay of depressive symptoms. More severe brain injuries include a longer period of unconsciousness, as well as a period of posttraumatic amnesia. In severe TBI the individual may remain unconscious, or in a coma, for a much longer period. Many, but not all, individuals with TBI may eventually begin to regain some awareness and response to extraneous stimuli, but the return to consciousness is generally accompanied by a state of deep confusion and cognitive dysfunction. Over time, there may be improvement in symptomatology, but the degree of improvement is related to a number of considerations, including severity of injury, general health, availability of rehabilitation services, and other factors not completely understood.

Because the mechanisms and site of brain injury are unique to each individual, there is not a single set of predictable symptoms. There are, however, a number of commonly seen areas of function affected by cognitive impairment. These include difficulties in attention, concentration, information sequencing, organization, perception, short-term memory, self-awareness, problem solving, and judgment. In addition to these cognitively mediated functions, many individuals with TBI also exhibit irritability, low frustration tolerance, and emotional lability or dyscontrol. Taken together with the cognitive symptoms, individuals with TBI may exhibit emotional reactions that appear out of proportion to the precipitating stressor. They may become easily overwhelmed and easily fatigued. Because of their impaired decision-making skills and a lack of self-awareness regarding their own limitations, many individuals exhibit poor judgment and may engage in questionable or potentially harmful behaviors. Many observers note that individuals with TBI seem to exhibit personality changes that are particularly challenging to friends and family. Many people with TBI have increased difficulty in recognizing social cues and may appear socially immature or insensitive, creating difficulties in forming and sustaining social and intimate relationships.

As improvements occur in self-awareness and memory, it is not unusual to see the onset of depression and a loss of self-esteem as the person with TBI realizes the enormity of his or her losses. It is also common for individuals with TBI to experience physical symptoms, including impairments in balance, impaired mobility, and other injuries sustained at the same time as the TBI. People with TBI also commonly have disturbances in their vision, which can be difficult for the observer to detect because they often have lost vision in part of their visual field. Some individuals may also have sensorineural loss and cortical blindness. Other senses may also be affected, including touch, taste, and smell. Appetite and sleep disturbances are common, and eating and swallowing disorders may be present. Many individuals with TBI will experience some degree of language dysfunction, including both expressive and receptive aphasia (the inability to accurately receive and communicate information). Many individuals will have difficulty learning new information in academic pursuits because of these communication and cognitive challenges, although old learning may remain relatively intact.

DEMENTIA

The cognitive changes described above associated with TBI are often referred to as *dementia*. Dementia can result from a variety of causes in addition to TBI, however. As the Alzheimer's Association (2015) has noted, dementia is not a specific disease but rather an overall term that describes a wide range of symptoms associated with a decline in cognitive abilities that is severe enough to reduce a person's ability to perform everyday activities. Alzheimer's disease accounts for 60% to 80% of cases. Vascular dementia, which can occur after a stroke, is the second most common dementia type. But there are many other conditions that can cause symptoms of dementia. One of the hallmark symptoms is a loss of short-term memory; however, many other cognitive skills may be affected, including communication and language, ability to attend and concentrate, reasoning and judgment skills, visual perceptions, and others as discussed above.

It is important to note that dementia is often incorrectly referred to as "senility" or "senile dementia," which reflects the formerly widespread but incorrect belief that serious mental decline is a normal part of aging. This is an understandable misperception, because the incidence of many dementias increases with age, but it is a dangerous fallacy, because the view of dementia as "normal" may discourage family members and caretakers from seeking medical help in a timely fashion. Additionally, for those whose dementia results from a health condition associated with aging, many of the other issues associated with aging may complicate and may further affect functioning with this disability. As with TBI (discussed above), any condition resulting in dementia poses significant challenges to family members and caregivers, and support for the entire social system is recommended.

RATIONALE FOR GROUP WORK
AND TYPES OF GROUPS

Group work for people with disabilities is a powerful vehicle for change and growth. Many individuals with disabilities share common experiences and reactions from the nondisabled world, ranging from uncomfortable avoidance to outright harassment and discrimination. Unfortunately, the onus is often placed on individuals with disabilities to place their nondisabled peers and colleagues at ease and to find ways to correct misperceptions and increase interaction, all while managing the many frustrations brought about by fears, lack of knowledge, and lack of access. Interactions with others who share a common experience can result in a number of benefits, including a sense of acceptance, group support, sharing information about various aspects of managing with a disability, vicarious learning through modeling, and others. Wright (1983) noted that in a group comprising children with disabilities,

> the fact that the children could hear each other complain about some of the annoyances on the "outside" and the fact that they could laugh about some of the misunderstandings undoubtedly serve to relieve some of the burden. When this is bolstered by a new understanding of

one's own feelings and the feelings of others, important preparation for subsequent changes in the management of social relationships has taken place. (p. 349)

For individuals with cognitive disabilities, common experiences may include the following:

- having been bullied or laughed at;
- often having been called "dumb" or "stupid" or "crazy";
- feeling frightened, ashamed, or angered by their inability to perform as they once did, or as they perceive others are able to do;
- feelings of loneliness or isolation related to social skills or behavioral issues;
- relationships and sexuality concerns;
- experiencing depression or self-esteem issues;
- frustrations with low expectations; and
- difficulties in obtaining, or lack of knowledge about, accommodations for school, work, or public services.

Those with communication issues due to stroke or TBI will often share frustrations in accurately perceiving and comprehending communications, communicating needs, and picking up on social cues. Additionally, groups often provide a safe social outlet for individuals with cognitive disabilities and are valued as a supportive atmosphere in which meaningful relationships can be experienced.

ADDRESSING THE NEEDS OF GROUP MEMBERS WITH COGNITIVE DISABILITIES

Obviously, there is great variability in the population of individuals whose disability includes cognitive symptoms, and group facilitators need, first and foremost, to recognize that each group member is unique and will have adapted in his or her unique fashion. Nevertheless, there are some common considerations that will enhance the group experience for these group participants. These considerations can be divided into considerations in planning the group, group structure, common challenges, and topics for exploration.

Planning the Group

Do your homework: When planning a group for or including individuals with cognitive disabilities, the facilitator will need to learn about the disability so that he or she is maximally prepared to be an effective facilitator. Olkin (1999) recommended that the clinician may need to spend extra time to "find national organizations with information and resources, to read about the disability, and to preview relevant reading material in order to make more client specific and well-timed recommendations" (p. 161).

Group Composition

Group facilitators should resist the urge to assume that individuals with cognitive disabilities will share a common identity and benefit by inclusion in group together. In fact, many individuals with cognitive disabilities without behavioral symptoms (e.g., mild IDs) may resist being categorized with individuals viewed as "crazy" or "weird." Similarly, individuals with TBI have long resisted the perception that they are "mentally retarded" and may object to being lumped in together (Shapiro, 1994). This is not to say that individuals with these diagnoses should not participate in groups together, because they may have a great deal to learn about and from each other. Rather, the facilitator will have to be aware of this possible consideration and discuss his or her rationale, with reassurances that he or she is making no assumptions about the nature of the disability by mixing members with different diagnoses that may share some similarities. Of greater importance is the need to ensure that individuals with mild cognitive disabilities do not become frustrated by the slow pace or frequent redirecting that may be needed when working with others with very markedly different processing speeds or serious difficulties in sustaining or shifting attention. Similarly, individuals with higher levels of emotional lability, frustration tolerance, or behavioral dysfunction may create elevated levels of anxiety in other group members and become disruptive to the group process (Marshak & Seligman, 1993). Such members may also become targets or scapegoats, especially if they are in the minority, and should be carefully screened for inclusion. Indeed, Stone (1996) recommended that "obvious singletons," or individuals who differ in some functional ability from the other members, be screened out. One way to create a sense of belonging in a very heterogeneous group is to create a buddy system, pairing members who share functional levels or other characteristics in common.

Simple Is Better

Many individuals with cognitive impairments experience difficulty with complex directions, abstractions, and multipart instructions. When providing printed or verbal guidelines regarding group rules, norms, expectations, and so on, the facilitator should try to keep language and vocabulary simple and straightforward. Many individuals will not ask for clarification of information that they do not understand because they may be overwhelmed and feel that asking questions makes them look dumb or calls attention to their lack of ability. Consequently, the facilitator should also discuss important information in person, providing an opportunity for questions, and take additional steps to ensure understanding of any printed materials rather than relying solely on comprehension of written materials. Although this is particularly helpful for individuals with cognitive disabilities, there may be nondisabled group members with varying reading levels and cognitive skills, and stressful situations may impair anyone's comprehension. Thus this practice is helpful for all and consistent with the principles of universal design.

Involve Caregivers

When eliciting needed information during screening, it may be helpful to involve caregivers. This is particularly true in situations in which deficits in self-awareness, memory, or general funds of knowledge are present. Individuals with TBI may not be aware of some of their health conditions or areas in which they have particular needs, and they may provide erroneous or incomplete information. Others may simply not have ever learned the names of medications or health conditions or have difficulty retrieving and communicating critical information. Individuals with ASD tend to provide only the minimum amount of information possible and may omit important details. More important, one should never assume that a potential participant is unable to independently provide the needed information. Rather, one should use careful observation and use clinical judgment in requesting involvement from caregivers or family members. Of course, family members should be contacted only with the consent of the potential participant if the participant is legally an adult. With children and adolescents, parental permission and informed consent are required, and the consenting process provides an opportunity to gather information. Later on, family members may also be helpful in between-groups homework assignments and in helping with processing group experiences.

Group Structure

No distractions, please! Because some group members with cognitive disabilities may be distractible, have difficulties with attention and concentration, or both, group locations should be as free from distractions as possible.

Accommodations

Because some individuals with cognitive disabilities may also have co-occurring physical or orthopedic disabilities, the setting should be comfortable, and group members should be encouraged to request specific accommodations (special seating, etc.) prior to initiation of the group and be provided with a variety of choices for seating.

Size and Length

Typically, groups for individuals with cognitive disabilities should be shorter in length, because it may be challenging to sustain attention for long periods. Most experts in group counseling suggest that sessions for adults last at least 90 minutes and can last up to 3 hours. When members have difficulties with attention and concentration, however, groups should generally last no longer than 90 minutes, and in the case of significant difficulty in sustaining attention or concentration, no more than 60 minutes. Because of the shorter time period, coupled with the need to allow for more time for redirection and the increased tangentiality often seen with individuals with cognitive disabilities, the need to ensure that each member of the group has time to contribute and to receive the attention that he or she deserves, groups will also need to be smaller than the recommended size of 6–12. Although groups that are too small are in danger of losing the valuable group dynamic that is so potentially helpful to this population, keeping the group on the small side, between four and six, is advisable. To sustain involvement and continuity, groups may benefit by occurring more frequently, for example two to three times per week, rather than once per week, and homework comprising concrete, active tasks with clear outcomes is advisable.

Group Rules

Members with slowed processing or aphasia will be greatly helped by some ground rules that stipulate that group members will speak one at a time. This rule helps members who may have some difficulty with following rapid conversations with multiple participants and allows member's to focus on one message at a time without the distractions of interruptions and rapid-fire changes in speakers. For adolescents and some adults, a "talking stick" can be a visual reminder of who has the floor. The person will relinquish the stick when she or he has finished speaking. It is also helpful if members agree to allow speakers time to get their thoughts together and their words out. This is important to enforce, and facilitators will have to be careful not only to provide reminders to group members but also to model this behavior themselves. It can be tempting to try to be helpful by finishing the sentences of one who is struggling to find the right words (Roth, 2013), but this robs the speaker of his or her freedom and autonomy to express him- or herself. A better approach is to wait patiently. If the speaker cannot find the words to express him- or herself after allowing a little time, the facilitator may wish to provide a prompt, such as "Can you say it another way?" or "Describe how the thing you're trying to name looks."

Facilitator Responsibilities

Provide Structure

Groups that include members with significant cognitive disabilities will require a greater degree of structure. Task-oriented activities tend to be more effective at sustaining attention. It is helpful to plan some continuity in activities over all sessions. For example, Huebner (2004) recommended that providing predictability increases the sense of self-control and empowerment and recommended that each session start and end with a particular activity such as a "group share." Additionally, she suggested that visual cues are helpful in assisting members to anticipate and prepare for novel group activities. She provided an example of a schedule being displayed in pictures attached with Velcro; as each item is completed, the picture is taken down.

Provide Redirection

Limited attention spans and distractibility may cause group members to lose focus and become disengaged from the work of the group. Facilitators should be much attuned to indications of wandering attention, such as loss of eye contact, decreased participation, and facial expression. It is not unusual for facilitators to see that glazed-over expression descending. In this case, the facilitator may wish to address the person by name, quickly summarize the current issue or activity, and invite the member to participate in the discussion or activity. Depending on the group's composition, this may become a frequent and very important function of the group leader.

Group Topics

Some topics that might be particularly helpful in groups for persons with cognitive disabilities include the following:

- education about specific disabilities and sharing about how to deal with specific common challenges, for example, how to organize schedules or schoolwork and how to use memory aids;
- disability rights and legal protections, including accommodations and explorations about whether and how to disclose a disability;
- empowerment groups focusing on common assaults on self-image and self-concept, information sharing about how to react and respond to demeaning or insulting behaviors or attitudes, and group activities that focus on contributions;
- life review groups for individuals with Alzheimer's disease or other progressive, late-onset forms of dementia;
- anger management and social skills groups, including active strategies such as role play, and providing visual and audio cues, such as videotaping and group feedback;
- dating, sex, and healthy and unhealthy romantic relationships, including opportunities to share experiences; worries about not being able to find a girlfriend or boyfriend; providing information about sex, birth control, sexually transmitted diseases, and safe sex; sharing ideas about how to meet someone; discussions of healthy and unhealthy relationships; and discussions about abuse and what to do if a relationship becomes abusive;
- vocational or prevocational groups, including work behaviors, looking for jobs, applying for jobs, interviewing skills, professional appearance, and work expectations; and
- issues specific to certain disabilities or groups of participants, for example, substance abuse prevention or intervention for individuals with TBI, issues related to parenting and independence and transition for teens, and so on.

SUMMARY

Group counseling can be a valuable approach to addressing some of the common challenges encountered by individuals with disabilities that include a cognitive disability. There are a number of ways in which the group structure and preparation should be altered, and the facilitator will often need to provide a greater degree of structure and direction. The sharing of common experiences and the opportunity to help other group members by sharing information and problem-solving strategies are extremely valuable. The opportunities for peer feedback in a supportive environment and the opportunities for socialization afforded by groups can have significant impacts beyond the limitations of individual counseling approaches.

KEY TERMS

Axonal tissue: the tissue sheaths that contain bundles of axons (nerves).

Developmental disabilities: disabilities that are present prior to the age of 22 years and involve deficits in general intellectual functioning and adaptive functioning. Mental retardation and other conditions that result in intellectual impairment are developmental disabilities.

Disequilibrium: a term used in economics and psychology that also refers to an inability to maintain a stable posture, that is, loss of balance.

Dysregulation: a disturbance in the ability to regulate or control emotions (also known as labile mood).

Echolalia: repeating others' spoken words.

Emotional dyscontrol: inability to control one's emotions.

Receptive/expressive language: Receptive language refers to the ability to understand the language of others, and *expressive language* describes one's production of language to communicate.

Subdural hematoma: bleeding in the space between the dura (cover of the brain) and the brain itself. This increases pressure on the brain.

Scapegoat: In a counseling group, this refers to a person who is repeatedly attacked or criticized by other members.

RECOMMENDATIONS FOR PRACTICE

1. When designing and planning the group, consider the variety of IDs as well as their severity in deciding on criteria for membership.
2. A predictable structure is generally best for groups with this clientele. You may wish to begin with a brief go-around in which each member contributes something (e.g., something you are happy about, what you like about the group), followed by a structured exercise in which each step is explained separately. A closing ritual is also helpful.
3. The size and duration of the group will be determined by the capacities of members. The screening interview is critical for evaluating the ability to sustain attention, remain in one place physically, follow a conversation, and so on.

For those with limited abilities, a short session with fewer members is needed.

4. The topics and goals of the group should be determined according to the needs of the members. Members with TBI may have different needs than do those with a developmental disability, for example.

5. Because a portion of these groups is likely to be psychoeducational, create handouts or visuals that focus on one concept at a time and use basic concrete language. It is better to have several handouts or posters with less content than one handout with too much information. It is also helpful if members take these handouts home to review with family or caregivers.

6. Consider offering groups to family or caregivers of persons with cognitive disabilities, because they also need support and can benefit from sharing with others in similar situations.

7. You may want to offer time-limited groups on specific topics of interest to these clients (see suggestions in this chapter) while allowing members to reenroll in subsequent topics once they complete a particular group. The narrowed foci of such groups may help the members to absorb more content. Review and repetition are helpful in that regard.

chapter 11
PHYSICAL DISABILITIES

Gabrielle Ficchi,[1] Linda R. Shaw, and Sheri Bauman

Physical disabilities are those that affect physical functioning, in contrast to disabilities that are primarily sensory or cognitive. In that general category are a range of disabilities and varying degrees of impairment. We summarize the major types of physical disabilities, noting both the bodily systems affected and the range of functional abilities.

ORTHOPEDIC DISABILITIES

Orthopedic disabilities are physical disabilities that encompass neuromotor impairments, degenerative diseases, and musculoskeletal disorders. Neuromotor impairments are those caused by an injury or disruption in the functioning of the brain, spinal cord, or nervous system. Degenerative diseases affect motor development, and musculoskeletal disorders include a variety of conditions that affect muscles, bones, and joints.

---

[1]Gabrielle Ficchi is a doctoral student in the Department of Disability and Psychoeducational Studies at the University of Arizona in Tucson, Arizona.

Neuromotor Disorders

These disorders often originate in utero, during birth, or in the first few years of life and interfere with or disrupt the brain's ability to control the muscles of the body (deBettencourt, 2002). The most common of these are cerebral palsy, spina bifada, and SCI. Persons with these disabilities may experience varying degrees of spasticity, which refers to muscle stiffness and problems with voluntary movements. They may also experience involuntary movements and problems with balance. Some persons may be atonic, or without muscle tone or muscular control. Infants and children may be unable to master motor developmental milestones such as sitting up without support, crawling, and walking. They may also have difficulty coordinating movements, so that activities of daily living are impaired and affect the ability to attend school and gain employment (O'Neil et al., 2006).

Degenerative diseases affect motor development, so that the person's organs and tissues gradually decrease in function. These diseases can be caused by congenital conditions or can be hereditary. The most common of these disorders is muscular dystrophy, which is a hereditary muscle-destroying disorder with wide variability in age of onset, initial muscles attacked, and the rate of progression. The disease also varies in terms of which muscles are affected and the degree of impairment (Bushby et al., 2010).

Musculoskeletal disorders, such as scoliosis and rheumatoid arthritis, are often accompanied by chronic pain and discomfort when engaging in everyday activities. Generally, treatment focuses on managing pain and reducing inflammation to restore the person's range of motion and function in the affected area. Physical conditioning may also be helpful in improving functional abilities (Hagberg, 1996).

Amputation

The loss of a body part is known as amputation. Sometimes, a person is born without a limb, which is a congenital amputation, but most amputations are the result of disease or traumatic injury. In the United States, there are approximately 1.9 million persons with amputations; 185,000 surgical amputations are performed each year (Amputee Coalition, n.d.). The largest number of amputations are related to vascular disease (including diabetes and arterial disease) and the next largest are trauma-related injuries. A small percentage of amputations are cancer related. Men and boys and

African Americans are more likely to have had amputations than are women and girls and Whites.

The location and level of the amputation affects the feasibility of a prosthesis (artificial replacement of the missing part), as does the overall health and condition of the remaining body part. For those whose amputation is necessary because of disease, there may be some time to prepare psychologically for the changes that will occur; for those whose amputation is the result of a traumatic injury, the absence of time to prepare can make the adjustment quite difficult. Individuals who experience an amputation will have to confront a change in functional capacity and body image and may struggle to grieve the loss and adapt to the changed situation. Many amputees will be able to use a prosthesis, but the use of a prosthesis is a process more than an event, requiring multiple fittings and sometimes additional assistive devices. Not all prostheses restore function; some are cosmetic (more often upper-limb amputations than lower limb). In addition, most amputations are accompanied by phantom pain, at least initially, which adds to the problems that must be managed.

There are few studies that address emotional issues subsequent to amputation. In one study (Price & Fisher, 2002), records of 100 patients who received counseling services and raised emotional issues were reviewed. Of those, the most common concern was depressive symptoms, followed by body image problems. Although mentioned by fewer patients, relationships and sex and anger and resentment were brought up most often in the sessions.

No articles were located that focused on group work with this population. The currently available evidence is only anecdotal (Healio O&P News, 2005). However, the Amputee Coalition offers many support groups around the country. Group support is likely to benefit members by providing a safe place to discuss practical issues (caring for the stump, basic self-care [e.g., bathing], and adapted recreational activities), as well as changes in relationships following the amputation, concerns about sexual functioning, and feelings of anger and resentment. Amputees can encourage each other to undertake those physical or adaptive activities of which they are capable. Many will be able to drive a car but may be fearful of doing so because of the changed mechanics of the task. Group members who have mastered that skill can serve as role models, encouragers, and sources of advice regarding specific concerns. In addition, wheelchair basketball, wheelchair tennis, and wheelchair racing and other adapted sports may be possible after sufficient healing has taken place. For those who were athletic and competitive prior to the amputation, these might be important activities to resume. Those who are able to use a prosthesis can engage in walking or running for cardiovascular conditioning. Depending on the location and level of the amputation, many people who have lost limbs are able to bicycle, swim, and dance, and the example of other group members who are doing those things can inspire those who are reluctant to take the risk.

Some amputees who are experiencing depression may find that participation in groups, especially cognitive behavior groups, assists them in reducing symptoms of that disorder. Depression can be extremely debilitating and can interfere with the process of adaptation; treatment in group or individual settings should be provided. Phantom limb pain can be responsive to relaxation or mindfulness approaches, and learning these techniques can occur in group formats.

Spinal Cord Injuries

Although there are some congenital SCIs (e.g., spina bifida) and some that are the result of disease (e.g., polio), the vast majority of SCIs are the result of accidents or some kind of violence. The degree of impairment that results is a function of the location of the injury and whether the spinal cord is severed, bruised, or compressed. When the spinal cord is severed, there is no nerve function below the level of the injury, but some functions may exist if the injury is incomplete. There is loss of both movement and sensation below the level of the injury.

There are numerous complications that can occur with a SCI; the interested reader might refer to Falvo (2014) for details. For the purposes of group work, we note that especially for those who become paraplegic or quadriplegic, adjustment usually involves a loss of independence along with the loss of mobility, and this can be very difficult for adults to accept. That loss of independence may also limit the person's ability to participate in many groups, particularly for individuals with quadriplegia: Transportation may be very difficult; the individual may require a personal care assistant; the time involved in basic hygiene and bladder and bowel routines can make it hard to keep appointments. For persons with limited access to in-person groups, online groups may be a good option. Access to technology, and adaptations to technology (e.g., voice recognition software to enable the individual to participate in an online chat), may be necessary. A Google search will quickly generate a list of online opportunities for support; many are password protected with screening of members to avoid trolls and others who might disrupt the group process.

The changes in a person who sustains a SCI also affect family members, and they should also have options to join groups of other family members. The person with the injury will likely require considerable resources of both time and money that will change the lives of family members. The roles and responsibilities previously assumed by the injured person will have to be undertaken by other family members. The stress on family members is considerable, and knowing other families that also struggle can be quite therapeutic. For some family members, the anger they experience may cause feelings of guilt to emerge. Family members may believe they should be understanding and compassionate at all times, and when they do not feel that way, they may experience guilt. Hearing from other family members of other spinal cord–injured persons can validate and normalize their experience, bringing some relief.

Groups for family members of persons with SCIs should include techniques for stress management because stress can be high in those families. In addition, a complete list of available resources and assistance in the community should be provided, and group members can share those that they have found most helpful.

CONGENITAL VERSUS ACQUIRED DISABILITIES

As has been noted above, some persons are born with the disability, and others acquire it later in life, often as a result of injury or illness. This distinction is important for adjustment and requires thoughtful consideration for a group facilitator about whether these two situations can be effectively combined in a single group. Those with congenital disabilities are likely to have adapted to the disability from the beginning, because that is the only condition that they have known. Although that may appear to be an advantage for adjustment, someone with a congenital disability has also likely experienced negative attitudes and discriminatory experiences on the basis of the disability, and he or she may have internalized some of those judgments. Furthermore, the expectations of others (parents, teachers) may have been low, sending the message that the child is incapable of attaining independence.

Those who acquire a disability will have their lives turned upside down. Many of their ways of functioning prior to the disability will no longer be possible, and they are faced with enormous physical, emotional, and perhaps existential challenges. This group of persons with physical disabilities may struggle to integrate a disability identity into their ideas of self, to the point that some may deny the condition and avoid associating with the disability community.

On one hand, it may be that persons with acquired disabilities can learn much from those in the group with congenital disabilities, especially if those members are enjoying full and satisfying lives. The instillation of hope is one of the therapeutic factors in groups and may be particularly relevant in these cases. On the other hand, the facilitators may decide that the struggles of each group are so different that having both as members of the same group would make cohesiveness difficult to achieve. In addition, some of the concerns of the two groups will be quite different. Members with congenital disabilities may have concerns about relationships, family, grief, or other themes that do not revolve around the disability, whereas those with recently acquired disabilities may need help with pragmatic issues such as pain, medication and side effects; use of assistive devices; mobility difficulties; and perhaps finding a new career. Although members with congenital disabilities may have much to offer members who are newly disabled, they may find that their own needs are treated as less urgent.

Facilitators must also consider that a minimum number of members is necessary to form a group, and it may not be possible to form a group of persons with only congenital or only acquired disabilities. We caution the reader that if the group combines both, it is important not to have one isolate and to explain the composition of the group during the screening interview so members have an idea of the situation of other members.

Group experiences for persons with physical disabilities can have a major impact via discovering that they are not alone, either in the presence of the disability or in the feelings and challenges that may be associated with the disability. The ability to share their stories and frustrations in a nonjudgmental environment with supportive others can be a great relief.

GROUP CONSIDERATIONS

Group Composition and Screening

When designing a group for individuals with physical disabilities, the group facilitators must determine the degree to which the individual is likely to benefit and ensure that the group is appropriate to the needs of the individual and that the individual will not detract from the total group experience. When groups include persons with physical disabilities, facilitators must keep in mind that some of these disabilities are accompanied by cognitive impairments. We discuss accommodations that may be appropriate in groups with members with cognitive disabilities (see Chapter 10), but when there are two types of disabilities, the facilitators must determine which is the more appropriate setting for the client.

During the screening interview, the facilitators need to determine the time since onset of an acquired disability. If it is quite recent, a group may not be the best form of treatment. The person may need time to obtain accurate information about the condition and the prognosis and investigate medication, assistive devices, and so on. Moreover, if the group includes many members with severe impairments, the person might be frightened that he or she will also become more impaired. However, some newly injured individuals may be eager to learn how others in similar circumstances have adapted and welcome the group for the information and shared experiences it can offer. The point at which the person is ready to participate in a group will be determined jointly by the facilitator and the client.

Logistics
These concerns are very relevant to groups that include persons with physical disabilities. The facilitators need to minimize potential barriers to participation. For example, the room where the group meetings are held needs to be large enough to accommodate all members' adaptive equipment and allow people to move around as needed. Wheelchairs have a wide turning radius, which must be taken into account. Wheelchairs are wider than chairs, and the sidewalks, building entrance, doorways, restrooms, and so on all need to be able to accommodate them. For some physical disabilities, individuals may have limitations in regulating body temperature, so that facilitators need to ask potential members about their needs and discuss potential ways to manage them in the group.

Some persons with physical disabilities may be unable to sit for extended periods of time and need to be able to move around during the meeting. Facilitators will want to consider inserting breaks into the meeting to allow this to happen without disrupting group process.

In groups that include able-bodied members and members with physical disabilities, the facilitator might wish to discuss with the potential member how and when he or she would like to tell the group about any accommodations that will be made in the group.

They also should be made aware that other members may be curious about the disability, so that they are prepared to provide information if they are willing and able to protect their privacy at the same time.

Topics or Themes

Although in Chapter 2 we discussed themes that frequently emerge in groups for persons with disabilities, we mention here those that might be particularly important for those with physical disabilities. Accessibility problems are likely to be prominent and should be explored with the goal of gaining information about options and exploring options to advocacy when accessibility is denied. Career and education are also topics that may be important, particularly because members need accurate information about available supports and required accommodations in education and on the job. Those with acquired physical disabilities that force a change in careers may grieve the loss of their previous work and need support as they gain the courage to explore new, realistic options. Another topic of importance is self-care for both physical and mental health. Although members may focus on the disability, it is important that they recognize the importance of following a healthy diet, getting whatever exercise they can, and managing such conditions as pressure sores and preventing bladder infections. Recreation and entertainment are part of a full life, and members should investigate opportunities for those and help each other find activities that are rewarding.

SUMMARY

Consistent with our position throughout this book, we believe that groups for those with physical disabilities can be very helpful as members struggle to adapt to their circumstances. The group milieu provides therapeutic factors not possible in individual counseling. As with other disabilities, it is probably best for the facilitator to have a disability as well, but when that is not possible, the facilitator will have to demonstrate his or her credibility via knowledge of the disabilities, laws, resources, and the disability community. In addition, able-bodied facilitators of groups for persons with physical disabilities need to model acceptance and care for group members in all their interactions.

Persons with physical disabilities also share other challenges with able-bodied persons: grief and loss, divorce, relationships, violence, and depression and anxiety, and they should be encouraged to join those groups as needed. Facilitators must familiarize themselves with the accommodations that may be necessary to enable the person to participate and work with the client to decide the best way to accomplish this to achieve full inclusion.

KEY TERMS

Acquired disability: a disability that was not present a birth. Generally, disabilities are acquired because of effects of illness or accident.

Amputation: loss of a body part.

Congenital disability: a disability present from birth.

Spasticity: a condition in which muscles are tight and stiff (extreme muscle contraction) and knee-jerk reflex may be exaggerated. Spasticity can interfere with movement or speech.

RECOMMENDATIONS FOR PRACTICE

1. We again stress the importance of the screening interview. The facilitator can check for necessary accommodations and determine whether there are any cognitive impairments during this important meeting and plan accordingly.
2. The facilitator will want to consider whether a group with both congenital and acquired physical disabilities is appropriate. She or he will want to consider the stages of adaptation of potential members in making the decision.
3. Stress is an everyday experience for those living in environments not adapted to their needs. Consequently, incorporating stress reduction training in the groups is a good idea. Because some physical disabilities will preclude progressive muscle relaxation, you might want to focus on deep breathing, visualization, and other methods that can be taught and practiced in group and encouraged for homework.
4. When a member of a group has a physical disability, or when the group consists of persons with physical disabilities, ensuring adequate accommodations of the physical setting is essential. A large room with no obstacles is necessary to allow for movement.

chapter 12
CHRONIC HEALTH CONDITIONS

In a sense, all of the disabilities addressed in this book are chronic. In this chapter, however, we address some of the disabling conditions that are quite common and have not been addressed elsewhere but have unique considerations for group facilitators. Most of these conditions are invisible, that is, the disability is not obvious or apparent to others. Persons with these disabilities may not appear to require much by way of accommodations or to have much functional impairment related to their disabilities. This may be because there are effective medications that manage the symptoms well, or because in the early years of progressive disabilities, functional impairments have not yet become disabling. However, in all cases, significant management and medication issues create needs for education, information sharing, and support. Consequently, a group format may be the perfect vehicle to address these needs. This chapter highlights several common disabilities—diabetes, epilepsy, and HIV/AIDS—and discusses group implications for each.

DIABETES

Diabetes mellitus, usually referred to simply as "diabetes," results from the dysfunction or destruction of the cells in the pancreas that are responsible for insulin production. When we eat, our body converts food into glucose, which nourishes all of the cells of the body. Insulin is essential for the body to use the glucose, and when insulin is absent or insufficient, glucose accumulates in the blood, leading to hyperglycemia. In an attempt to cleanse the body of glucose, the kidneys produce large amounts of water and glucose is excreted in the urine. Consequently, many individuals with diabetes may drink copious amounts of water and need to urinate frequently.

Ketones are byproducts of metabolism and are produced when the body begins to break down fat and protein as a source of energy. When too many ketones accumulate, a condition called ketosis or ketoacidosis results, and without insulin, the individual may experience diabetic coma, a life-threatening condition. Diabetic ketoacidosis results in fatigue and lethargy, and as the condition worsens, it may also result in nausea, flushed dry skin, confusion, and eventually unconsciousness (coma). To manage the disease, most individuals take insulin—in pill form, as injections, or by using an insulin pump, which delivers insulin subcutaneously in a slow, continuous delivery method through a needle in the abdomen. The pump must be worn continuously and is programmed to deliver insulin at the estimated times and amount needed, timed to regularly occurring meals and activities. The method used (pill, injection, pump) will depend on a number of factors, such as degree of insulin insufficiency and other medical and personal considerations.

Ideally, the amount and type of insulin will be balanced with the number and type of calories consumed, activity levels, and other factors that affect metabolism, such as sleep, sickness, and stress. Unfortunately, this is challenging, as life often does not work in a perfectly regulated fashion, and the interplay of factors affecting metabolism are complex and not easily predicted. Consequently, if an individual has taken insulin and there is an insufficient amount of glucose in the body to balance it, that individual may experience hypoglycemic shock, sometimes called insulin shock. Hypoglycemia is the opposite of diabetic coma and manifests as acute hunger, shakiness, acute anxiety, and sometimes confusion or irritation. Whereas the treatment for ketoacidosis is an injection of insulin, individuals with hyperglycemia will need to ingest food that can rapidly be converted by the body into glucose. Orange juice works quickly but is not very portable. Many people with diabetes carry candy bars as a ready source of potential glucose, if needed.

If not treated, hypoglycemia can be life threatening. Some individuals with diabetes use assistance dogs or other animals who are able to sense the onset of a health emergency and alert the individual to take action early enough to prevent serious problems. Although careful monitoring of blood levels and careful control of diet and other factors can lessen the long-term risk of onset of health problems related to diabetes, it cannot perfectly prevent them. Diabetes affects every body system, and common long-term complications include diabetic retinopathy (affecting vision), kidney failure, peripheral neuropathy (nerve damage) resulting in pain and numbness, and circulatory problems with ulceration of skin wounds, sometimes leading to amputation (Inzucchi & Sherwin, 2012). Although sexual functioning is not generally affected, neuropathy can create impotence or loss of sensation in women.

Diabetes is usually classified as Type 1 (producing little or no insulin and often, but not always, present in childhood) or Type 2 (producing insulin, but in insufficient amounts, often with a later onset (American Diabetes Association; http://www.diabetes.org). Type 2 diabetes can often be managed with oral medications. Obesity is a common risk factor, and weight loss can sometimes result in improvements and reductions or even elimination of medications (Gregg, 2010). Type 1 and Type 2 diabetes used to be called juvenile and adult diabetes, respectively; however, these terms are no longer used by medical professionals, because onset can occur at any age.

Obviously, careful management of diabetes is essential, both for ongoing day-to-day functioning and prevention of serious side effects. The need to carefully regulate diet and exercise and to manage stress and health is essential, but inconvenient, and sometimes embarrassing (particularly for younger people) and limiting. Jobs with work schedules requiring shiftwork, unpredictable energy outputs, or irregular meal schedules make management extremely difficult. For young adults, in particular, the desire to fit in can lead to risky behaviors such as drinking, late nights, and unhealthy diets. The support of family and friends is essential, both to good management and to safety.

EPILEPSY

Epilepsy is the all-inclusive term used to describe several different types of seizure activity that result in irregular activity in the brain

(Falvo, 2014). Onset of epilepsy can occur at any time, due to such factors as injuries to the brain and congenital health conditions, but often the cause is not known. Seizures are described by the area of the brain affected, as well as the behaviors associated with the seizure. Epilepsy is usually classified as (1) generalized tonic–clonic seizures, previously termed *grand mal*; (2) absence seizures, previously termed *petit mal*; (3) partial seizures, which include simple (previously termed *focal seizures*) and complex (previously termed *psychomotor seizures*); and (4) status epilepticus, in which multiple seizures occur one after another. Status seizures are life threatening and require immediate medical attention (Pedley, 2004). Generalized tonic–clonic seizures consist of behaviors most typically thought of when people think of a seizure. The seizure often will begin with an aura (warning sign). The individual will then become rigid, followed by rapid, jerky movements. Seizures usually last only a couple of minutes, and then the individual regains consciousness but often experiences extreme fatigue and sometimes headache or some confusion. Although bystanders often feel some alarm when witnessing a seizure, there is generally no danger. The only action that should be taken is to remove any nearby objects on which the individual might harm him- or herself, place the individual on his or her side, if possible, and wait for the seizure to pass. No effort should be made to put anything in the mouth, despite a commonly held belief that the individual needs a block placed to ensure that he or she does not bite his or her tongue. Medical help is generally not needed, and most individuals would prefer not to have to deal with medical personnel. However, if the seizure lasts for more than 5 or 6 minutes, medical help should be sought promptly, because the individual may be experiencing status seizures.

Absence seizures are most commonly seen in children and manifest as brief periods with absent expressions, or blank stares, and during them, the child has no awareness of activity around him or her. Most absence seizures last only a few seconds, but some children may have many seizures throughout the day. Because they are so brief, they are often undiagnosed and may instead be interpreted as daydreaming or not paying attention. School performance can suffer, because the child is unaware of what is happening around him or her during the seizure. Absence seizures usually disappear as the child grows older.

Simple partial seizures are localized to one part of the body, and the individual does not lose consciousness. Complex partial seizures are more complex, as the name suggests. They often involve random movements such as pacing, gesturing, and making grunts and nonverbal sounds. Because of the activity associated with complex partial seizures, they are often mistaken for substance abuse or mental illness. These seizures usually last about 20 minutes.

Epilepsy is usually managed with various medicines that decrease the frequency and severity of seizures. Many of these medicines have unpleasant side effects, such as nausea, gum problems, and fatigue, causing adherence to the medication regimen to be challenging, especially for children. However, individuals considering stopping or decreasing their medications should always consult their physician, because some medicines are only effective at certain concentrations in the bloodstream, and some may be dangerous to abruptly discontinue. For a small number of individuals, medicine will not be effective in managing the seizures. In these cases, surgery may be considered. Alcohol and illness can lower seizure thresholds and result in medication interactions.

People with poorly controlled epilepsy must take care not to engage in activities that may put them at risk should a seizure occur. For example, swimming alone, operating dangerous equipment, and driving are all contraindicated for people who experience seizures. Because the time and place of a seizure cannot be predicted, people with epilepsy often describe feeling as though they have little control over their lives and may find themselves in the embarrassing situation of alarming those in the immediate vicinity when a seizure occurs. Historically, epilepsy was sometimes associated with evil or with possession by the devil. Coupled with the extreme discomfort that can be produced in bystanders when they witness a seizure, there remains considerable stigma associated with the condition, which persons with epilepsy often describe as challenges in forming relationships.

Although most people with epilepsy have reliable treatment regimens that control their seizure activity effectively, their ability to participate fully in social and community roles may still be restricted. Jobs may be limited because of safety concerns, and drivers' licenses may be revoked, if the length of time between seizures is deemed too short, causing many of the same transportation dilemmas described in Chapter 11. Children and adults are often prevented from engaging in sports and recreational activities because of overly restrictive rules aimed at safety.

As with diabetes, the need to avoid situations that might be dangerous should a seizure occur can create additional restrictions on freedom that are stressful and upsetting, particularly for teens and young adults. Additionally, some environmental stressors are known to trigger seizures in some individuals (e.g., strobe lights, lack of sleep) and must be avoided. Again, for young people trying to fit in, the stress associated with all of these concerns may lead to an overlay of anxiety or depression and result in medication noncompliance or acting-out behaviors. The help and support of family and friends is essential, and sharing experiences with others who have developed strategies to deal with the associated difficulties can be invaluable. Groups can be particularly helpful for this population.

HIV INFECTION

At one time, HIV was considered to be a death sentence, and treatment was focused on acceptance, management, and general support until death inevitably resulted. With the development of new medications, however, HIV is more properly considered a chronic health condition, and most individuals who receive prompt diagnosis and treatment will live long, productive lives (Donnell et al., 2010; Westergaard & Gupta, 2012). It is caused by a virus that is transmitted through blood and body secretions. Because many people associate HIV with transmission by homosexual contact or unclean needles shared by intravenous drug users, and because of the historical perception that HIV can be easily caught, resulting in a swift death, there is a great deal of stigma associated with it. In actuality, HIV can be transmitted by any direct blood-to-blood transmission, including accidental needle sticks, heterosexual intercourse, or in utero fetal transmission. More importantly, there is no evidence that it can be transmitted by any other casual contact, such as toilet seats, shaking hands, coughing, or sneezing. Because the virus cannot live long outside of the body, the risk of transmission in casual contact is very minimal. Nevertheless, many people continue to believe that HIV is easy to catch and avoid any contact with an infected person.

HIV affects the entire body and, if untreated, can result in a wider variety of health conditions. Individuals with HIV are at risk for opportunistic infections (resulting from depressed immune system functioning) that can become serious health concerns. Currently, medications are often given in a "cocktail," meaning that several drugs are combined together. If begun early, this can restore some compromised functioning and decrease the risks of infection to others. Additional management involves taking care to support the immune system and prevent opportunistic infections. This means that individuals with HIV should be careful to adhere to a wellness-oriented regimen with healthy exercise, sleep, and good nutrition.

Some individuals with advanced HIV may fatigue easily or feel lacking in energy. In older age groups or among individuals without access to good health care and a healthy lifestyle, a wide variety of health conditions may result. These frequently include HIV dementia, lymphoma, peripheral neuropathy, weakness of extremities, gait difficulties, sensory loss, skin infections, and various complications to the pulmonary, cardiac, gastrointestinal, ophthalmologic, renal, and musculoskeletal systems. HIV is also strongly associated with several cancers, including Kaposi's sarcoma and others.

The psychosocial stressors associated with HIV are considerable. There remains a powerful social stigma tied to fears of contagion, homophobia, and a perception that HIV is associated with drug use or immoral activity. Most people with HIV have stories of social rejection and judgmental attitudes that can be difficult to hear, let alone to experience. Many more share stories about being subtly shut out of activities, clubs, or social groups or having experienced subtle and not-so-subtle discrimination. Additionally, people with HIV must confront and come to terms with the uncertainty of their future prognosis and the somewhat variable response that some people have to available treatments. Because of the risk of transmission, sexual and intimate relationships can be difficult and complicated. The individual with HIV must grapple with decisions about how and when to disclose his or her HIV status with potential partners and the very real risks of rejection and abandonment due to that disclosure. Women who are HIV positive will need to consider the risks associated with transmission to their children and may choose not to have children, a very difficult decision to come to terms with in itself.

CONSIDERATIONS FOR GROUP

For all three of the conditions discussed above, groups can be a powerful place to share stories and to benefit from discussing the stressors associated with these invisible disabilities. Because people do not look disabled, they often feel that they need to act not disabled, but there are very real needs and worries that they have to manage. For example, when accommodations are needed, persons with chronic health conditions may be concerned that others will think that they are getting unnecessary special treatment, because the condition is not apparent to an outsider. They may also be embarrassed about some of the ways in which they manage their conditions (e.g., riding public transportation when they are able to afford a vehicle). Groups are safe places in which members can share information, feelings, and strategies, all within the context of shared experiences and social support.

Information about benefits or assistance available to persons with these disabilities can be provided in the group setting. For example, many chronic health conditions are considered legally protected disabilities, and thus clients should be aware of programs for which they may qualify. They could be eligible for Social Security Disability Insurance, available to people who have accumulated the required number of work credits, or for Supplemental Security Income for low-income persons with disabilities who have not earned the required number of work credits. Useful information is available at http://www.disabilitysecrets.com/page5-13.html.

Planning the Group

Meeting times should take the management needs of members into consideration. Individuals with diabetes will not be well served by groups that meet at mealtimes. However, some support groups might wish to deliberately combine a group with a meal. This would combine the advantages of convenient scheduling after work, the educational benefits of sharing healthy recipes, and the sense of camaraderie and fellowship that comes with sharing a meal. For example, the advantages of low-glycemic foods in the diabetic diet could be reinforced by sampling recipes that feature these foods.

Because transportation may well be a concern for some members with epilepsy, the facilitator will want to make sure that the group is scheduled at a time when public transportation is available and that the location of the group is near bus stops, train stations, and so on. If members have visual difficulties associated with retinitis (HIV) or retinopathy (diabetes), written materials associated with the group may need to be prepared in large type or using software easily enlarged or used with a text reader. For individuals with mobility concerns secondary to amputations or other complications of diabetes or HIV, physical accessibility concerns will need to be addressed. As is always the case in working with people with disabilities, the individual needs of all members should be ascertained and accommodated. As always, the facilitator should consider whether a group that mixes newly diagnosed members with members whose symptoms and health concerns are more advanced is wise. As discussed in Chapter 13, members newly diagnosed may become overwhelmed in groups with individuals with amputations or blindness due to diabetes, or any of the many health conditions associated with having lived with HIV for many years. The needs of individuals in the early stages of coming to grips with a diagnosis should be individually discussed and ascertained.

Facilitator Responsibilities

Facilitators working with individuals with these health issues should make sure to become familiar with the management and psychosocial issues associated with the disability. When facilitating a group with only one person who has diabetes or epilepsy, the facilitator should have a discussion ahead of time with the member about how he or she would like to address the group's curiosity or desire to understand the needs of the member. It should be the right of the member to disclose if and when he or she chooses. A discussion about this ahead of time might help to allay any worries on the part of the member about how this might occur.

In a heterogeneous high school group that focused on personal growth and developing positive relationships, one male member talked about how awful it was to have insulin-dependent diabetes. He blamed his friendship difficulties on the diabetes. He believed he could not go drinking as "everyone else" did, that he had to pay attention to having regular meals and getting enough sleep, and so on, and thus believed that no one would want him as a friend. In an early session, he said something like, "You just can't imagine what it's like to have to give yourself an insulin injection every morning," and a female member of the group who had not disclosed that she had diabetes mellitus responded, "Oh yes I can, because I do it every day too." The young man was speechless, with his mouth agape. He realized that for her, the condition did not define her and she enjoyed a full social life. He learned a great deal in the course of that group, not only from her, but from all members.

When a member of a heterogeneous group has diabetes, epilepsy, or HIV, the facilitator may find that many group members will have inaccurate information and will believe common misperceptions about all three of these disabilities. Many people believe that you get diabetes from eating too many sweets and that it is the fault of the person for overeating or not losing weight. In fact, some people still refer to it as "sugar diabetes" or just "sugar." Few people understand the experience of ketoacidosis or hyperglycemia and may misunderstand the mood changes that can accompany hyperglycemia. As was mentioned previously, many people fear individuals with epilepsy and are intensely curious what it is like. Group members will likely want to know what they should do if the member has a seizure. Many people are completely unaware of the existence of any type of seizure except generalized tonic–clonic seizures, and almost all will use the outdated nomenclature for seizures, if they know any terms at all. Some may still harbor suspicions that there is something otherworldly about epilepsy and may wonder whether there is some degree of mental instability that accompanies it. They may be appalled that someone with epilepsy would ever drive and consider it dangerous and inconsiderate to other drivers, even when no seizure activity has been present for many years. Finally, for both diabetes and epilepsy, there is a fairly widespread belief that because there are medications to treat it, it is not really a problem and that talking about it is attention-seeking behavior or that the individual is exaggerating its impact.

Particularly when a group member has HIV, the facilitator should be prepared for the possibility of a negative reaction, including fear and rejection on the part of a member or members who lack accurate information or have strong biases or homophobia. Often, a frank discussion about common misconceptions regarding transmission will help, but there may still be hesitancy on the part of some members or even outright hostility. If you are aware of intense negative emotions and outright hostility toward a group member for any reason during screening, you will have already considered whether this composition of group members is in the best interests of the group members as a whole as well as the group member with HIV who could become a target. Sometimes, however, the group member will not have discussed his or her HIV status ahead of time and will disclose it in group. If confronted with a situation in which the member is attacked or scapegoated or is in a situation of substantial harm, the group leader will need to intervene and actively protect the individual attacked.

Topics

The topics of interest to group participants who have chronic health disabilities are likely to vary, depending on the type of disability, time since diagnosis, age group of participants, the degree to which the group is homogeneous or heterogeneous, and other factors.

Consequently, the content of the group should be determined by the needs of its members. That said, there are certainly some common issues that are likely to be of interest or benefit to group participants. For psychoeducational groups and groups that are more highly structured, groups may be structured around some of the more common topics. Even for those that are less structured, the group facilitator should consider inviting discussion or prepare activities in some of the areas that are likely to be of common interest. These may include such topics as those listed below.

Understanding the Disability

This topic is especially important for newly diagnosed members, although it can be extremely helpful even years later. Many individuals have had their disabilities discussed with them in "medical-ese" with technical language and using difficult-to-comprehend medical concepts. Even when receiving clear and easily understandable information, it can be difficult for a newly diagnosed person to take it all in, because stress adversely affects information processing. Additionally, some information makes sense only as the individual acquires a personal understanding of how the disability affects his or her function. For example, few children under the age of 10 years have reason to retain information about the effects of alcohol on seizure thresholds. As they enter young adulthood and experience peer pressures to party, the information becomes highly relevant and has consequences that are easy to understand: If you drink and have a seizure, you may lose your license. Children with disabilities may have received explanations geared to their age at the time the initial conversation took place and will need to continually reeducate themselves as they grow older and as their grasp of more complex information improves. Specific information that will likely be of interest includes basic medical information related to what the disability is, how it affects health and functioning, how to manage the disability effectively, medication and treatment options, and research updates on prevention and treatment.

Practical Health Management Issues (Diet, Exercise, Stress)

The advantages of sharing information and strategies for day-to-day management have been discussed above and elsewhere in this book. For these disabilities, this information is invaluable. One of the enormous benefits of group is the instant credibility of group members who have been there themselves. Teens are particularly likely to be especially receptive to information that comes from another teen who understands their challenges.

Handling Difficult Social Situations

Although the specific social situations might vary from group to group and disability to disability, this topic will be of interest to all. For teens, the primary concern may be making friends and putting up with overbearing parents, whereas for older adults it may be fearing increased dependence on adult children associated with aging with a disability. For individuals with HIV, social ostracism may be a fairly commonplace occurrence, and individuals with diabetes may struggle with presumptions that insulin takes care of all of their problems. For all, however, there are likely to be many shared incidents, reactions, worries, and emotions that can be shared and processed together.

Stress Management and Wellness

Devoting a group to learning the basics of stress management benefits virtually everyone but particularly individuals who deal with the stresses of managing their lives with a disability and for whom stress can exacerbate symptoms and contribute to the development of complications. Learning to use relaxation and mindfulness techniques is helpful. Introducing members to the benefits of stress-relieving activities such as yoga or tai chi may open them to healthful pastimes with direct health benefits. Discussing the interaction of disability and healthy diet, exercise, and adequate sleep will be helpful, accompanied by practical, useful information on how to make changes in members' lives that will benefit overall health.

Sex, Relationships, and Parenthood

As is stated above, virtually everyone has concerns about intimacy, and the presence of a chronic disability will often introduce additional concerns around this topic. For example, members with diabetes might worry about finding partners who can put up with insulin pumps, injections, and working schedules around the routines required to effectively manage diabetes. Fears about embarrassing friends and potential partners with a seizure or restrictions in activities might create concerns among people with epilepsy. Individuals who have disabilities that affect sexual functioning, because of either the disability itself or medications affecting sexual functioning, will likely be relieved to have someone with whom to discuss these issues, because they may be embarrassing and taboo subjects in many families. As is noted above, individuals with HIV may share worries and trade experiences in how they handle issues of disclosure and sexual intimacy. For teenagers, worries about fitting in, having friends, and dating are paramount. Individuals whose disabilities are progressive may worry about whether a partner will stick in for the long haul. The ability to have and to raise children will also be a topic of discussion for many. People with epilepsy may worry about how they can guarantee the safety of their children if they have a seizure, and for individuals whose disabilities are genetically linked, the question of whether or not to have children is important and can be highly emotionally charged. Access to information about genetic counseling, parenting with a disability, and the opportunity to process emotions connected to these concerns can be extremely helpful.

Safety Issues

When a disability imposes limitations on function, there is always a risk–safety judgment that needs to be made. Never taking a risk may increase the likelihood of safety, but it also might limit access to the world and to the thrill of stretching one's boundaries. However, there are real safety risks that have to be weighed when making decisions to engage in activities such as sports, social drinking, and recreational drugs or participating in trials of new drugs. For someone with epilepsy, driving or starting a trial off of anticonvulsants after an extended seizure-free period may be risky but have potential benefits. Decisions about where one's comfort level lies around this issue have to be made individually, but many people with disabilities have received the message loud and clear from family, friends, and the media that there are many things that they just should not try to do. Frank and open discussions related to safety and the benefits of risk can be very empowering and promote healthy self-evaluation.

Empowerment and Advocacy

Discussions about self-advocacy, as well as advocacy for others with disabilities in public policy and in daily life, can be extremely beneficial. Again, each individual must find his or her own comfort level with this topic. However, many people are unaware that they have rights as people with disabilities, let alone how and whether to assert those rights in any given situation. Education about laws regarding access and disability rights, as well as discussions about values and comfort levels with these issues, can be productive and empowering. For individuals with disabilities that are not apparent—those we have referred to as "invisible" disabilities—"passing" or not acknowledging their disability status may confer some benefits—avoiding the stigma associated with disability or job discrimination—but it may also come at a cost: denying a very real part of who one is and the energy and stress of protecting an inauthentic identity. Discussing these issues with others who may or may not share one's perspective can be enlightening and challenging.

SUMMARY

The needs of individuals with chronic health conditions will vary. We have selected a few disabilities for closer examination; however, the kinds of concerns and topics discussed above are issues that may be important for many people with a wide variety of disabilities.

KEY TERMS

In this chapter, the important medical terms are defined in the text. We note here a few terms that may require a bit more explanation.

Assistance animals: generally associated with guide dogs for persons who are blind, but they can assist with a variety of conditions. In this chapter, we refer to animals that can be trained to detect an impending seizure, so the person is alerted and can move to a safe environment to avoid injuries from objects in the area.

Glucose: the form of sugar found in the blood that provides energy (fuel) for the cells in the body.

Hyperglycemia: too much glucose in the blood. The opposite condition is hypoglycemia, in which glucose levels are below normal.

Insulin: a hormone produced by the pancreas that controls the level of glucose in the blood. The cells cannot use the glucose without insulin.

Ketone: a chemical that breaks down fat for energy. It appears in the blood when there is not enough sugar in the blood to use for energy, so the body turns to fat to supply energy.

Lymphoma: a type of cancer that starts in the lymphatic system, which produces, stores, and transports white blood cells to areas of the body to fight infections.

Seizures: uncontrolled or abnormal electrical activity in the brain. There may be convulsions (the body shakes uncontrollably), sensory disturbances, and confusion that occurs when the electrical disturbance is happening.

RECOMMENDATIONS FOR PRACTICE

1. Include questions about invisible disabilities in your screening interview.

2. If you have a member of a heterogeneous group who has a chronic medical condition, inquire privately about that member's preference for telling the group. Doing so may ease fears that others misunderstand the condition and provide an opportunity to correct any misinformation, but this is a personal decision, and the facilitator should respect the right of the individual to control the decision and the timing of any self-disclosures.

3. Groups for children with these conditions will need more structure and are likely to be psychoeducational. The facilitator might want to cofacilitate with a school nurse, who can provide some age-appropriate medical information and quickly detect misinformation. For high school students, a straightforward explanation of how alcohol affects diabetes is important. For epilepsy, high school students will want to discuss the issue of driving and feeling socially limited by their condition.

4. For groups of persons with HIV, members may wish to discuss the question of disclosure to others, especially potential sexual partners. It is common for them to fear rejection once their condition is known, and this is not without a basis in reality. Practicing ways to disclose may be helpful, and engaging in advocacy efforts to better inform the public about the disease, including the many ways in which one can be infected, may give them a sense of purpose.

5. Group facilitators may become advocates for members of these groups. For example, although a child may not need or qualify for special education, he or she might need and qualify for a 504 Plan that provides accommodations for medical conditions. For example, a child with diabetes may need to have candy or orange juice available when needed, even if school rules prohibit eating in class. Students with epilepsy who have an aura (a feeling that a seizure is coming on) should be allowed to go to a nurse's office without delay in order to avoid having a seizure in front of other children. For adults, the advocacy may relate to employment issues.

part III
RESOURCES

chapter 13
RECAP AND CONCLUSIONS

The various forms of group work (psychoeducational, counseling, and therapy) are both effective and efficient ways of promoting change in members. When members include persons with disabilities, those benefits may be even more powerful. People with disabilities are frequently socially isolated and marginalized in society, and groups can have a profound impact on those who do not have social support available.

In some ways, one might argue that this population is also marginalized by the counseling profession. The flagship professional organization for counselors, ACA, has a list of competencies that are expected of practitioners (http://www.counseling.org/knowledge-center/competencies), but working with persons with disabilities is not among them. Within the 2014 *ACA Code of Ethics*, there is a section on multiculturalism and diversity, but the focus remains on racial and ethnic minorities, although disability was added to the list of groups facing discrimination and stigma in many places within the *Code*. The Multicultural and Social Justice Principles (www.asgw.org) document does mention disability in the list of differences that are important for group leaders to attend to, and the document also reminds facilitators that intragroup differences must be recognized to avoid stereotyping. But that is the only mention in the 15-page document. One might argue that ARCA provides guidance and in fact is all about working with persons with disabilities, but persons with disabilities seek counseling from a variety of sources for a variety of reasons, and it is important for all counselors who facilitate groups to be as prepared to serve members with disabilities as they are to serve ethnic minority clients. The requirements of the ADA mandate that counselors serve clients with disabilities, and although many groups will likely be facilitated by rehabilitation counselors, others will be organized around an issue that is not disability specific, and all counselors must be prepared to provide services.

Given that counselors must be inclusive, what kinds of training are needed to reach competency to work with this population? First, we stress that it is not just skills alone that are necessary. One hopes that all counselors will have had didactic education and practical supervised experience in facilitating groups. They will also need solid knowledge of the disabilities represented in their members. At a minimum, counselors need access to resources, both print and online, that cover the essential information, including onset, symptoms, levels of impairment, treatment options, and psychosocial aspects of the disability. Finally, facilitators must have an attitude of acceptance toward persons with disabilities. They must not pity them, fear them, avoid them, or display discomfort. Displaying interest and concern is important; treating the person as a curiosity is not (see Chapter 7). Inquiring about the kinds of accommodations the client needs is necessary, but probing for intimate details about the disability is not.

The client may seek to educate you, however, and that should be welcome. For example, one of the authors of this book had a referral from an agency that provided services to clients with TBI. The client was depressed because of a divorce. I explained that I did not have specialized training in working with TBI, but I was persuaded to have a consultation with the potential client because she had been having difficulty finding a clinician. During that meeting, I explained that I had no training in TBI and was concerned about that. She was undeterred and told me that she would ensure that I was well informed. During our first session, she provided me with a pile of reading material and in future sessions was diligent about noting when a particular problem or situation was related to her disability. We worked together for several years, and she stated on termination that she received help not just with the relationship issue but with the associated TBI symptoms.

Group facilitators (and all counselors) must recognize that persons with disabilities may have multiple minority identities (see Chapter 4). It is the intersection of these identities that is present in the group. As with any other client, the person with disabilities should choose the way that he or she identifies. Biracial people often identify with one or the other of their parents' races, although recently biracial has become a distinct identity category. Persons with disabilities may belong to a minority racial group, religious persuasion, sexual orientation, and socioeconomic status, and all these categories affect their ways of being and interacting. The facilitator must guard against members attempting to pigeonhole the person with disabilities and assist them, if necessary, in clarifying why such attempts might be offensive or hurtful.

In addition to some level of expertise in group facilitation and disabilities, group facilitators need to be prepared to address topics of high interest to many groups for persons with disabilities. In Chapter 2, we provide overviews of issues, including social relationships and dating, sexuality, overprotection, abuse, maintaining health, accessibility issues, and substance abuse.

The therapeutic factors identified by Yalom (1995) are the mechanisms by which change occurs in groups. The first of those is universality, the discovery that others share similar circumstances and, more important, that others experience similar feelings in response to those circumstances, and one is not alone. Altruism, or the concern for others, is demonstrated when members are helpful to one another in the group. The opportunity to be helpful, despite one's own struggles, can provide a boost to one's self-esteem. Groups also instill hope; by getting to know and understand others who have perhaps made great progress, an individual can imagine making progress in his or her own journey. There are more practical advantages for groups as well: Information is shared, social skills are taught or modeled, and one develops greater self-awareness via interpersonal and intrapersonal learning. For those who are marginalized, the sense of cohesion—or belonging to, being part of, the group—can be a very curative factor. Persons who are in psychological pain often attempt to mask that because they fear burdening significant others. In persons with acquired disabilities, relationship dynamics often need to readjust to the new reality, and those with the disability may feel that they are already a burden to loved ones. In the group, catharsis, or emotional release, is a safe place to express those emotions, which can provide considerable relief. The opportunity for imitative behavior, or observing and modeling the behaviors of persons whose skills and behaviors one sees as effective, is also part of the dynamics that unfold in groups. A more psychodynamic therapeutic factor is the corrective recapitulation of family-of-origin issues. Groups display dynamics that are similar to those of a family, and particularly when there are male and female coleaders, one may recognize patterns of interaction that mimic those developed in the family of origin. But in recognizing the patterns, one has the opportunity to use the group as a laboratory to test new, healthy behaviors. Finally, the existential issues are always present: the inevitability of death, finding meaning in a meaningless universe, the freedom to choose one's course and accepting responsibility for those choices, and the ultimate loneliness and isolation of the human condition. These may come to the forefront more readily in a group for persons with disabilities, especially if the disability has been recently acquired. The safety of the group allows members to ponder these profound dilemmas and perhaps find a way forward in light of the human condition.

We reiterate here that the social or minority model of disability provides a perspective for group facilitators' thinking about clients. In essence, this model proposes that the problems encountered by persons with disabilities are due to societal barriers. The lack of accessible facilities coupled with negative and demeaning attitudes toward persons with a disability restrict their participation in all aspects of society. Persons with disabilities are viewed as a minority group, along with racial and ethnic minorities, that experiences oppression, denial of civil rights, social isolation, unequal treatment, unemployment, and other disparities associated with minority status (Olkin, 1999). Some would refer to disability as a culture, as in Deaf culture. What is important to group facilitators is that the social isolation and mistreatment that persons with disabilities have experienced is part of their worldview and must be respected and understood. It is likely that frustrations with inaccessibility, mistreatment, and discrimination will surface in the group setting, and those must not be dismissed as irrelevant. Adaptation to disability (the goal of many groups) cannot occur without acknowledging the barriers that are outside the individual's control. Some members might be activists, working toward changing the physical and attitudinal structures in society. Such activism often provides meaning (in the existential sense) and purpose to their lives and must be appreciated.

It is also important, according to Shakespeare (2013), to distinguish between disability, which is a social category, and impairment, which is a physical limitation. He argued that we must accept impairment and remove disability. He also addressed the language issue: *person with disabilities*, he says, is mainstream language, whereas *disabled people* is more fitting to the social model. We recognize that this issue is still contentious, and we do not pretend to have an answer as to which usage is more correct. We reiterate here that our goal is to communicate clearly without offending anyone unintentionally.

We mention throughout the book that prescreening interviews are extremely important, and we wish to emphasize that again. Whether groups are going to be homogeneous for a disability (which means that there will be heterogeneity on many other characteristics), it is crucial to assess whether a potential client is a good fit for the group. One must assess for psychosis, potential for violence, ability to communicate, interest in the topic, and understanding of the format and structure of the group. The screening interview should be conducted by both facilitators if the group is co-led, because it is closer to the group environment and one can observe how the person reacts to the different leaders. This is also an opportunity to learn what impact the disabilities might have on participation and what accommodations would facilitate engagement. While screening the potential member, you are also setting the tone, introducing yourselves as facilitators, and articulating expectations for the group. If mandated clients are seeking membership, we urge the facilitator to consider the effect the person might have on other group members. If a mandated client is adamantly opposed to the group and does not believe that there is anything he or she might gain from participation, we urge facilitators not to accept him or her. Unless the facilitators are under a contract with an agency to provide groups for their clients, the mandate falls on the client, not the facilitators, and you must consider the importance of all members of the group.

In Chapter 7, we reviewed the principles for etiquette when interacting with persons with disabilities. Although some of them may seem self-evident, unless one is completely immersed in disability culture, it is easy to overlook something that matters. A colleague who is blind mentioned that people often speak to him, assuming that he recognizes their voice even if they have had minimal contact. A Deaf friend reminds us that people tend to look at the interpreter rather than her when interacting; after all, we are repeatedly told to make eye contact with the speaker. We need to remember that the speaker is the Deaf person; the interpreter is providing the sounds. It really does take vigilance to observe these behaviors, and when one inevitably forgets, it is important to apologize.

A final point we wish to reiterate here is regarding the use of exercises in groups for persons with disabilities. First, the facilitators need to carefully think about ways in which members' disabilities might interfere with their full participation. An experienced group facilitator who had not worked with Deaf clients before used a popular activity in which members were blindfolded. The activity was consistent with the goal of that particular group. The Deaf student could not see the interpreter, and so could not get the instructions and information the other members got and could not participate. The facilitator was distressed when she realized that she had not considered this issue. We hope that readers of this book will take time to consider these possibilities as part of their planning process.

Second, we stress that exercises serve a purpose, but they are not the purpose. That is, using exercises in a group can reassure facilitators that something will happen. It is admittedly a bit daunting to be in a group without the structure that a series of exercises can provide. But exercises are selected by the facilitators in advance of the meeting in order to prepare. The energy and dynamics of the group might suggest that another direction would be more beneficial. If the facilitators are willing to discard the exercise in favor of the immediate process, the exercise is being used (or not used) to further the goals of the group. When facilitators are excited about the exercise and determined to use it, regardless of what emerges in the group, that rigidity is detrimental to the group.

Exercises must be selected to be consistent with the goals and nature of the group, appropriate for the age of the participants, accessible to all members, and introduced very carefully to members. The meat of the exercises is in the processing, discussing members' experiences during the exercise, exploring their feelings that emerged during the exercise, noting reactions to others, linking members, and so on. When this is done adequately (with sufficient time allowed), exercises can be quite useful. We encourage facilitators to also gain experience with process-oriented groups, in which members rather than facilitators provide the material. When facilitators are able to see how productive and meaningful such groups can be, they are more inclined to use that approach. With persons with disabilities, having some control over the direction of their group can be empowering, because lack of control over many areas of their lives is a frequent consequence of the disability.

No discussion about groups and people with disabilities is complete without the very important topic of ethics. Generally speaking, the same ethical principles and standards that guide counselors in providing groups are the same, regardless of whether or not a member or members have disabilities. Some considerations that are particularly important for group facilitators who work with individuals with disabilities include ensuring that informed consent processes take cognitive or intellectual barriers into consideration, issues around confidentiality and exceptions to confidentiality that are commonly seen in working with individuals with disabilities, as well as the ethical issues involved in online group counseling with people with disabilities. We discussed issues involved in screening and competency and argued for an inclusion bias, while discussing the need to have exclusion criteria. We referred throughout to the codes of ethics of ACA and CRCC, as well as the ASGW *Best Practice Guidelines* and multicultural competencies, and we recommended that group facilitators keep the guidance contained in them close by and ever present in everything they do.

In Part II of this book, we discussed groups for persons with specific types of disabilities. We recognize that there are many disabilities that did not receive individual attention, but we chose to focus on several that are particularly common or for which there are substantial implications for the group facilitator. It is beyond the scope of this book to cover all disabilities in detail, but it is hoped that the central message was received: that it is important to learn a little about the disabilities of prospective members of your group and to consider the ways in which you need to ensure that the group will meet the needs of all of its members, including the member who has a disability. Once again, we wish to remind readers that often they have access to the best consultant possible: the individual who is living with the disability himself or herself, and facilitators should take advantage of that expertise. In the preceding chapters we provided specific but basic information about several disabilities; however, we encourage readers to access additional resources to enhance their knowledge of those disabilities so that if a client presents for a group, you will already know where to go for more information.

In conclusion, we are strong advocates both of group work and for persons with disabilities. We hope this book has inspired readers to share those passions with us.

RECOMMENDATIONS FOR PRACTICE

1. Although a facilitator cannot be an expert on every disability, it is recommended that at least one basic text be read (such as Falvo, 2014) to get an overview of medical and psychosocial issues associated with any disability that members may have.

2. We also recommend that facilitators peruse the resources in Chapter 14 and build a library not only for their own use but also to recommend to clients books that might provide a new perspective on their disability. Bibliotherapy can be implemented in a group or with individual clients.

3. We strongly recommend a cofacilitation model in groups for persons with disabilities. This requires time to plan and process group sessions, but it also provides a more effective mode of facilitation.

4. The screening interview is essential. This is an opportunity for facilitators to both give information and prepare potential members for the group experience, and also to gather information about the nature of the disability, necessary accommodations, and fit within the group.

5. Facilitators should familiarize themselves with agencies in the area that can be sources of information to which they may refer group members who need further assistance.

6. Because online groups are so convenient for many persons with disabilities, it is important to understand how they work and how privacy and security can be implemented if one chooses to offer online groups.

7. Ethical issues are of paramount importance, and facilitators should keep current on changes to ethical codes. They should also read journals or association magazine columns that offer commentary or examples of how to resolve common ethical dilemmas.

8. We also strongly recommend that facilitators make an effort to attend professional conferences during which relevant topics are covered. The counseling organizations listed in Chapter 14 generally have annual or biennial conferences, and one can check this list of programs offered when deciding whether to attend.

chapter 14
EXERCISES AND RESOURCES

Below are exercises that can be used in any group but could be particularly helpful in a group with persons with disabilities. Exercises need to be consistent with the goals of the group, and because the activities are not the goal but the vehicle to increase understanding and interaction, it is essential to allocate sufficient time for processing. These exercises can be in a group comprising able-bodied persons and persons with disabilities, with the goal of increasing understanding of disabilities, and are particularly useful in counselor training.

Facilitators will need to modify some of the exercises to accommodate the disabilities that members have. If paper and pencil are used, but the members have motor impairment that precludes writing, the exercises can be done orally. If members are blind, handouts can be prepared in advance for members who read Braille or could use a large-print version. If members use assistive technology to facilitate communication, let them know in the screening interview that they will want to have the technology with them for group sessions.

We apologize in advance for not crediting sources of all activities. We have used them for so long, we often forget where we originally learned them, and in many cases, we have modified them so often that the resemblance to the original is marginal.

With that said, we offer some exercises that you might want to incorporate into your repertoire.

WHO AM I?

This exercise can lead to awareness about the self, but it is also interesting to ask members to note the ways in which their responses are similar to and different from others' and what that might reveal. The instructions are quite simple. Tell members that you will give them incomplete sentences, which they are to complete with whatever makes sense to them. We usually have them number from 1 to 10 on the paper and then start with Number 1. The sentence stem is "I am _____." Use the same stem for Numbers 2–10.

It is fascinating to see how different individuals approach this activity. For example, some will fill in all roles (I am a mother, I am a student, I am a worker), and others will use descriptions (I am someone who likes to laugh, I am someone with a quick temper). Still others describe their feelings in the moment (I am annoyed at this activity, I am stuck, I am tired). Some find it very difficult after the first few items, others want more space or time to add. In a group for persons with disabilities, it is interesting to see how prominent disability-related items are in the list. The same is true for other minority statuses. It has been our experience that no one says "I am able-bodied," but those with disabilities typically mention their disability in one of the sentences. In the same vein, racial minority students are more likely to mention their race in the list than are White students. There is much to process in this exercise.

SENTENCE STEMS

A popular exercise is one that can be modified in an infinite number of ways by varying the stems to suit the needs and goals of your group. The list below comes from Pfieffer and Jones (1970) and is still a good one. To do the exercise, it is helpful to ask each person to write his or her sentence completions and then share verbally in a go-around, then do a bit of processing after each round: How similar or different were the endings for the same stem? Who surprised you? Who seems most like you? One of the processing questions is whether they shared exactly what they wrote, and if they did not, what caused them to change their mind or to keep what they wrote to themselves. We often ask the person who is last to share a particular stem to decide which stem to share next, so we do not go in a predictable order.

1. Other people usually _____.
2. The best measure of personal success is _____.
3. Anybody will work hard if _____.
4. People think of me as _____.
5. When I let go _____.
6. Marriage is _____.
7. Nothing is as frightening as _____.
8. I miss _____.
9. People in charge should _____.
10. The thing I like best about myself is _____.
11. There are times when I _____.
12. I would like to be _____.
13. When I have something to say _____.
14. As a child, I _____.
15. The teacher I liked best was a person who _____.
16. It is fun to _____.
17. My body is _____.
18. When it comes to men/women _____.
19. Loving someone _____.
20. Two years from now, I _____.

Items 12 and 17 can provide meaningful discussion in a group with both able-bodied persons and persons with disabilities. Able-bodied people often expect those with disabilities to say something about not having their disability for Item 12 and wanting to be able-bodied in Item 17. Persons with disabilities often do not say those things, and it is fruitful to talk about the expectations of the other and what that reveals to themselves and others about their understanding of disabilities.

FIRST IMPRESSIONS

There are many ways to encourage members to share their initial reactions to each other. This can be particularly useful in a group with both able-bodied persons and members with disabilities. It involves some movement, so facilitators will need to be mindful of what might have to change. This activity can be quite risky for some groups; facilitators can reduce the number of steps to make it less anxiety provoking. We suggest prefacing this with a discussion of how groups are unique in that people can get honest feedback about the way others perceive them, and this is an opportunity for significant growth.

Again, this is presented below as a written exercise, so modify it as needed.

1. At the beginning of the first session of the group, members are asked to share their name and one or two facts about themselves.
2. Then, participants turn their chairs away from the group (or some other means to keep them from seeing each other) and list the names that they remember.
3. They turn around again to face each other and discover who they forgot. They may ask for more information about each other to help them remember going forward.
4. Talk about names—how members feel about their name, if they know how or why their name was chosen, and also how they felt about not being able to remember some names and not being remembered if that happened in this activity.
5. The facilitators pass around a list of members in the group. Members are asked to write down their first impressions of each of the other members. A facilitator collects these and reads all the impressions of a member without disclosing who provided them. As each member's impressions are shared, they are asked to comment on how accurate they are and feelings about hearing them. This continues until everyone has had a turn.

When processing, note how many first impressions of the member with a disability were or were not disability related and discuss. Often members will deliberately try to think past the disability because they do not think mentioning it would be polite, and this can open the door to fruitful conversations about avoiding the topic of disability (the elephant in the room) and how this is perceived by the person who has the disability.

AUTOBIOGRAPHY

There are various ways to do this. If the facilitators believe that some personal history would be helpful—particularly if some or all members have an acquired disability—here are some ways to get pertinent information without moving the group into a focus on the past.

Each person gets to write and share his or her autobiography; the limit is five sentences. This requires that they determine the most critical events.

Members are told to think about a book that they could write about their lives. They list the titles of the chapters, and share those.

Members are asked to draw a roadmap of their lives, and share. They may share detours, forks in the roads, and so on.

Processing is important, including why members are curious about the paths that others' lives have taken. How will this information affect the group? Who surprised you? Who are you curious to learn more about? Who is most like you? Who can you most learn from?

EMPTY CHAIR

The empty chair exercise is a tool from the Gestalt framework and is used to work on unfinished business or to integrate two contradictory aspects of the self. It can be extremely powerful and should not be done by facilitators who are not well versed in this technique, prepared to manage strong emotions, and to follow up as needed.

In this exercise, a member of the group will have a dialogue with an empty chair, which can represent a person with whom there is unfinished business, or the disability, or another side of self, or a side of a dilemma. During the exercise, the facilitator guides the member to share what he or she is feeling, then switch positions and respond as the other person or entity, repeating this until the dialogue has reached a conclusion. When this is done in a group, the other members are spectators, but they can learn to be shrewd observers who offer their insights when the member indicates that he or she is ready to receive them. The member should explore how he or she felt during the exercise.

This should not be done as a go-around, in which each member takes a turn in the chair. It should be used when a member is struggling to understand a relationship, resolve an internal conflict, or address a concern (the disability) in a creative way that may allow feelings and ideas to emerge that are not forthcoming by using other means.

GROUP TASKS

An activity that can be used in a variety of ways is a group consensus-building activity. We prefer to use those with "expert" solutions, such as the Winter Survival or Stranded in the Desert scenarios that can be found in Johnson and Johnson's (2012) *Joining Together* book, now in its 11th edition. If at least 8 people in the group are mobile, Traffic Jam (from *Silver Bullets*, by Rohnke, 1984) is a great activity to demonstrate the importance of different perspectives, points of view, assertiveness, and so on. What is important when doing this activity is careful observation to highlight the ways in which the group worked together, who listened well, who spoke up despite opposition, who contributed, who took leadership, and so on. The point of the exercise is to illuminate how different members of the group bring to the group different styles of interaction, different types of knowledge, different ideas, and so on—all of which combine to bring about a better conclusion than each person's individual solution. If a member uses a wheelchair, whether he or she chooses to be an observer or an active participant, and the group's reaction to either choice, is important to discuss.

ADJECTIVES

Ask members to write five descriptive terms or phrases that best describe them. The leader collects and reads them aloud, and the group members try to determine whom they describe. What is important are the reasons that people give for their guesses. At the end, discuss whether people were easy or difficult to match with their descriptors, how accurate they seemed, whether important adjectives were omitted, how it felt to be known by others, and so on.

FEEDBACK

Sometimes, group members struggle to give feedback to other members and may be very careful not to hurt anyone's feelings by focusing only on positive feedback. Although that is often very welcome, it may lead to an unspoken norm that members give only positive feedback in this group. That deprives members of important information that can be the most growth enhancing of the experience. One activity that we have used to encourage the exchange of both kinds of information is "Who in the Group?" This involves a series of descriptors under the heading, "Who in the group . . . ?" with items such as "Who would you choose to bring to a family dinner at your house?" "To be trapped in a dangerous situation with?" "To be with you after a funeral?" "To be your lawyer?" "To tell you bad news?" "To tell you good news?" "To tell a secret to?" "To care for you when you are ill?" "To go on vacation with?" "To help you with a difficult task?" "To make a bank deposit for you?"

The items can be chosen to fit the group's situation. What is important in processing is noting who got chosen repeatedly for the same thing, who did not get chosen, how people felt about being chosen or not chosen, whether people changed whom they chose when they realized some people had not been chosen as many times as others, and so on.

SELF-DISCLOSURE

These are activities that encourage self-disclosure. Some groups will benefit from a structured way to share about themselves, and these exercises help that occur. One exercise is to ask each member to share something in a wallet, purse, backpack, or pocket that has some significance for that individual. Encourage dialogue about the item and what it reveals about the member who shared. This can be taken a step further by asking members in advance to bring something of significance to share on a specified day. These choices can be very moving and often encourage important dialogue, which the facilitators of course will encourage. If a member in the group forgets to bring an item, he or she can be asked to either draw it or describe it in great detail. When processing, talk about how sharing affects the cohesion of the group.

Another self-disclosure exercise is to provide an outline of a human to each member. Then ask members to draw or write the following: "In the head, put your earliest memory; in the eyes, put what you wish others could see about you; in your ears, put inspirational things you have heard; in the mouth, put what you want to speak up about; in the hands, put things you want to reach for in your life; in the feet, put what you stand for; in the heart, put people or things that are close to your heart; in the gut, put things that upset you." You can revise and add, as needed. Take the time to have each member share his or her drawing and for other members to reflect on each person's drawing and how they were affected by learning about the person. What did members learn about themselves, others, and the group from the activity?

SOURCES OF ACTIVITIES

- The Indiana Governor's Council for People With Disabilities has a booklet that has activities that might be useful in some groups. It can be retrieved from www.indianadisabilityawareness.org/assets/docs/ActivitiesBooklet.pdf.

- An excellent booklet on disability etiquette is available from https://www.unitedspinal.org/pdf/DisabilityEtiquette.pdf. It has clever illustrations that emphasize specific points.
- A manual for treatment of combat-related PTSD can be retrieved from www.mirecc.va.gov (*PTSD Recovery Group Client Manual*). The main site has links to handouts that go with the activities.
- A useful set of exercises that are designed for a disability awareness workshop that can be easily converted to a psychoeducation group format can be found at www.projectvision.net.
- The video referred to in Chapter 7 on the Ten Commandments for interacting with persons with disabilities is available for purchase at http://www.disabilitytraining.com/product-info. php?Ten_Commandments_of_Communicating_With_People_ With_Disabilities_DVD-pid111.html. There is a clip on the site previewing the first 5 minutes so that you can decide whether this is something you would like to have on hand. Or you can request that a local library obtain a copy.

RESOURCES

Throughout the book, we have mentioned various resources in relation to the content. Below, we list additional resources that facilitators of groups with persons with disabilities may find helpful and informative. The list is far from exhaustive and should not be considered an endorsement by us of these particular groups. We wish to provide a starting place for facilitators who would like more information.

Many of the resources we list are websites. If you use a website to disseminate information, you should ensure that your site is accessible to persons with disabilities. This site is an excellent place to start: http://ncdj.org/resources/educators/web-accessibility/.

Group Work

- www.agpa.org is an organization dedicated to group therapy and has extensive publications available for practitioners. Links to important articles are on the site. This organization publishes the *International Journal of Group Psychotherapy*.
- www.apadivisions.org/division-49/index.aspx is the home of Division 49 (Society of Group Psychology and Group Psychotherapy) of the American Psychological Association. Their scholarly publication is *Group Dynamics: Theory, Research, and*

Practice; a newsletter is also published (*The Group Psychologist*), which includes a Diversity Column. The website has a link to the July 2009 newsletter, which has a useful article on a model of group therapy for persons with IDs, along with other psychiatric disorders.

- www.asgw.org is the website for the Association for Specialists in Group Work, a division of ACA. One can find standards, practices, and resources for group work facilitators. They have books and media for sale and a self-rated inventory of confidence in group work skills. This association publishes the *Journal for Specialists in Group Work* and a newsletter.

General Disability Information

- www.aapd.com is the home site for the American Association of People With Disabilities. It has a good video featuring members with disabilities talking about their work and careers. There is also a 30-second video on bullying of children with disabilities, with actual children as the only speakers.
- http://abledbody.com/ is a source of news and media about disability-related materials. The variety of materials on the site makes it worth a visit. The site has been online since March 2009.
- www.disability.gov has information about all manner of resources (employment, housing, civil right, benefits, etc.) for persons with disabilities and their families. It is an accessible website and is an excellent source of information about the ADA. Disability.gov can also be contacted by telephone at 1-800-514-0301.
- www.disabilityscoop.com is a similar site focused on developmental disabilities. There are sections of the website specific to autism, cerebral palsy, Down syndrome, and IDs.
- www.ndrn.org is the National Disability Rights Network website, which also has a wide range of information and is an accessible site. There are several helpful videos to raise awareness of disabilities. *Wipe Out Stigma* is presented by persons with mental illness, and another video on protection and advocacy is narrated by Geraldo Rivera. This organization is involved in issues such as juvenile justice, in which youth with disabilities are disproportionately represented.
- www.nod.org is the website of the National Organization on Disability, which focuses on employment opportunities for persons with disabilities.

- www.selfadvocacyonline.org is a great resource for clients. It has short video tutorials on a variety of basic skills, all featuring persons with disabilities.

Specific Disabilities

- http://www.aadb.org. We have not discussed in this book those persons who are both deaf and blind. This site has good information and links.
- http://www.aaidd.org. This is the site for the American Association on Intellectual and Developmental Disabilities. It is geared toward professionals who work with this population. It hosts teleconferences and webinars and includes information about conferences.
- http://www.afb.org is the site of the American Federation for the Blind (including vision loss).
- http://www.amputee-coalition.org/support-groups-peer-support/support-group-network/ is a useful site for finding information and services for persons with amputations.
- http://www.brainline.org specializes in TBI and has numerous links and other resources that can be accessed from the site.
- https://www.gallaudet.edu/clerc-center/info-to-go.html is associated with Gallaudet University and has a very comprehensive list of links and information for persons who are deaf and hard of hearing. It is an excellent place to start if seeking information on this population.
- http://www.nad.org is the site for the National Association of the Deaf.
- http://www.nami.org. This is the site of the well-known organization that focuses on mental illness. It has news items, a helpline, personal stories, and online support groups for family members, peers, and others. It also has information about specific mental disorders. This is definitely the site to begin with on this topic.
- http://www.nfb.org. The National Federation of the Blind recently celebrated 75 years of existence.
- http://www.nih.gov/about/almanac/organization/NIDA. htm is the location of the National Institute on Drug Abuse. This site is primarily for professionals, as is www.samhsa.gov.
- http://www.ninds.nih.gov/index.htm. Although much of this site would be of interest to neuroscientists, there are links to information about every brain disorder, which are quite thorough and written in layperson's language. Each page of

information also has links to organizations and publications on that particular disorder.

- http://www.ptsd.va.gov is an essential resource maintained by the U.S. Department of Veterans Affairs (VA). It has information for the public as well as for professionals and has a lengthy list of organizations that deal with trauma. Because PTSD can be caused by combat trauma, the VA has a vested interest in providing accurate and up-to-date information.
- https://recovergateway.org/substance-abuse-resources/. This site on substance abuse is geared toward the public and includes a helpline number as well as information on a number of substances that are often misused.
- http://www.spinalcord.org/spinal-network/support-groups/11105/spinal-cord-injury-support-group-16/. This site has good links to support groups both for individuals with SCIs and for their family members. Other information is also available on the site.
- http://www.thearc.org. This is a well-known organization formed more than 60 years ago to focus on persons with IDs. They are a strong advocacy group, and one can find links to the state and local chapters on this site.

Books

We observed earlier that the best way to become comfortable around people with disabilities is to be around people with disabilities. Second best might be reading about persons with disabilities, so we include some titles below. Many are first-person accounts, so we get to know the individuals intimately. This list is not by any means exhaustive but may provide a jumping-off point for introducing yourself to the narratives of people with disabilities in their own voices. You may also wish to recommend some of these books to group members. Full information is in the References section at the end of the book.

The Child Who Never Grew (Buck, 1992). This personal story is by the author of the classic *The Good Earth*. It is unique in that it provides a picture of how children with disabilities were regarded and treated 50 years ago. Institutionalizing a child is no longer the norm, but readers will benefit from understanding this mother's struggle.

Deaf Again (Drolsbaugh, 2008) is a fascinating perspective on deafness, because the author is a child of deaf parents who is initially raised to be in the hearing world. He eventually becomes

Deaf himself, and his experiences in both the hearing and Deaf worlds, and the pressure to maintain a hearing identity (he does not), are very revealing.

The Diving Bell and the Butterfly (Bauby, 1998) is the memoir of a 43-year-old magazine editor who suffers a massive stroke, which leaves him paralyzed. He is able to communicate by blinking his left eye and manages to write this account. The story was also made into a movie.

Expecting Adam: A True Story of Birth, Rebirth, and Everyday Magic (M. Beck, 2011). Martha Beck was working on her doctorate when she became pregnant and learned that the child would have Down syndrome. She and her husband agreed to have the child, and the book chronicles that time period and the time after his birth.

Far From the Tree: Parents, Children and the Search for Identity (Solomon, 2012) is a collection of accounts of children with disabilities and other differences born into families without experience with their conditions. There are chapters on autism, deafness, Down syndrome, schizophrenia, criminality, and transgenderism. The focus is on how the family copes with children with these disorders.

The Hidden Kennedy Daughter (Larson, 2015) is a brand-new account of the life of Rosemary Kennedy. The story is horrific and reveals the attitudes and beliefs about IDs in the first half of the 20th century. A strength of the book is the account of the ways in which family members responded to their child and sibling. Reviews indicate that there is new material about her life and that the book is extremely worthwhile.

Life as We Know It: A Father, a Family, and an Exceptional Child (Berube, 1998) describes the experiences of the author's second child, who was born with Down syndrome. In addition to the personal account, the author describes the social context of raising a child with a disability.

Life on Wheels (Karp, 2008) is written by a person who uses a wheelchair for mobility. Reviewers find it to be useful for both new and long-term wheelchair users and their families. This is a second edition, revised in response to reader feedback and with a strong emphasis on empowerment.

Mindstorms (Cassidy, 2009) is written for family and caregivers of someone with a TBI, although some persons with TBI also found it valuable. The author is a neuropsychiatrist who founded a TBI program at McLean Hospital in Boston, Massachusetts. The book has important information and is written for the general public, although there is less focus on mild TBI than on more serious injuries.

My Left Foot (C. Brown, 1955) also a major movie, is the autobiography of a man with severe cerebral palsy who develops a way to communicate. He is highly intelligent, and reviewers who have disabilities have high praise for this book's honesty. It has been described as inspirational.

Sight Unseen (Kleege, 1999). Georgina Kleege began losing her sight at age 11 from macular degeneration and is legally blind, although she has some residual vision (10%). She describes her experiences with visual impairment and also attacks cultural stereotypes about blindness.

There's a Boy in Here (Barron & Barron, 2002) is told by the mother of a son with autism and recounts their struggles as he was growing up. The two perspectives make the book particularly illuminating regarding the dynamics of parenting an autistic child.

Travelling to Infinity: The True Story Behind the Theory of Everything (Hawking, 2014). The film based on this memoir is also quite moving. Jane Hawking tells the story of Stephen Hawking's struggle with amyotrophic lateral sclerosis (Lou Gehrig's disease) and its impact on the lives of the family. Stephen Hawking was given a life expectancy of 2 years in 1965, but he continues to be a productive scientist.

Online Materials

Practice Guidelines for Group Psychotherapy
(American Group Psychotherapy Association, Science to Service Task Force, 2007). Download this resource from the link on this page: http://209.190.242.22/guidelines/index.html.

Substance Abuse Treatment: Group Therapy:
Treatment Improvement Protocol, TIP 41
This is invaluable for counselors conducting groups for persons with substance abuse problems and is available at no cost from http://store.samhsa.gov/product/TIP-41-Substance-Abuse-Treatment-Group-Therapy/SMA12-3991

REFERENCES

Adams, Z. W., & Boyd, S. W. E. (2010). Ethical challenges in the treatment of individuals with intellectual disabilities. *Ethics & Behavior, 20,* 407–418.

Adler, M. (1995). Homogeneity or heterogeneity of groups: When, and along what dimensions? *Canadian Journal of Counselling, 29,* 14–21.

Agency for Healthcare Research and Quality. (2010). *National healthcare disparities report, 2009* (AHRQ Publication No. 10-0004). Rockville, MD: U.S. Department of Health and Human Services.

Agrawal, Y., Platz, E. A., & Niparko, J. K. (2008). Prevalence of hearing loss and differences by demographic characteristics among US adults: Data from the National Health and Examination Survey, 1999–2004. *JAMA Internal Medicine, 168,* 1522–1530.

Alzheimer's Association. (2015). *What is dementia?* Retrieved from http://www.alz.org/what-is-dementia.asp

American Counseling Association. (2014). *ACA code of ethics.* Alexandria, VA: Author.

American Group Psychotherapy Association. (2002). *Oractice guidelines for group psychotherapy. The American Psychotherapy Association Science to Service Task Force.* New York, NY: Author.

American Psychiatric Association. (1980). *Diagnostic and statistical manual of mental disorders* (3rd ed.). Washington, DC: Author.

American Psychiatric Association. (2013). *Diagnostic and statistical manual of mental disorders* (5th ed.). Arlington, VA: American Psychiatric Publishing.

Americans With Disabilities Act of 1990, 42 U.S.C. §§ 12101–12213 (2000).

Amputee Coalition (n.d.). *Limb loss statistics*. Rerieved from http://www.amputee-coalition.org/limb-loss-resource-center/resources-by-topic/limb-loss-statistics/limb-loss-statistics/

Aunos, M., & Feldman, M. A. (2002). Attitudes towards sexuality, sterilization and parenting rights of persons with intellectual disabilities. *Journal of Applied Research in Intellectual Disabilities, 15*, 285–296.

Avery, D. M. (1998, January). Electronic parenting or, it takes a (listserv) village to raise families with disabilities. *CMC Magazine, 5*. Retrieved August 13, 2015, from http://www.december.com/cmc/mag/1998/jan/avery.html

Bailey, D. (1991). Guideline for authors. *Journal of Early Intervention, 15*, 118–119.

Baladerian, N., Coleman, T. F., & Stream, J. (2013). *Abuse of people with disabilities: Victims and their families speak out. A report on the 2012 National Survey on Abuse of People With Disabilities.* Los Angeles, CA: Spectrum Institute Disability and Abuse Project.

Balsam, K. F., Lehavot, K., Beadnell, B., & Circo, E. (2010). Childhood abuse and mental health indicators among ethnically diverse lesbian, gay, and bisexual adults. *Journal of Consulting and Clinical Psychology, 78*, 459–468.

Barron, J., & Barron, S. (2002). *There's a boy in here: Emerging from the bonds of autism.* Arlington, TX: Future Horizons.

Bass, J. K., Annan, J., Murray, S. M., Kaysen, D., Griffiths, S., Cetinoglu, T., . . . Bolton, P. A. (2013). Controlled trial of psychotherapy for Congolese survivors of sexual violence. *New England Journal of Medicine, 368*, 2182–2191.

Bauby, J. (1998). *The diving bell and the butterfly.* New York, NY: Vintage Books.

Bauman, S. (2008). *Essential topics for the helping professional.* Boston, MA: Pearson.

Bauman, S., & Rivers, I. (2015). *Mental health in the digital age.* London, England: Palgrave.

Bauman, S., & Thorbergson, A. (2011). Reflections on an experience: Preparing deaf counselors in a graduate program for hearing students to do group work. *Group Worker, 40*, 9–11.

Beck, J. G., & Coffey, S. F. (2005). Group cognitive behavioral treatment for PTSD: Treatment of motor vehicle accident survivors. *Cognitive and Behavioral Practice, 12,* 267–277.

Beck, M. (2011). *Expecting Adam: A true story of birth, rebirth, and everyday magic.* Panorama City, CA: Harmony.

Bedell, J. R., Hunter, R. H., & Corrigan, P. W. (1997). Current approaches to assessment and treatment of serious mental illness. *Professional Psychology: Research and Practice, 28,* 217–228.

Behler, G. T. (1993). Disability simulations as a teaching tool: Some ethical issues and implications. *Journal of Postsecondary Education and Disability, 10,* 3–8.

Berger, M. T., & Guidroz, K. (Eds.). (2009). *The intersectional approach: Transforming the academy through race, class, and gender.* Chapel Hill: University of North Carolina Press.

Berube, M. (1998). *Life as we know it: A father, a family, and an exceptional child.* New York, NY: Vintage Books.

Better Health Channel.vic.gov.au (0000). *Title of article.* Retrieved from http://www.betterhealth.vic.gov.au/bhcv2/bhcarticles.nsf/pages/Disability_managing_overweight_and_obesity?open

Block, P., Balcazar, F., & Keys, C. (2001). From pathology to power: Rethinking race, poverty, and disability. *Journal of Disability Policy Studies, 12,* 18–39.

Bonovitz, S. (2005). Locating culture in the psychic field: Transference and countertransference as cultural products. *Contemporary Psychoanalysis, 41,* 55–76.

Boyle, C., Boulet, S., Schieve, L., Cohen, R., Blumberg, S., Yeargin-Allsepp, M., . . . Kogan, M. (2011). Trends in the prevalence of developmental disability in US children, 1997–2008. *Pediatrics, 127,* 1034–1042.

Brabender, V. A., Fallon, A. E., & Smolar, A. I. (2004). *Essentials of group therapy.* Hoboken, NJ: Wiley.

Braithwaite, D. O., Waldron, V. R., & Finn, J. (1999). Communication of social support in computer-mediated groups for people with disabilities. *Health Communication, 11,* 123–151.

Brown, B. (1995). The process of inclusion and accommodation: A Bill of Rights for people with disabilities in group work. *Journal for Specialists in Group Work, 20,* 71–75. doi:10.1080/01933929508411328

Brown, C. (1955). *My left foot.* New York, NY: Simon & Schuster.

Buck, P. (1992). *The girl who never grew.* Bethesda, MD: Woodbine House.

Burgstahler, S., & Doe, T. (2004). Disability-related simulations: If, when, and how to use them in professional development. *Review of Disability Studies, 1,* 4–17.

Burlingame, G. M., Fuhriman, A., & Mosier, J. (2003). The differential effectiveness of group psychotherapy: A meta-analytic perspective. *Group Dynamics: Theory, Research, and Practice, 7*, 2–12.

Bushby, K., Finkel, R., Birnkrant, D. J., Case, L. E., Clemens, P. R., Cripe, L., . . . Constantin, C. (2010). Diagnosis and management of Duchenne muscular dystrophy: Part 1. Diagnosis, and pharmacological and psychosocial management. *Lancet Neurology, 9*, 77–93.

Card, K. J., & Schmider, L. (1995). Group work with members who have hearing impairments. *Journal for Specialists in Group Work, 20*, 83–90.

Cassidy, J. W. (2009). *Mindstorms: Living with traumatic brain injury.* Boston, MA: De Capo Lifelong Books.

Center for Parent Information and Resources. (2015, July). *Visual impairment, including blindness. Disability Fact Sheet 13.* Retrieved from http://www.parentcenterhub.org/repository/visualimpairment/

Center for Substance Abuse Treatment. (2005). *Substance abuse treatment: Group therapy* (Report No. SMA 05-3991). Rockville, MD: Substance Abuse and Mental Health Services Administration.

Chamberlain, K., & Zika, S. (1990). The minor events approach to stress: Support for the use of daily hassles. *British Journal of Psychology, 81*, 469–481. doi:10.1111/j.2044-8295.1990.tb02373.x

Chard, K. M. (2005). An evaluation of cognitive processing therapy for the treatment of posttraumatic stress disorder related to childhood sexual abuse. *Journal of Counsulting and Clinical Psychology, 73*, 965–971. doi:10.1037/0022.006X.73.5.965

Chima, F. O. (1998). Workplace and disabilities: Opinions on work, interpersonal, and intrapersonal factors. *Journal of Applied Rehabilitation Counseling, 29*, 31–37.

Clarke, M. (2016, February). *Social Security disability benefits for the legally blind.* Retrievd from http://www.allaboutvision.com/lowvision/social-security.htm

Cochran, S. D., Mays, V. M., Alegria, M., Ortega, A. N., & Takeuchi, D. (2007). Mental health and substance use disorders among Latino and Asian American lesbian, gay, and bisexual adults. *Journal of Consulting and Clinical Psychology, 75*, 785–794.

Commission on Rehabilitation Counselor Certification. (2009). *Code of professional ethics for rehabilitation counselors.* Schaumburg, IL: Author.

Corey, G. (2016). *Theory and practice of group counseling.* Independence, KY: Cengage Learning.

Corey, M. S., Corey, G., & Corey, C. (2013*). Groups: Process and practice* (9th ed.). Belmont, CA: Brooks-Cole.

Crenshaw, K. (1989). Demarginalizing the intersection of race and sex: A Black feminist critique of antidiscrimination doctrine, feminist theory and antiracist politics. *University of Chicago Legal Forum, 140,* 139–167.

Crenshaw, K. (1991). Mapping the margins: Intersectionality, identity politics, and violence against women of color. *Stanford Law Review, 43,* 1241–1299.

Cross, W. E., Jr. (1971). Negro-to-Black conversion experience: Toward a psychology of Black liberation. *Black World, 20,* 13–27.

Cuskelly, M., & Bryde, R. (2004). Attitudes towards the sexuality of adults with an intellectual disability: Parents, support staff, and a community sample. *Journal of Intellectual and Developmental Disability, 29,* 255–264.

Danesco, E. R. (2006). Parental beliefs on childhood disability: Insights on culture, child development, and intervention. *International Journal of Disability, Development, and Education, 44,* 41–52.

deBettencourt, L. U. (2002). Understanding the differences between IDEA and Section 504. *Teaching Exceptional Children, 34,* 16–23.

Disabled-World.com. (2016, January 16). *Disability: Definition, types and models.* Retrieved from http://www.disabled-world.com/disability/types/

Disabled-World.com. (2013, July 22). *Substance abuse and persons with disabilities.* Retrieved from http://www.disabled-world.com/medical/pharmaceutical/addiction/serious.php

Donnell, D., Baeten, J. M., Kiare, J., Thomas, K. K., Stevens, W., & Cohen, C. R. (2010). Heterosexual HIV-1 transmission after initiation of antiretroviral therapy: A prospective cohort analysis. *Lancet, 375,* 2092–2098.

Drolsbaugh, D. (2008). *Deaf again.* Springhouse, PA: Handwave.

Dunn, D. S., & Andrews, E. E. (2015). Person-first and identity-first language: Developing psychologists' cultural competence using disability language. *American Psychologist, 70,* 255–264. doi:10.1037/a0038636

Easton, A. (2013). *Autism and sexuality presentation.* Palatine, IL: South Campus Day School.

Eifert, D. R. (n.d.). *Delusional disorder.* Retrieved from http://www.minddisorders.com/Br-Del/Delusional-disorder.html

Ellis, S. K., Simpson, C. G., Rose, C. A., & Plotner, A. J. (2015). Group counseling services for people with disabilities. In J. L. DeLucia-Waack, C. R. Kalodner, & M. Riva (Eds.), *Handbook of group counseling and psychotherapy* (2nd ed., pp. 264–275). Thousand Oaks, CA: Sage.

Embry, R. A., & Grossman, F. D. (2006). The Los Angeles County response to child abuse and deafness: A social movement theory analysis. *American Annals of the Deaf, 151,* 488–498.

Erevelles, N., & Minear, A. (2010). Unspeakable offenses: Untangling race and disability in discourses of intersectionality. *Journal of Literary & Cultural Disability Studies, 4,* 127–145.

Erickson, W., Lee, C., & von Schrader, S. (2014). *2012 Disability status report for the United States.* Ithaca, NY: Cornell University Employment and Disabilities Institute.

Erford, B. T. (2011). *Group work process and applications.* Upper Saddle River, NJ: Pearson.

Evans, R. L., Smith, K. M., Werkhoven, W. S., Fox, H. R., & Pritzl, D. O. (1986). Cognitive telephone group therapy with physically disabled elderly persons. *Gerontologist, 26,* 8–11. doi:10.1093/geront/26.1.8

Falvo, D. (2014). *Medical and psychosocial aspects of chronic illness and disability* (5th ed.). Burlington, MA: Jones & Bartlett Learning.

Finn, J. (1999). An exploration of helping processes in an online self-help group focusing on issues of disability. *Health & Social Work, 24,* 220–231.

Foy, D. W., Ruzek, J. I., Glynn, S. M., Riney, S. J., & Gusman, F. D. (2002). Trauma focus group therapy for combat-related PTSD: An update. *Psychotherapy in Practice, 58,* 907–918. doi:10.1002.jclp.1066

Foy, D. W., Unger, W. S., & Wattenberg, M. S. (2004). *Module 4: An overview of evidence-based group approaches to trauma with adults.* New York, NY: American Group Psychotherapy Association.

French, S. (1992). Simulation exercises in disability awareness training: A critique. *Disability, Handicap & Society, 7,* 257–266.

Garcia, S. B., Mendez-Perez, A., & Ortiz, A. A. (2000). Mexican-American mothers' beliefs about disabilities: Implications for early childhood intervention. *Remedial & Special Education, 21,* 90–102.

Gill, C., J., Kerotoski, M., A., & Turk, N., M. A. (1996). Becoming visible: Personal health experiences of women with disabilities. In D. Krostoski, M. Nosek, & M. Turk (Eds). Women with physical disabilities: Achieving and maintaining health and well-being (pp. 5–16). Baltimore, MD: Brookes.

Gladding, S. T. (2015*). Groups: A counseling specialty* (7th ed.). Upper Saddle River, NJ: Pearson.

Glickman, N. (1996). The development of culturally deaf identities. In N. Glickman & M. Harvey (Eds.), *Culturally affirmative psychotherapy with deaf persons* (pp. 115–153). Mahwah, NJ: Erlbaum.

Greene, B. (2003). What difference does a difference make? Societal privilege, disadvantage, and discord in human relationships. In J. D. Robinson & L. C. James (Eds.), *Diversity in human interactions: The tapestry of America* (pp. 3–20). New York, NY: Oxford University Press.

Greer, S. (2002). Psychological intervention: The gap between research and practice. *Acta Oncologica, 41,* 228–243.

Gregg, W. (2010). Are children the future of Type 2 diabetes prevention? *New England Journal of Medicine, 362,* 548–552.

Hagberg, M. (1996). ABC of work-related disorders: Neck and arm disorders. *BMJ, 313,* 419. Retrieved from http://www.bmj.com/content/313/7054/419

Haley, T. J., & Dowd, E. T. (1988). Responses of deaf adolescent to differences in counselor method of communication and disability status. *Journal of Counseling Psychology, 35,* 258–262.

Harley, D. A., Nowak, T. M., Gassaway, L. J., & Savage, T. A. (2002). Lesbian, gay, bisexual, and transgender college students with disabilities: A look at multiple cultural minorities. *Psychology in the Schools, 39,* 525–538. doi:10.1002/pits.10052

Hawking, J. (2014). *Traveling to infinity: The true story behind the theory of everything.* Richmond, England: Alma Books.

Hays, P. A. (1996). Addressing the complexities of culture and gender in counseling. *Journal of Counseling & Development, 74,* 332–338.

Hearing Loss Association of America (n.d.). *Cochlear implants.* Retrieved from http://www.hearingloss.org/content/cochlear-implants

Heasley, S. (2013). *Survey finds disability abuse widespread.* Retrieved from https://www.disabilityscoop.com/2013/09/04/survey-abuse-widespread/18652/

Healio O&P News. (2005, November 1). *Support groups provide many benefits for amputees.* Retrieved from http://www.healio.com/orthotics-prosthetics/prosthetics/news/online/%7B997eb430-b141-427a-bc5b-b93567bae7d3%7D/support-groups-provide-many-benefits-for-amputees

Hellem, A. (2015, November). What does "legally blind" mean? Retrieved from http://www.allaboutvision.com/lowvision/legally-blind.htm

Hopps, S. L., Pépin, M., & Boisvert, J. (2003). The effectiveness of cognitive behavioral group therapy for loneliness via inter relaychat among people with physical disabilities. *Psychotherapy: Theory, Research, Practice, Training, 40,* 136–147. doi:10.1037/0033-3204.40.1/2.136

Huebner, R. A. (2004). Group procedures. In F. Chan, N. L. Berven, & K. R. Thomas (Eds.), *Counseling theories and techniques for rehabilitation professionals* (pp. 244–263). New York, NY: Springer.

Hughes, M. C., & Cohn, L. K. (1990). Group therapy with chronically ill children. In M. Seligman & L. Marshak (Eds.), *Group therapy: Interventions with special populations* (pp. 127–146). Needham Heights, MA: Allyn & Bacon.

Ibrahim, S. (2012, August 14). Over protection: The real enemy. *Blind Issues, Independent Living, Blind Daily Life.* Retrieved from https://letusspeakup.wordpress.com/2012/08/14/over-protection-the-real-enemy/

Inzucchi, S. E., & Sherwin, R. S. (2012). Type I diabetes mellitus. In L. Goldman & A. I. Shafer (Eds.), *Goldman's Cecil medicine* (4th ed., pp. 1475–1489). Philadelphia, PA: W. B. Saunders.

Johnson, D. W., & Johnson, F. P. (2012). *Joining together: Group theory and group skill* (11th ed.). Upper Saddle River, NJ: Pearson.

Jones, S. (1997). *The archaeology of ethnicity: Constructing identities in the past and present.* New York, NY: Psychology Press.

Jones, S. R. (2009). Constructing identities at the intersections: An autoethnographic exploration of multiple dimensions of identity. *Journal of College Student Development, 50,* 287–304.

Kanas, N. (1996). *Group therapy for schizophrenic patients.* Washington, DC: American Psychological Association.

Karp, G. (2008). *Life on wheels* (2nd ed.). New York, NY: Demos Health.

Kessler, R. C. (2004). Epidemiology of dual diagnosis. *Biological Psychiatry, 56,* 730–737. doi:10.1016/j.biopsych.2004

Kissane, D. W., Bloch, S., Miach, P., Smith, G. C., Seddon, A., & Keks, N. (1997). Cognitive–existential group therapy for patients with primary breast cancer—Techniques and themes. *Psycho-Oncology, 6,* 25–33.

Kleege, G. (1999). *Sight unseen.* New Haven, CT: Yale University Press.

Kolakowsky-Hayner, S. A., Gourley III, E. V., Kreutzer, J. S., Marwitz, J. H., Cifu, D. X., & McKinley, W. O. (1999). Pre-injury substance abuse among persons with brain injury and persons with spinal cord injury. *Brain Injury, 13,* 571–581.

Krahn, G., Farrell, N., Gabriel, R., & Deck, D. (2006). Access barriers to substance abuse treatment for persons with disabilities: An exploratory study. *Journal of Substance Abuse Treatment, 31,* 375–384.

Kvam, M. H. (2004). Sexual abuse of deaf children: A retrospective analysis of the prevalence and characteristics of childhood sexual abuse among deaf adults in Norway. *Child Abuse & Neglect, 28,* 241–251. doi:10.1016/j.chiabu.2003.09.017

Ladeau, E. (2015, July 20). *Why person-first language doesn't-always put the person first.* Retrieved from http://www.thinkinclusive.us/why-person-first-language-doesnt-always-put-the-person-first/

Ladau, E. (2014, March 11). I won't pretend that disability simulation works. *Huffington Post.* Retrieved from http://www.huffingtonpost.com/emily-ladau/i-wont-disability-simulation_b_4936801.html

Laitmon, E. (1979). Group counseling: Sexuality and the hearing impaired adolescent. *Sexuality and Disability, 2,* 469–177. doi:10.1007/BF01100788

Larson, K. C. (2015). *Rosemary: The hidden Kennedy daughter.* Boston, MA: Houghton Mifflin Harcourt.

Leigh, I. W. (2009). Deaf identities: Perspectives from theory and research. In I. W. Leigh (Ed.), *A lens on deaf identities* (pp. 23–42). New York, NY: Oxford University Press.

Lieberman, M. A. (1990). A group therapist perspective on self-help groups. *International Journal of Group Psychotherapy, 40*(3), 251–278. doi:10.1080/00207284.1990.11490608.

Lieberman, M. A., Wizlenberg, A., Golant, M., & DiMinno, M. (2005). The impact of group composition on Internet support groups: Homogeneous versus heterogeneous Parkinson's groups. *Group Dynamics: Theory, Research, and Practice, 9,* 239–250.

Lincourt, P., Kuettel, T. J., & Bombardier, C. H. (2002). Motivational interviewing in a group setting with mandated clients: A pilot study. *Addictive Behaviors, 27,* 381–391.

Livneh, H. (1986). A unified approach to existing models of adaptation to disability: Part I. A model adaptation. *Journal of Applied Rehabilitation Counseling, 17,* 5–16.

Livneh, H., Wilson, L. M., & Pullo, R. E. (2004). Group counseling for people with physical disabilities. *Focus on Exceptional Children, 36,* 1–18.

Lohr, C. (2012, February 22). Isolating a child with disabilities can do life-long damage. *HuffPost Parents.* Retrieved from http://www.huffingtonpost.com/carla-lohr/isolating-a-child-with-di_b_1289693.html

Lubin, H., Loris, M., Burt, J., & Johnson, D. R. (1998). Efficacy of psychoeducational group therapy in reducing symptoms of posttraumatic stress disorder among multiply traumatized women. *American Journal of Psychiatry, 155,* 1172–1177.

Mackelprang, R. W. (1993). A holistic social work approach to providing sexuality education and counseling for persons with severe disabilities. *Journal of Social Work & Human Sexuality, 8,* 63–87. doi:10.1300/J291v08n02_04

Madell, J. (2015). *Counseling and support for children with hearing loss.* Retrieved from http://www.audiologyonline.com/articles/counseling-support-for-children-with-13758

Mardiros, M. (1989). Conception of childhood disability among Mexican-American parents. *Medical Anthropology, 12,* 55–68.

Marshak, L. (1990). Outpatient group psychotherapy for persons with chronic mental illnesses. In M. Seligman & L. Marshak (Eds.), *Group psychotherapy: Interventions with special populations* (pp. 88–104). Boston, MA: Allyn & Bacon.

Marshak, L. E., & Seligman, M. (1993). *Counseling persons with physical disabilities: Theoretical and clinical perspectives.* Austin, TX: Pro-Ed.

Mason, J. (2007). The provision of psychological therapy to people with intellectual disabilities: An investigation into some of the relevant factors. *Journal of Intellectual Disability Research, 51,* 244–249.

Mayers, K. S. (1978). Sexual and social concerns of the disabled: A group counseling approach. *Sexuality and Disability, 1,* 100–111. doi:10.1007/BF01101771

McCallion, P., & Janicki, M. (1997). Exploring the impact of culture and acculturation on older families' care giving for persons with developmental disabilities. *Family Relations, 46,* 347–358.

Mehra, S., Eavey, R. D., & Keamy, D. G., Jr. (2009). The epidemiology of hearing impairment in the United States: Newborns, children, and adolescents. *Otolaryngology—Head and Neck Surgery, 140,* 461–472.

Mejias, N. J., Gill, C. J., & Shpigelman, C. (2014). Influence of a support group for young women with disabilities on sense of belonging. *Journal of Counseling Psychology, 61,* 208–220. doi:10.1037/a0035462

Merchant, N. (2013). Multicultural diversity—Competent group work. In J. Trotzer (Ed.), *The counselor and the group* (4th ed., pp. 319–350). Philadelphia, PA: Taylor & Francis.

Miller, W. R., & Rollnick, S. (1991). *Motivational interviewing: Preparing people to change addictive behavior.* New York, NY: Guilford Press.

Mpofu, E., & Conyers, L. M. (2004). A representational theory perspective of minority status and people with disabilities: Implications for rehabilitation education and practice. *Rehabilitation Counseling Bulletin, 47,* 142–151.

National Center on Elder Abuse. (n.d.). *Fact sheet: Elder abuse prevalence and incidence.* Washington, DC: Author.

National Council on Disability (2009). *The current state of health care for people with disabilities.* Retrieved from http://www.ncd.gov/publications/2009/Sept302009#Gaps

National Federation of the Blind (2016, March). *Blindness statistics.* Retrieved from https://nfb.org/blindness-statistics

National Eye Institute. (2004). Causes and prevalence of visual impairment among adults in the United States. *Opthalmology, 122,* 477–485. Retrieved from https://nei.nih.gov/eyedata/pbd1

National Institute of Mental Health. (n.d.) *Schizophrenia.* Retrieved from http://www.nimh.nih.gov/health/statistics/prevalence/schizophrenia.shtml

National Institute of Mental Health. (2007, October 18). *National survey tracks prevalence of personality disorders in U. S.* population. Retrieved from http://www.nimh.nih.gov/news/science-news/2007/national-survey-tracks-prevalence-of-personality-disorders-in-us-population.shtml

National Institute of Mental Health. (2014). *Major depression among adults.* Retrieved from http://www.nimh.nih.gov/health/statistics/prevalence/major-depression-among-adults.shtml

Nettles, R. (2012). Multiple minority identities in group psychotherapy: Within and between. In R. Nettles & N. Balter (Eds.), *Multiple minority identities: Applications for practice, research, and training* (pp. 95–115). New York, NY: Springer.

Nettles, R., & Balter, R. (2012). *Multiple minority identities: Applications for practice, research, and training.* New York, NY: Springer.

Olkin, R. (1999). *What psychotherapists should know about disability.* New York, NY: Guilford Press.

Olson, T. (2014, January). How disability simulations promote stereotypes. *Braille Monitor, 57.* Retrieved from https://nfb.org/images/nfb/publications/bm/bm14/bm1401/bm140107.htm

O'Neil, M. E., Fragala-Pinkham, M. A., Westcott, S. L., Martin, K., Chiarello, L. A., Valvano, J., & Rose, R. A. (2006). Physical therapy clinical management recommendations for children with cerebral palsy–spastic diplegia: Achieving functional mobility. *Pediatric Physical Therapy, 18,* 49–72.

Patient Protection and Affordable Care Act, 42 U.S.C. §§ 18001-18121 (2010).

Pedley, T. A. (2004). The epilepsies. In L. Goldman & D. Ausiello (Eds.), *Cecil textbook of medicine* (22nd ed., pp. 2257–2268). Philadelphia, PA: W. B. Saunders.

Pfeiffer, J. W., & Jones, J. E. (1970). *A handbook of structured experiences for human relations training* (Vol. II). Iowa City, IA: University Associates Press.

Piper, W., Ogrodniczuk, J., Joyce, A., Weidman, R., & Rosie, J. (2007). Group composition and group therapy for complicated grief. *Journal of Consulting and Clinical Psychology, 75,* 116–125.

Pope, M., Pangelinan, J. S., & Coker, A. D. (2011). *Experiential activities for teaching multicultural competence in counseling.* Alexandria, VA: American Counseling Association.

Price, E. M., & Fisher, K. (2002). How does counseling help people with amputation? *Journal of Prosthetics and Orthotics, 14,* 102–106.

Ratts, M. J., Singh, A. A., Nassar-McMillan, S., Butler, S. K., McCullough, J. R., & Hipolito-Delgado, C. (2015). *Multicultural and social justice counseling competencies.* Alexandria, VA: Association for Multicultural Counseling and Development.

Reeve, D. (2000). Oppression within the counseling room. *Disability and Society, 14,* 669–682.

Rehabilitation Act of 1973 § 501, as amended, 29 U.S.C. § 791 and § 504, as amended, 29 U.S.C. § 794 (2014).

Reiter, S., & Lapidot-Lefler, N. (2007). Bullying among special education students with intellectual disabilities: Differences in social adjustment and social skills. *Intellectual and Developmental Disabilities, 45,* 174–181.

Reiter, S., Mar'i, S., & Rosenberg, Y. (1986). Parental attitudes toward the developmentally disabled among Arab communities in Israel: A cross-cultural study. *International Journal of Rehabilitation Research, 9,* 355–362.

Riva, M. T. (1990). Group treatment with sexually abused children. In M. Seligman & L. Marshak (Eds.), *Group psychotherapy: Interventions with special populations* (pp. 174–194). Boston, MA: Allyn & Bacon.

Rohnke, K. E. (1984). *Silver bullets: A guide to initiative problems, adventure games, and trust activities.* Beverly, MA: Project Adventure.

Rose, J., West, C., & Clifford, D. (2000). Group interventions for anger in people with intellectual disabilities. *Research in Developmental Disabilities, 21,* 174–181.

Rosenberg, M. B. (2013, April 15). LGBT's living with disabilities: Also here, also queer. *Huffpost Gay Voices.* Retrieved from http://www.huffingtonpost.com/mark-brennan-rosenberg/lgbts-living-with-disabil_b_3016564.html

Roth, J. (2013). Inclusive group facilitation strategies for all abilities. *Counseling Today, 56,* 52–56.

Ruzek, J. I. (2003, August 1). Group treatment of posttraumatic stress disorder and other trauma-related problems. *Primary Psychiatry.* Retrieved from http://primarypsychiatry.com/group-treatment-of-posttraumatic-stress-disorder-and-other-trauma-related-problems/

Sakellariou, D. (2006). If not the disability, then what? Barriers to reclaiming sexuality following spinal cord injury. *Sexuality and Disability, 24,* 101–111.

Salazar, C. (2009). *Group work experts share their favorite multicultural activities: A guide to diversity-competent choosing, planning, conducting, and processing.* Alexandria, VA: Association for Specialists in Group Work.

Sandel, M. E., Williams, K. S., Dellapietra, L., & Derogatis, L. R. (1996). Sexual functioning following traumatic brain injury. *Brain Injury, 10,* 719–728.

Sanders, K. Y. (2006). Overprotection and lowered expectations of persons with disabilities: The unforeseen consequences. *Work, 27,* 181–188.

Seligman, M. (1993). Group work with parents of children with disabilities. *Journal for Specialists in Group Work, 18,* 115–126.

Serido, J., Almeida, D. M., & Wethington, E. (2004). Chronic stressors and daily hassles: Unique and interactive relationships with psychological distress. *Journal of Health and Social Behavior, 45,* 17–33.

Shakespeare, T. (2013). The social model of disability. In L. J. Davis (Ed.), *The disability studies reader* (4th ed., pp. 214–221). New York, NY: Routledge.

Shapiro, J. (1994). *No pity.* New York, NY: Broadway Books.

Shaw, L. R., Chan, F., & Lam, C. (2004). Professional disclosure practices of rehabilitation counselors. *Rehabilitation Counseling Bulletin, 48,* 38–50.

Shaw, L. R., & Tarvydas, V. (2001). The use of professional disclosure in rehabilitation counseling. *Rehabilitation Counseling Bulletin, 45,* 40–47.

Shea, M. T., McDevitt-Murphy, M., Ready, D. J., & Schnurr, P. P. (2008). Group therapy. In E. B. Foa, T. M. Keane, M. J. Friedman, & J. A. Cohen (Eds.), *Effective treatments for PTSD: Practice guidelines from the International Society for Traumatic Stress Studies* (2nd ed., pp. 306–326). New York, NY: Guilford Press.

Silverman, A. M., Gwinn, J. D., & Van Boven, L. (2015). Stumbling in their shoes: Disability simulations reduced judged capabilities of disabled people. *Social, Psychological, and Personality Science, 6,* 464–471.

Singh, A., Merchant, N., Skudrzyk, B., & Ingene, D. (2012). *Association for Specialists in Group Work: Multicultural and social justice competence principles for group workers*. Retrieved from http://static1.squarespace.com/static/55cea634e4b083e448c3dd50/t/55d3f911e4b0ac4433ebd4cd/1439955217809/ASGW_MC_SJ_Priniciples_Final_ASGW.pdf

Sloan, D. M., Bovin, M. J., & Schnurr, P. P. (2012). Review of group treatment for PTSD. *Journal of Rehabilitation Research and Development, 49*, 689–702. doi:10.1682/JRRD.2011.07.0123

Small, A., & Cripps, J. (2012). On becoming: Developing an empowering culture identity framework for deaf youth and adults. In A. Small, J. Cripps, & J. Côté (Eds.), *Cultural space and self/identity development among deaf youth* (pp. 29–41). Toronto, Ontario, Canada: Canadian Cultural Society of the Deaf.

Smeltzer, S. C. (2010). Improving health and wellness of people with disabilities. In J. H. Stone & M. Blouin (Eds.), *International encyclopedia of rehabilitation*. Retrieved from http://cirrie.buffalo.edu/encyclopedia/en/article/300

Sobsey, D., & Doe, T. (1991). Patterns of sexual abuse and assault. *Sexuality and Disability, 9*, 243–259.

Solomon, A. (2012). *Far from the tree: Parents, children, and the search for identity*. New York, NY: Scribner.

Special Olympics. (2003). *Multinational study of attitudes toward individuals with intellectual disabilities*. Washington, DC: Author.

Spiegel, D., Morrow, G. R., Classen, C., Raubertas, R., Stott, P. B., Mudaliar, N., . . . Riggs, G. (1999). Group psychotherapy for recently diagnosed breast cancer patients: A multicenter feasibility study. *Psycho-Oncology, 8*, 482–493.

Stone, W. N. (1996). *Group psychotherapy for people with chronic mental illness*. New York, NY: Guilford Press.

Stringer, K., & Molnos, A. (n.d.). *Narcissistic defenses*. Retrieved from http://www.toddlertime.com/mh/terms/narcissistic-defenses.htm

Strohmer, D. C., & Biggs, D. A. (1983). Effects of counselor disability status on disabled subjects' perceptions of counselor attractiveness and expertness. *Journal of Counseling Psychology, 30*, 202–208.

Stuart, O. (1993). Double oppression: An appropriate starting point. In J. Swain, V. Finkelstein, S. French, & M. Oliver (Eds.), *Disabling barriers—Enabling environments* (pp. 93–100). London, England: Sage.

Substance Abuse and Mental Health Services Administration. (2011, August). Substance use disorders in people with physical and sensory disabilities. *In Brief, 6*(1).

Sue, D. W., & Sue, D. (2015). *Counseling the culturally diverse: Theory and practice* (7th ed.). Hoboken, NJ: Wiley.

Suler, J. (2004). The online disinhibition effect. *Cyberpsychology & Behavior, 7,* 321–326. doi: 10.1089/1094931041291295

Teaster, P. B. (n.d.). *A response to the abuse of vulnerable adults: The 2000 survey of state adult protective services.* Washington, DC: National Center on Elder Abuse.

Tepper, M. S. (2000). Sexuality and disability: The missing discourse on pleasure. *Sexuality and Disability, 18,* 283–290.

The Ten Commandments of Disability. (2014, August 14). [video]. Available from https://www.youtube.com/watch?v=G_v4tZ9GLHY&spfreload=10

Thomas, R. V., & Pender, V. A. (2008). Association for Specialists in Group Work: Best practice guidelines 2007 revisions. *Journal for Specialists in Group Work, 33,* 111–117.

Thornberry, C., & Olsen, K. (2005). The abuse of individuals with developmental disabilities. *Developmental Disabilities Bulletin, 33*(1-2), 1–19.

Tsau, G. (2000). *Growing up Asian American with a disability.* Retrieved from http://www.colorado.edu/journals/standards/V7N1/FIRSTPERSON/tsao.html

Tutty, L., & Giurgiu, B. (2010). *No longer silent: Persons with disabilities who have been abused identify their service needs.* Calgary, Alberta, Canada: University of Calgary. Retrieved from http://www.academia.edu/1601259/No_Longer_Silent_Persons_with_disabilities_who_have_been_abused_identify_their_service_needs

Unger, R. (1989). Selection and composition criteria in group psychotherapy. *Journal for Specialists in Group Work, 14,* 151–157.

U.S. Census Bureau Reports (2012, July 25). *Nearly 1 in 5 people have a disability in the U. S.* [press release]. Retrieved from https://www.census.gov/newsroom/releases/archives/miscellaneous/cb12-134.html

U. S. Department of Justice, Civil Rights Division, Disability Rights Section. (n.d.). *Project Civic Access: Cities and Counties: First steps toward solving common ADA problems.* [project report]. Retrieved from http://www.ada.gov/civiccommonprobs.htm

U. S. Department of Labor. (2015). *Occupational outlook handbook,* 2014–2015 ed. St. Paul, MN: Jist Publishing.

Vernon, A. (1999). The dialectics of multiple identities and the disabled people's movement. *Disability & Society, 14,* 385–398.

Walther, J. B. (1996). Group and interpersonal effects in international computer-mediated collaboration. *Human Communication Research, 23,* 324–369.

Webb, M. (2014). Accessing Canal pride: The intersection of identities for LGBT people with physical disabilities at a global event. *Independent Study Project (ISP) Collection* (Paper No. 1983). Available at http://digitalcollections.sit.edu/isp_collection/1983

Westergaard, R., & Gupta, A. (2012). The patient with HIV disease. In E. T. Bope & R. D. Kellerman (Eds.), *Conn's current therapy* (pp. 86–104). Philadelphia, PA: Elsevier Saunders.

Whitehouse, M. A., & McCabe, M. P. (1997). Sex education programs for people with intellectual disability: How effective are they? *Education and Training in Mental Retardation and Developmental Disabilities, 32,* 229–240.

Whyte, A. K., Aubrecht, A. L., McCullough, C. A., Lewis, J. W., & Thompson-Ochoa, D. (2013, October 1). Understanding deaf people in counseling contexts. *Counseling Today.* Retrieved from http://ct.counseling.org/2013/10/understanding-deaf-people-in-counseling-contexts/

Wolf, A. (1999). The foundation of psychodynamic group therapy: The fallacy of the group as a whole. In S. de Schill & S. Libovici (Eds.), *The challenge of psychoanalysis and psychotherapy* (pp. 213–230). London, England: Jessica Kingsley.

Wolfsdorf, B. A., & Zlotnick, C. (2001). Affect management in group therapy for women with posttraumatic stress disorder and histories of childhood sexual abuse. *Psychotherapy in Practice, 57,* 169–181.

World Health Organization. (2006). *Defining sexual health.* Geneva, Switzerland: Author. Retrieved from http://www.who.int/reproductivehealth/topics/sexual_health/sh_definitions/en/

World Health Organization. (2011). *World report on disability.* Geneva, Switzerland: WHO Press.

Wright, B. A. (1983). *Physical disability: A psychosocial approach.* New York, NY: Harper & Row.

Yalom, I. (1995). *The theory and practice of group psychotherapy* (4th ed.). New York, NY: Basic Books.

Yalom, I. D., & Leszcz, M. (2005). *Theory and practice of group psychotherapy* (5th ed.). New York, NY: Basic Books.

Yelin, E. H. (1991). The recent history and immediate future of employment among persons with disabilities. *Milbank Quarterly, 69,* 129–149.

Young, M. E., Nosek, M. A., Chapping, G. F., & Rintala, D. (1998). Prevalence of abuse of women with physical disabilities. *Archives of Physical Medicine and Rehabilitation, 78,* 34–38.

INDEX

Tables are indicated by "t" following the page number.

V

W

Y

Z